Getting to the Core of Writing

Essential Lessons for Every Fourth Grade Student

Richard Gentry, Ph.D.

Jan McNeel, M.A.Ed.

Vickie Wallace-Nesler, M.A.Ed.

SHELL EDUCATION

Publishing Credits

Dona Herweck Rice, *Editor-in-Chief*; Robin Erickson, *Production Director*;
Lee Aucoin, *Creative Director;* Timothy J. Bradley, *Illustration Manager;*
Sara Johnson, M.S.Ed., *Senior Editor*; Jodene Smith, M.A., *Editor;*
Jennifer Kim, M.A.Ed., *Associate Education Editor;* Tracy Edmunds, *Editor;*
Leah Quillian, *Assistant Editor;* Grace Alba, *Designer;* Corinne Burton, *M.A.Ed., Publisher*

Standards

© 2004 Mid-continent Research for Education and Learning (McREL)
© 2007 Teachers of English to Speakers of Other Languages, Inc. (TESOL)
© 2010 National Governors Association Center for Best Practices and Council of Chief State School Officers (CCSS)

Shell Education

5301 Oceanus Drive
Huntington Beach, CA 92649-1030
http://www.shelleducation.com

ISBN 978-1-4258-0918-8

© 2012 Shell Educational Publishing, Inc.
Reprinted 2013

Table of Contents

Introduction 5
  The Importance of Writing 5
  Traits of Quality Writing 6
  The Reading and Writing Connection . . 7
  The Purpose of Assessment 10
How to Use This Book 11
  Planning Writing Instruction 11
  Components of Writer's Workshop 14
  Implementing the Lessons 15
  Implementing Writer's Workshop 18
  The Writing Conference 19
  The Writer's Notebook 21
  Top 10 Tips for Creating
    Successful Writers 23
  Correlation to Standards 24
Acknowledgments 31
About the Authors 32
Managing Writer's Workshop 33
  Lesson 1: Components of
    Writer's Workshop 35
  Lesson 2: Our Group Meeting 38
  Lesson 3: The Writing Folder 41
  Lesson 4: The Writer's Notebook 50
  Lesson 5: Organizing the
    Writer's Notebook 52
  Lesson 6: Sharing 58
  Lesson 7: Turn and Talk 62
  Lesson 8: Guidelines for
    Writer's Workshop 65
  Lesson 9: Teacher and
    Peer Conferences 68
  Lesson 10: The Five-Step
    Writing Process 71

Ideas 75
  Lesson 1: My Authority List 77
  Lesson 2: Authors as Mentors 80
  Lesson 3: Interesting Places 83
  Lesson 4: The Best Times!
    The Worst Times! 86
  Lesson 5: Brainstorming Boxes 89
  Lesson 6: What Should We Write? 92
  Lesson 7: Pocket of Picture Topics 95
  Lesson 8: I Wonder List 98
Sentence Fluency 101
  Lesson 1: Circle and Count 103
  Lesson 2: Subject + Predicate =
    Sentence 106
  Lesson 3: Sentence Search 110
  Lesson 4: Appositive Action 117
  Lesson 5: Compound Sentences 121
  Lesson 6: Writing Complex
    Sentences 126
  Lesson 7: Stepping Up Sentences 131
  Lesson 8: Building Triangle
    Sentences 134
Organization 137
  Lesson 1: Creating Cinquains 139
  Lesson 2: Powerful Paragraphs 142
  Lesson 3: Narrative Notes 145
  Lesson 4: Build-a-Character 148
  Lesson 5: Story Building Blocks 151
  Lesson 6: It's a Bear Beginning 154
  Lesson 7: Don't You Agree? 158
  Lesson 8: It's Your Business 161
  Lesson 9: How-To Writing 165
  Lesson 10: Composition Planner 168
  Lesson 11: A Cache of Poetry 172

Table of Contents (cont.)

Word Choice. 175

    Lesson 1: Stupendous Similes 177

    Lesson 2: Be a Word Wizard 180

    Lesson 3: Connecting Ideas 183

    Lesson 4: Put "Said" to Bed 187

    Lesson 5: COW to WOW. 190

    Lesson 6: Auspicious Adjectives 193

    Lesson 7: Be Explicitly Specific 196

    Lesson 8: Adverb Alert 199

    Lesson 9: Alliteration Action 203

Voice 207

    Lesson 1: Show Me Your Voice. 209

    Lesson 2: What's My Voice?. 215

    Lesson 3: The Voices on the Bus 217

    Lesson 4: Various Voices. 220

Conventions 223

    Lesson 1: Capital Creations. 225

    Lesson 2: Super Spellers 228

    Lesson 3: Common Comma
        Conventions 231

    Lesson 4: The Color of CUPS. 235

    Lesson 5: Dandy Dialogue 239

    Lesson 6: Show Me Editing. 242

    Lesson 7: Traits Team Checklist 245

    Lesson 8: Digging into Editing 248

Appendices 253

    Appendix A: Conferring Resources. . . . 253

    Appendix B: Assessment Resources . . . 261

    Appendix C: Mentor Text List 273

    Appendix D: Additional Resources 282

    Appendix E: References 287

    Appendix F: Contents of the Teacher
        Resource CD 290

The Importance of Writing

In recent years, many school districts and teachers referred to writing as the "Neglected R" and viewed reading as the path to literacy success. Today, as research has revealed more information about the fundamental connection between reading success and writing competency, we are realizing that the road to literacy is a two-way street (Graham and Hebert 2010). While working as literacy consultants, we encountered numerous, capable teachers struggling with the complexity of implementing rigorous writing instruction. We wrote this book to enable all teachers to implement a successful writing program with a high degree of teaching competency. The success enjoyed by many of the teachers using the materials in this book has relieved frustrations, rejuvenated careers, and rekindled enthusiasm for teaching.

This book was written to fulfill two major objectives. The first objective involves motivating teachers to value and incorporate writing instruction as an essential element of literacy development. It should help them implement best practices and simplify the planning of writing instruction. New writing standards have been applied by education leaders at every level. Ultimately, the responsibility for implementing these standards is placed on the classroom teacher. Historically, the lack of emphasis on writing instruction in teacher education programs has left teachers feeling woefully unprepared to teach primary students to write, particularly at a level which meets the expectations of the standards for writing. The burden of this responsibility and feelings of inadequacy have left both experienced and novice teachers feeling empty-handed and unprepared.

Since 2010, most states have adopted the Common Core State Standards (CCSS), which are designed to provide teachers and parents with a clear understanding of what students are expected to learn. Since the CCSS are newly adopted, many teachers have not received professional development to become familiar with the standards nor have they received resources for their instruction, particularly in the area of writing. Therefore, the second objective of this book is to assist teachers in becoming familiar with these standards for writing and provide resources to support the implementation of these standards in their classrooms. *Getting to the Core of Writing* provides lessons outlining four key areas of writing: Text Types and Purposes, Production and Distribution of Writing, Research, and Range of Writing. It offers suggestions to meet those standards in instruction during Writer's Workshop. It also addresses how speaking and listening standards are easily practiced by engaging students in an interactive lesson format.

It is no secret that students become better writers by writing every day. This book contains the foundational structure and best practices that will guide teachers as they establish a daily Writer's Workshop that includes consistent, structured instruction to engage students in the writing process. Beyond that, a flexible pacing guide is provided to aid in planning writing instruction.

It is our hope that this book provides teachers with all the tools needed to inspire and equip young writers in today's classrooms.

—Richard, Jan, and Vickie

Traits of Quality Writing

The traits of quality writing continue to gain recognition as the language of successful writers. Educators at the Northwest Regional Educational Laboratory, now Education Northwest, searched for an accurate, reliable method of measuring student writing performance. Six attributes of good writing are identified in *Seeing with New Eyes* (Spandel 2005). These characteristics are used to inform and guide writing instruction:

- **Ideas** are the heart of the message, the content of the piece, and the main theme.

- **Sentence fluency** is the rhythm and flow of the language, the sound of word patterns, and the way in which the writing plays to the ear, not just to the eye.

- **Organization** is the internal structure, the thread of central meaning, and the logical and sometimes intriguing pattern of ideas within a piece of writing.

- **Word choice** is the use of rich, colorful, precise language that moves and enlightens the reader.

- **Voice** is the heart and soul, the magic, and the wit, along with the feeling and conviction of the individual writer that emerge through the words.

- **Conventions** are how the writer uses mechanical correctness in the piece— spelling, paragraphing, grammar and usage, punctuation, and capitalization.

Knowing and understanding the traits of quality writing supports teachers, students, and parents in thinking about writing and understanding what makes for writing success. Even in the early grades, students can communicate and recognize the characteristics of quality writing. The works of Ruth Culham (2008) and Vicki Spandel (2008) emphasize the value and benefits of using these traits to provide a common language—"a writer's vocabulary for thinking, speaking, and working like writers" (Spandel 2008, 7)—to enrich instruction and assessment in primary classrooms.

The value and importance of using this trait language in writing instruction is well supported by research (Gentry 2006). It is particularly important when working with students in the early grades to provide instructional tools to support students' different learning styles. In *Getting to the Core of Writing*, the traits are personified through student-friendly characters. Each of the characters represents a different writing trait, and collectively they are referred to as the Traits Team (traitsteam.pdf). Students are introduced to the individual team members through the mini-lessons. The Traits Team becomes a valuable tool for a Writer's Workshop experience. A more detailed description and poster of each Traits Team member is provided in the introduction to each trait section.

The Reading and Writing Connection

Students' writing abilities often shift in third through sixth grade as student readers make a giant cognitive leap from learning to read to reading to learn. Students have likely advanced through all five phases of beginning reading and writing development, attaining a degree of independence as both readers and writers by the time they enter third grade.

In some ways, reading advances faster than writing, and the complexity of writing is accentuated during third through sixth grade. It becomes apparent that writing is more demanding and, in some ways, harder than reading for third, fourth, fifth, and sixth graders. For example, fourth graders can read fairly complex novels, but they would not be able to write novels at that same level of complexity. In the words of writing expert Ralph Fletcher, "Reading is up here and writing is down there. Probably the smartest fourth grader in the country cannot write a novel" (Fletcher 2000).

One expectation of the reading and writing connection in third through sixth grade is that students gain facility in reading a book like a writer (Yates 1995). During this period, students likely begin viewing writing more from the author's perspective, bringing structure and organization to pieces they create based on the reading they do and the study of literary authors' crafts.

In earlier grades, young writers often have a linear sense of writing; they follow a story map or a simple structure, such as *first*, *then*, *next*, and *last*, or *beginning*, *middle,* and *end*. Younger writers often move purposely straight through their composition in a step-by-step approach, rarely rereading or reflecting as they write. Rereading and reflecting as they move through a text becomes more important in the intermediate grades, helping students make sense of what they have written (Gentry 2002).

Not only do they read like a writer, the Common Core State Standards help them think like a writer.

Moving from Concrete to Abstract Thinking

Third-, fourth-, fifth-, and sixth-grade writing often mirrors how children think. Initially in this period of elementary school, students' writing can reflect thinking "limited to concrete phenomena and their own past experiences: that is, thinking is not abstract" (Bjorklund 1999). A third-grade writer following a clear-cut, step-by-step sequence may reflect thinking "limited to tangible facts and objects and not to hypotheses" (Bjorklund 1999). During third grade through sixth grade, students will learn to shift back and forth during drafting to survey the piece from both the reader's and writer's perspective. This includes responding to varying demands of audience, purpose, task, and genre, often guided by the Common Core State Standards and based on a rich array of appropriate models for writing.

The Reading and Writing Connection *(cont.)*

As third- through sixth-grade writers mature, they begin to reflect on their own thinking, pausing and rereading to see how the piece they have crafted sounds or discovering alternative routes for a story plot or other written presentation. They are more likely to begin to consider the reader before putting words down on paper. They gain greater mastery of paragraphing, revising, and editing.

Towards the end of elementary school, writers are much more likely "to introspect about their own thought processes, and generally, can think abstractly" (Bjorklund 1999). Moving from the constrains of story mapping or events in their immediate experience, they advance in ability to critique, consider the impact of specific details, choose just the right word, cite specific textural evidence to support their views, and make other appropriate choices for their writing. They demonstrate both deductive and inductive reasoning, moving from the general to the specific or moving from specific observations to broad generalizations, respectively. Their understanding of components and conventions of the writing process grows, and with the support of the Common Core State Standards, their writing becomes more sophisticated, moving along the grade-by-grade continuum that will eventually lead to college- and career-readiness.

As students move through third through sixth grade, the reading and writing connection likely changes them as thinkers, helping them develop abilities to assimilate information into abstract schemes, question their own thinking, test their own hypotheses, and develop deeper levels of knowledge and thinking (Mann 2002).

The Reading and Writing Connection (cont.)

Basic Common Core Goals for Writers

Students engage in a rich array of literature as models for writing.
Students continue to develop the ability to write both fiction and nonfiction.
Students' writing ties into a comprehensive, content-rich curriculum.
Students demonstrate independence as writers appropriate for their grade level.
Students demonstrate strong content knowledge through writing.
Student writers respond to the varying demands of audience, task, purpose, and discipline.
Students' writing demonstrates ability to both comprehend and critique.
Student writers cite specific textual evidence in their writing to support their views.
Students consider the impact of specific words and details and make appropriate choices.
Students bring structure and organization to their own writing based on studies of the literary authors' crafts.
Students use technology to enhance their writing.

Adapted from "College and Career Readiness Standards for Reading, Writing, and Speaking and Listening" (Shanahan 2009).

The Purpose of Assessment

Assessment plays an integral role in writing instruction. It may occur at the district or state level to measure the student's ability to meet specific standards. Many classrooms include self-assessment where students use rubrics and checklists to score and reflect on their own work. Writing assessment can also take place informally as we sit and confer with young writers, taking anecdotal notes. Maintaining student writing portfolios comprised of both spontaneous and directed writing provides assessment information of a student's writing development and performance over a specific time. No matter the type or form of assessment, it should enable you to determine students' strengths and weaknesses so you may revise your instruction to meet the needs of your writers.

> *Assessment must promote learning, not just measure it. When learners are well served, assessment becomes a learning experience that supports and improves instruction. The learners are not just the students but also the teachers, who learn something about their students.*
>
> —Regie Routman (1999, 559)

Monitoring students' writing over time provides valuable information about their growth and development. The samples, collected periodically throughout the year into student portfolios, reflect where the Writer's Workshop journey began and the student's ongoing progress and achievement relative to the instructional goals. Portfolios, along with your anecdotal notes, not only inform parents of their child's growth but also show students the variety of concepts and skills learned during Writer's Workshop.

In addition to ongoing classroom assessment, it is valuable to conduct benchmark assessments at the beginning, middle, and end of the year. The beginning of the year benchmark provides you with a baseline of data that represents the foundational skill level of the student writer. The middle and end of the year benchmarks show areas of achievement and needs as well as identify effective instructional strategies. *Getting to the Core of Writing* refers to these benchmarks as Benchmarks 1, 2, and 3 respectively. After each benchmark, it is important to analyze the student's work using the grade-level rubric (pages 263–264; writingrubric.pdf) in order to identify the additional support needed for the student.

Collaborating with other teachers encourages targeted conversations about student work and helps build confidence as you become more knowledgeable in interpreting and evaluating student writing. Although *Getting to the Core of Writing* includes a Suggested Pacing Guide (pages 12–13; pacingguide. pdf) and a Year-at-a-Glance plan of instruction (yearataglance.pdf) that provide benchmark prompt suggestions, it is not a one-size-fits-all classroom writing map. Your assessments and observations provide essential information to guide instructional decisions designed to meet the needs of all of your students. For additional assessment resources, including benchmark support information, a rubric, a scoring guide, a classroom grouping mat, and scored student writing samples, see Appendix B (pages 261– 272).

Planning Writing Instruction

Essential in any literacy development is planning and scheduling. *Getting to the Core of Writing* supports teachers as they learn and grow as writers along with their students while at the same time implementing Writer's Workshop. Growing requires nurturing like writing requires practice. The provided plan of instruction is based on the conviction that Writer's Workshop happens each and every day throughout the school year. Mini-lessons may be retaught, when necessary. Some mini-lessons may require more than one day for students to fully grasp an understanding of the writing concept. Additionally, teachers proficient in writing instruction may select individual mini-lessons and teach them in an order that meets the specific needs of their students.

When writing is shared consistently and enthusiastically, students learn, love, and choose to write. As always, instruction must also be guided by the developmental needs of the students as revealed through their daily writing. The structure provided by Writer's Workshop and the lessons in this book allow both students and teachers to recognize themselves as successful writers. Once the routines of Writer's Workshop are in place, it is much easier for the teacher to focus on a quality daily writing time. Things become so routine that teachers will find themselves feeling motivated and passionate about writing instruction instead of overwhelmed.

The pacing guide found on pages 12–13 provides a suggested sequence for when to teach the lessons in this book. It serves as a guide for consistent practice in the writing process and incorporates the traits of quality writing. It is suggested that some lessons be taught more than once throughout the year. When this occurs, if desired, the content of the student writing pieces can be modified slightly to provide students with opportunities to practice writing opinion-, informative-explanatory-, and narrative-based texts. By doing this, students get to write different genres in formats that are familiar to them. For example, in Ideas Lesson 1, students can change the content about which they brainstorm to create an opinion piece on why dogs are the best pet, a narrative on their summer vacation, and an informative piece on the types of plants around the school.

Planning Writing Instruction (cont.)

Suggested Pacing Guide

Month	Lesson
August/September	• Managing WW Lesson 1 (page 35) • Managing WW Lesson 2 (page 38) • **Administer Benchmark 1:** Sometimes it is fun to imagine what might happen if you found something while walking to school. What might happen if you found a bag and a shoe? Reveal the sequence in a natural way. Use dialogue to add interest. • Managing WW Lesson 3 (page 41) • Managing WW Lesson 4 (page 50) • Managing WW Lesson 5 (page 52) • Managing WW Lesson 6 (page 58) • Organization Lesson 1 (page 139) • Managing WW Lesson 7 (page 62) • Managing WW Lesson 8 (page 65) • Ideas Lesson 1 (page 77) • Conventions Lesson 1 (page 225) • Sentence Fluency Lesson 1 (page 103) • Word Choice Lesson 1 (page 177) • Conventions Lesson 2 (page 228) • Organization Lesson 2 (page 142) • Ideas Lesson 2 (page 80)

Month	Lesson
October	• Review Managing WW Lessons 1–8 as needed. • Managing WW Lesson 9 (page 68) • Managing WW Lesson 10 (page 71) • Ideas Lesson 3 (page 83) • Sentence Fluency Lesson 2 (page 106) • Word Choice Lesson 2 (page 180) • Organization Lesson 3 (page 145) • Voice Lesson 1 (page 209) • Organization Lesson 4 (page 148) • Word Choice Lesson 3 (page 183) • Conventions Lesson 3 (page 231) • Sentence Fluency Lesson 3 (page 110) • Conventions Lesson 4 (page 235) • Ideas Lesson 2 (page 80)

Month	Lesson
November	• Review Managing WW Lessons 1–10 as needed. • Ideas Lesson 4 (page 86) • Organization Lesson 5 (page 151) • Voice Lesson 1 (page 209) • Conventions Lesson 5 (page 239) • Word Choice Lesson 4 (page 187) • Sentence Fluency Lesson 4 (page 117) • Organization Lesson 6 (page 154) • Conventions Lesson 6 (page 242) • Ideas Lesson 2 (page 80) • Publish

Month	Lesson
December	• Review Managing WW Lessons 1–10 as needed. • Ideas Lesson 5 (page 89) • Sentence Fluency Lesson 5 (page 121) • Voice Lesson 2 (page 215) • Organization Lesson 7 (page 158) • Word Choice Lesson 5 (page 190) • Conventions Lesson 3 (page 231) • Word Choice Lesson 6 (page 193) • Conventions Lesson 1 (page 225) • Ideas Lesson 2 (page 80)

Planning Writing Instruction (cont.)

Suggested Pacing Guide (cont.)

Month	Lesson
January	• Review Managing WW Lessons 1–10 as needed. • Ideas Lesson 1 (page 77) • Word Choice Lesson 3 (page 183) • Sentence Fluency Lesson 3 (page 110) • Conventions Lesson 4 (page 235) • Voice Lesson 3 (page 217) • Organization Lesson 7 (page 158) • Word Choice Lesson 7 (page 196) • Sentence Fluency Lesson 6 (page 126) • Organization Lesson 8 (page 161) • Conventions Lesson 7 (page 245) • Ideas Lesson 2 (page 80) • **Administer Benchmark 2:** Eating healthy foods is important. Think about why it is important to eat healthy. What food do you consider to be healthy? Provide details and examples to support your topic.

Month	Lesson
February	• Review Managing WW Lessons 1–10 as needed. • Ideas Lesson 6 (page 92) • Sentence Fluency Lesson 1 (page 103) • Word Choice Lesson 8 (page 199) • Organization Lesson 9 (page 165) • Conventions Lesson 6 (page 242) • Voice Lesson 4 (page 220) • Sentence Fluency Lesson 7 (page 131) • Conventions Lesson 8 (page 248) • Ideas Lesson 2 (page 80)

Month	Lesson
March	• Review Managing WW Lessons 1–10 as needed. • Ideas Lesson 7 (page 95) • Word Choice Lesson 3 (page 183) • Sentence Fluency Lesson 8 (page 134) • Organization Lesson 10 (page 168) • Word Choice Lesson 1 (page 177) • Conventions Lesson 4 (page 235) • Conventions Lesson 7 (page 245) • Ideas Lesson 2 (page 80)

Month	Lesson
April	• Review Managing WW Lessons 1–10 as needed. • Review genre studies based on students' needs. • Ideas Lesson 8 (page 98) • Sentence Fluency Lesson 7 (page 131) • Word Choice Lesson 9 (page 203) • Conventions Lesson 2 (page 228) • Organization Lesson 11 (page 172) • Conventions Lesson 8 (page 248) • Publish Poetry • Ideas Lesson 2 (page 80)

Month	Lesson
May	By this time of the year, students will have mastery of many concepts. And although you may have completed your state writing assessment, it is important to continue writing workshop. Revisit mini-lessons based on students' needs and interests. **Administer Benchmark 3:** Your school is considering changes in the dress code, including requiring students to wear uniforms. What suggestions would you make concerning the dress code policy at your school? Write an essay to convince your readers to agree with your recommendations.

Components of Writer's Workshop

Writer's Workshop entails common characteristics that are essential to developing enthusiastic and successful student writers (Graves 1994, 2003; Fletcher 2001; Calkins 1994; Calkins, Hartman and Zoe 2005; Ray 2001; Ray and Cleaveland 2004; Gentry 2000, 2004, 2010). The guidelines that follow have been time-tested by years of classroom practice and collaboration with master writing teachers. The framework of this structure includes the following: the mini-lesson, writing practice time, and sharing time.

The Mini-Lesson

The mini-lesson is 5–15 minutes in length and begins the workshop. It is an opportunity to review past learning, introduce new writing strategies through modeling, and engage students in practicing those strategies through oral rehearsal. Each mini-lesson is focused on one specific topic that both addresses the needs of writers and reflects these skills as practiced by real authors. The mini-lesson is always energetic and challenges students to participate while building their confidence as writers. Students gather in a common area and become part of a comfortable, safe environment that provides guidance and encouragement.

In the appropriate mini-lessons, introduce the Traits Team poster as a visual reminder for students of the writing traits. The Traits Team includes *Ida, Idea Creator* (page 76); *Simon, Sentence Builder* (page 102); *Owen, Organization Conductor* (page 138); *Wally, Word Choice Dectective* (page 176); *Val and Van, Voice* (page 208); and *Callie, Super Conventions Checker* (page 224). These characters work as a team to show students that good writing is not built one skill at a time but with a team of strategies.

Writing Practice Time

During the 15–30 minute writing practice, students apply the skill, strategy, or craft taught in the mini-lesson. This part of the lesson gives students practice necessary in becoming proficient writers as they compose a message to share with a reader. Simultaneously, the teacher helps individual students or small groups of students compose through conferencing. These conferences provide teachers the opportunity to praise students for applying a strategy, followed by a short teaching point. Teachers document observations in a Conferring Notebook to be used for evaluating students' progress, planning new instruction, and meeting with parents. An important part of the writing practice time is the *Spotlight Strategy*. It calls attention to one or two students briefly each day by spotlighting their work, especially when attempting the focus skill presented in the mini-lesson.

Sharing Time

The 5–15 minutes of sharing echoes the mini-lesson across Writer's Workshop and provides an additional opportunity for student talk time. At the end of the writing practice time, students are invited to spend several minutes sharing with partners, in small groups, or individually in the Author's Chair. Teachers select students to share based on their observations during writing time. A variety of sharing methods is used to promote motivation and excitement. At the end of Writer's Workshop, homework suggestions are made to help students follow up on the mini-lesson ideas. Homework can be shared on the next workshop day.

Implementing the Lessons

Each lesson supports teachers in their writing instruction and encourages students to write like published authors. Consistent language builds a commonality between students as well as across grade levels. Talking about writers, studying other writers, and practicing the craft of writing give students the gift of being authors. While the focus of the lesson may change each day, the lesson routine remains constant. Building routines in any instruction yields smooth transitions between activities and fewer opportunities for distractions. Some mini-lessons may be taught daily while others might be explored across several days. Several mini-lessons can easily be adapted to multiple themes and various pieces of literature, including those listed in the Common Core State Standards Suggested Works. It is important to consider the specific developmental levels and needs of the students. The lesson format provides structure, support, and a framework for instruction for the busy classroom teacher.

Using consistent language during each section of Writer's Workshop is one structure that students will recognize and that will be helpful for smooth transitions. Suggested language for each section of Writer's Workshop is provided in the lessons. Each Writer's Workshop lesson includes the following sections:

- Think About Writing
- Teach
- Engage
- Apply
- Write/Conference
- Spotlight Strategy
- Share
- Homework

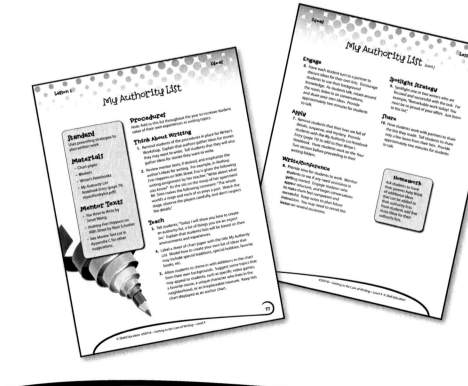

Implementing the Lessons (cont.)

Think About Writing—Students reconnect to past mini-lessons and teachers make authentic connections between reading and writing.

Procedures and **Notes**—Special information and teaching tips, followed by the explicit directions for teaching the lesson.

Standards and **Materials**—Indicates the areas of focus for the lesson and all materials needed.

Mentor Texts—Published writing that contains explicit and strong examples of the concepts addressed in the lesson. Use the recommended mentor text as a read-aloud during your reading block or quickly review it during Writer's Workshop. During the writing block, focus on small samples of text that match the mini-lesson skill. Recommended mentor texts are suggested as part of each lesson. Alternative suggestions can be found in Appendix C or on the Teacher Resource CD (mentortextlist.pdf).

Lesson 1   Ideas

My Authority List

Procedures

Note: Add to this list throughout the year to increase student value of their own experiences as writing topics.

Standard

Uses prewriting strategies to plan written work

Materials

- Chart paper
- Markers
- Writer's Notebooks
- *My Authority List Notebook Entry* (page 79; myauthoritylist.pdf)

Mentor Texts

- *You Have to Write* by Janet Wong
- *Nothing Ever Happens on 90th Street* by Roni Schotter
- See *Mentor Text List* in Appendix C for other suggestions.

Think About Writing

1. Remind students of the procedures in place for Writer's Workshop. Explain that authors gather ideas for stories they may want to write. Tell students that they will also gather ideas for stories they want to write.

2. Review mentor texts, if desired, and emphasize the author's ideas for writing. For example, in *Nothing Ever Happens on 90th Street*, Eva is given the following writing assignment by her teacher: "Write about what you know!" As she sits on the stoop of her apartment Mr. Sims makes the following comment: "The whole world's a stage and each of us plays a part. Watch the stage, observe the players carefully, and don't neglect the details."

Teach

3. Tell students, "Today I will show you how to create an authority list, a list of things you are an expert on." Explain that students' lists will be based on their environments and experiences.

4. Label a sheet of chart paper with the title *My Authority List*. Model how to create your own list of ideas that may include special traditions, special hobbies, favorite books, etc.

5. Allow students to chime in with additions to the chart from their own backgrounds. Suggest some topics that may appeal to students, such as specific video games, a favorite movie, a unique character who lives in the neighborhood, or an irreplaceable treasure. Keep this chart displayed as an anchor chart.

© Shell Education #50918—Getting to the Core of Writing—Level 4   77

Teach—Supports students through demonstration and modeling to help elevate their level of writing.

Implementing the Lessons (cont.)

Engage—Students will talk to each other about what they will apply in their writing. Talk time is short, intense, and focused. The teacher monitors, observes, and offers supportive comments.

Spotlight Strategy—The teacher points out students' efforts and successes, emphasizing a skill or specific task to further student understanding.

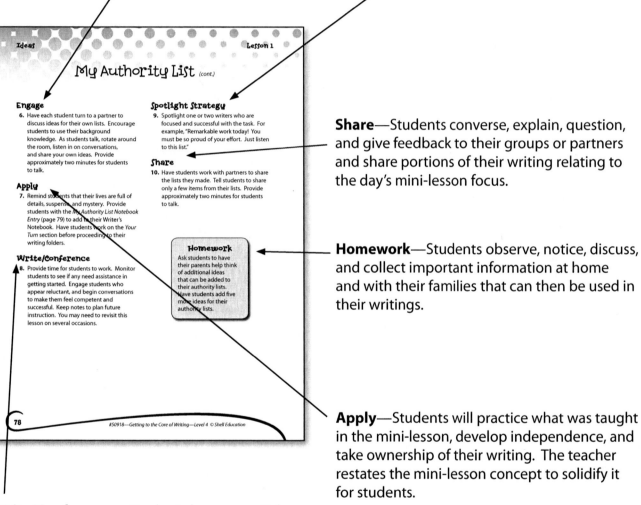

Share—Students converse, explain, question, and give feedback to their groups or partners and share portions of their writing relating to the day's mini-lesson focus.

Homework—Students observe, notice, discuss, and collect important information at home and with their families that can then be used in their writings.

Apply—Students will practice what was taught in the mini-lesson, develop independence, and take ownership of their writing. The teacher restates the mini-lesson concept to solidify it for students.

Write/Conference—Students have essential, independent practice time. The teacher confers with students in one-on-one or small-group settings.

Implementing Writer's Workshop

Writer's Workshop-at-a-Glance

This chart provides an at-a-glance overview of the Writer's Workshop format provided in *Getting to the Core of Writing*. It can be a helpful tool to use when planning instruction.

Component	Time	Description
Mini Lesson	5–15 minutes	Lesson plan subsections include: • Think About Writing • Teach • Engage • Apply

Writing Practice	15–30 minutes	Lesson plan subsections include:
		• Write/Conference
		  • Praise accomplishments
		  • Make a teaching point
		  • Use Conference Log
		• Spotlight Strategies

Sharing	5–15 minutes	Lesson plan subsections include:
		• Share
		  • Whole/small group
		  • Partners
		  • Compliment and comment
		• Homework

The Writing Conference

Writing conferences are most successful when they occur as a conversation between two writers who are simply talking about writing. It is a time to value students as writers, to differentiate instruction, to teach new strategies, and to gather information for forming instructional decisions. Anderson (2000) notes that a conference conversation basically includes two parts: conversation based upon the student's current writing and conversation based on what will help him or her become a better writer. Katie Wood Ray (2001) and Lucy Calkins, Amanda Hartman, and Zoe White (2003) tell us conferring is hard! It is one part of the day that is a bit unknown. When conferring one-on-one with young writers, there is no script—no specific plan developed prior to the meeting. That is a strong deterrent that can keep many teachers from stepping into the conferring role during Writer's Workshop.

Following Calkins, Hartman, and Zoe's dictum: "Conferring is the heart of Writer's Workshop" (2003, VIII), the sharing of information in conference conversation over the development of a specific writing piece is the very heart of teaching writing. Although difficult at times, especially at first, even the smallest conversation lets your students know you are interested in them as writers and helps nudge them forward in their writing development. Just as students become better writers by writing, you will only become better at conferring by conferring. The sincerity with which you approach this task will not only affect your students' writing future but also your sense of accomplishment as a teacher.

Although the content of the conference conversation is unknown, the conference structure is predictable. The four phases of a conference structure are:

1. Observe
2. Praise
3. Guide
4. Connect

First, study to determine what the writer knows, what the writer is trying to do, and what the writer needs to learn. Next, provide praise. Then, develop a teaching point and guide and encourage the writer to practice that teaching point. Lastly, stress the importance of using what was learned in future writing. For a more detailed explanation of each phase, see pages 258–260 in Appendix A.

The Writing Conference (cont.)

Included in Appendix A and on the Teacher Resource CD are additional resources dedicated to the subject of conferring with students.

- **Essential Materials**—Use this list to assemble a "toolkit" of items you can carry with you as you conference with students (page 253).

- **Mini-Lesson Log**—Keep a record of the mini-lessons taught to serve as a reminder of writing strategies and crafts students have been exposed to during whole-group instruction (page 255).

- **Conference Log**—This conference form serves as a good starting point and makes it easy to view your entire class at one glance. It is a simple summary of the conference listing the name, date, praise, and teaching point. See pages 258–260 in Appendix A for more information on conferring steps. Some teachers prefer a separate conference page for each student as they become more familiar with the conferring process (page 256).

- **Conference Countdown**—This page lists simple reminders of salient points to consider during writing conferences (page 257).

When you take the time to have a conversation, you are sending a message that you care enough to listen and communicate. With so much emphasis on testing achievement, it is important to stay committed to teaching the writer and not just the work of the writer. Carl Anderson (2000) tells us that student efforts and achievements are most likely not due to the questions we ask, the feedback we give, or our teaching. He states, "In the end, the success of a conference often rests on the extent to which students sense we are genuinely interested in them as writers—and as individuals."

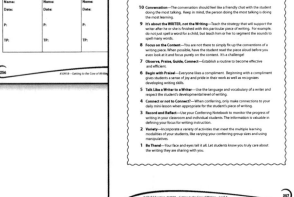

The Writer's Notebook

The Writer's Notebook can be a young writer's best friend, always at his or her side to help out. It is personalized, customized, and interactive. Students can refer back to any mini-lesson taught during the year in Writer's Workshop to refresh their memories or find a tip for moving forward. The Writer's Notebook is like a friend, giving student writers a helping hand when they need guidance or are struggling with a writing skill. Consider this scenario:

The student's pencil taps incessantly on his desk. He's stuck. He can't think of how to begin an informational piece following a jumpstart mini-lesson in Writer's Workshop. The teacher observes the problem, stops by his desk and asks, "How's your writing going?" The student's response is quick and to the point. "Not so good! I don't have anything to write about." Writer's Notebook to the rescue! The teacher invites the student to return to lessons presented months ago, with notebook entries to gather ideas for writing. As the student moves his finger down his customized expert list, his facial expression completely changes from confusion to a brilliant smile. "I've got it," he exclaims with relief. "It's in my list. I know a lot about model volcanoes." "Then off you go!" the teacher replies with a smile.

The notebook is intended as a resource that student writers revisit to dig deeper, gather old ideas, or return to an anthology of mini-lessons taught throughout the year. Previous lessons are readily available and students can return to any lesson at a moment's notice for support. The left side of the notebook holds a glued-in notebook entry sheet designed to help the student with a skill or strategy connected to the writing traits and coordinated to a daily mini lesson. The right side of the notebook is used for individual or partner practice of the specific skill or strategy that was taught. Students move from their Writer's Notebook to writing pieces in their writing folders and apply the notebook entry skills or strategies on their essays, stories, and compositions.

Here are some tips for creating the Writer's Notebook and using them with your students:

- Use inexpensive, well-constructed composition notebooks if possible; however, you may also use spiral-bound notebooks or three-ring binders. Aimee Buckner (2005) tells us to select notebooks that match our style of teaching, the space and time available, and the management of the notebooks. There are a variety of brands available that are often on sale during back-to-school season.

- Encourage students to decorate and personalize their notebooks. This activity can be done in class or you may provide directions and make this a student-and-parent activity for a home connection. Personalizing the notebook with pictures, words, and phrases develops ideas for writing projects. (See page 282 of Appendix D for a sample home connection letter.)

- Store notebooks in a location accessible to students, such as small baskets on desks or shelves. If the Writer's Notebook is easily available, students are more apt to use them as a writing resource.

The Writer's Notebook *(cont.)*

- Copy and cut notebook entry sheets in advance. Notebook entries are easily cut with a paper cutter and are then readily available for students to glue into their notebooks.

- Deliver specific instructions on adding notebook entries. Have materials available so students can add a few dots of glue and have the sheet in the notebook quickly. Develop expectations and routines to save valuable writing time.

- Set up a Table of Contents and create chapter sections:

  1. Managing Writer's Workshop: 10 pages

  2. Ideas: 15 pages

  3. Sentence Fluency: 15 pages

  4. Organization: 15 pages

  5. Word Choice: 15 pages

  6. Voice: 5 Pages

  7. Conventions: 15 pages

  8. Miscellaneous: 5 pages

- Have students number the chapters using flags for ease of management. When teaching a lesson, your prompt should be simple, such as, "Turn to Chapter 4—Organization." Extra pages may be included in each chapter to give teachers the prerogative to add additional lesson ideas for any chapter.

Students react positively to the use of the Writer's Notebook. Ralph Fletcher (1996), author and educational consultant, states, "…the most important tool I use: my writer's notebook. Keeping a writer's notebook is one of the best ways I know of living a writing kind of life." That is exactly the desired response from students as well.

Top 10 Tips for Creating Successful Writers

1. **Schedule Writer's Workshop Daily.** Scheduling Writer's Workshop daily grants valuable, necessary time for students to practice and grow as writers.

2. **Establish and Commit to Routines.** Life is good when everyone knows what to do and when to do it. Take the time to establish foundational routines that will impact your Writer's Workshop throughout the year. Revisit Managing Writer's Workshop lessons as the need arises.

3. **Model, Model, Model!** Modeling gives direct instruction while scaffolding for young writers. Use these steps to model specific skills and behaviors with students (*I* is the teacher and *you* is the student) (Pearson and Gallager 1983):

   - I do, you watch
   - I do, you help
   - You do, I help
   - You do, I watch

4. **Read, Read, Read!** Reading a variety of texts through the eyes of a writer exposes students to the craft of the author and encourages students to explore new avenues of writing.

5. **Display and Celebrate!** Walking down the hallway in a school setting, you can usually get a good idea of the writing that is going on in each classroom. The more students write, the more comfortable they become, and they will want to show off their work. Celebrate student writing and recognize students as writers.

6. **Confer Weekly.** This is your opportunity to learn about each student's writing development. Encourage, guide, and listen.

7. **Share, Share, Share!** Young children love to share everything. Sharing during Writer's Workshop enhances their sense of importance as writers.

8. **Involve and Inform Parents.** Writing is an automatic means of connecting with parents. Wall displays of writing samples show parents how you value their child's writing effort. Hold an Author's Tea and invite parents so they can see first-hand the important writing of their child.

9. **Be Flexible and Reflect.** A well-planned lesson may fall flat. So, go back to the drawing board and ask yourself, "Why?" "What happened?" How can you reteach to make the right connections for students? Take time to reflect on your teaching and student learning.

10. **Set High Expectations.** Be specific with your expectations and articulate clearly what you would like the students to accomplish. Believe in your students' abilities and challenge them to succeed. Every child can be an author.

Correlation to Standards

Shell Education is committed to producing educational materials that are research- and standards-based. In this effort, we have correlated all of our products to the academic standards of all 50 United States, the District of Columbia, the Department of Defense Dependent Schools, and all Canadian provinces. We have also correlated to the **Common Core State Standards**.

How To Find Standards Correlations

To print a customized correlation report of this product for your state, visit our website at **http://www.shelleducation.com** and follow the on-screen directions. If you require assistance in printing correlation reports, please contact Customer Service at 1-877-777-3450.

Purpose and Intent of Standards

Legislation mandates that all states adopt academic standards that identify the skills students will learn in kindergarten through grade twelve. Many states also have standards for Pre-K. This same legislation sets requirements to ensure the standards are detailed and comprehensive.

Standards are designed to focus instruction and guide adoption of curricula. Standards are statements that describe the criteria necessary for students to meet specific academic goals. They define the knowledge, skills, and content students should acquire at each level. Standards are also used to develop standardized tests to evaluate students' academic progress. Teachers are required to demonstrate how their lessons meet state standards. State standards are used in the development of all of our products, so educators can be assured they meet the academic requirements of each state.

McREL Compendium

We use the Mid-continent Research for Education and Learning (McREL) Compendium to create standards correlations. Each year, McREL analyzes state standards and revises the compendium. By following this procedure, McREL is able to produce a general compilation of national standards. Each lesson in this product is based on one or more McREL standard. The chart on pages 25–27 and on the Teacher Resource CD (standards.pdf) lists each standard taught in this product and the page number(s) for the corresponding lesson(s).

TESOL Standards

The lessons in this book promote English language development for English language learners. The standards listed on the Teacher Resource CD (standards.pdf) support the language objectives presented throughout the lessons.

Common Core State Standards

The lessons in this book are aligned to the Common Core State Standards (CCSS). The standards on pages 28–30 and on the Teacher Resource CD (standards.pdf) support the objectives presented throughout the lessons.

Correlation to Standards (cont.)

McREL Standards

Standard	Lesson
Understands the structure of Writer's Workshop	Components of Writer's Workshop (page 35); Our Group Meeting (page 38); The Writing Folder (page 41); The Writer's Notebook (page 50); Organizing the Writer's Notebook (page 52); Sharing (page 58); Turn and Talk (page 62); Guidelines for Writer's Workshop (page 65); Teacher and Peer Conferences (page 68); The Five-Step Writing Process (page 71)
Prewriting: Uses prewriting strategies to plan written work	My Authority List (page 77); Authors as Mentors (page 80); Interesting Places (page 83); The Best Times! The Worst Times! (page 86); Brainstorming Boxes (page 89); What Should We Write? (page 92); Pocket of Picture Topics (page 95); I Wonder List (page 98)
Drafting and Revising: Uses strategies to draft and revise written work	Circle and Count (page 103); Subject + Predicate = Sentence (page 106); Sentence Search (page 110); Appositive Action (page 117); Compound Sentences (page 121); Writing Complex Sentences (page 126); Stepping Up Sentences (page 131); Building Triangle Sentences (page 134); Creating Cinquains (page 139); Powerful Paragraphs (page 142); Narrative Notes (page 145); Build-a-Character (page 148); Story Building Blocks (page 151); It's a Bear Beginning (page 154); Don't You Agree? (page 158); It's Your Business (page 161); How-To Writing (page 165); Composition Planner (page 168); A Cache of Poetry (page 172); Digging into Editing (page 248)
Editing and Publishing: Uses strategies to edit and publish written work	The Color of CUPS (page 235); Show Me Editing (page 242); Traits Team Checklist (page 245); Digging into Editing (page 248)
Evaluates own and others' writing	All lessons
Writes expository compositions	How-To Writing (page 165); Composition Planner (page 168)
Writes narrative accounts, such as poems and stories	Creating Cinquains (page 139); Narrative Notes (page 145); Build-a-Character (page 148); Story Building Blocks (page 151) It's a Bear Beginning (page 154); A Cache of Poetry (page 172)

Correlation to Standards (cont.)

McREL Standards (cont.)

Standard	Lesson
Writes expressive compositions	Show Me Your Voice (page 209); What's My Voice? (page 215); The Voices on the Bus (page 217) Various Voices (page 220)
Writes personal letters	It's Your Business (page 161)
Writes opinion compositions	Don't You Agree? (page 158)
Uses descriptive and precise language that clarifies and enhances ideas	Stupendous Similes (page 177); Be a Word Wizard (page 180); Connecting Ideas (page 183); Put "Said" to Bed (page 187); COW to WOW (page 190); Auspicious Adjectives (page 193); Be Explicitly Specific (page 196); Adverb Alert (page 199); Alliteration Action (page 203); The Voices on the Bus (page 217)
Uses paragraph form in writing	Powerful Paragraphs (page 142)
Uses a variety of sentence structures in writing	Circle and Count (page 103); Subject + Predicate = Sentence (page 106); Sentence Search (page 110); Appositive Action (page 117); Compound Sentences (page 121); Writing Complex Sentences (page 126); Stepping Up Sentences (page 131); Building Triangle Sentences (page 134)
Uses nouns in written compositions	Be Explicitly Specific (page 196)
Uses adjectives in written compositions	Auspicious Adjectives (page 193); Be Explicitly Specific (page 196)
Uses adverbs in written compositions	Adverb Alert (page 199)
Links ideas using connecting words	Connecting Ideas (page 183)
Uses conventions of spelling in written compositions	Super Spellers (page 228); The Color of CUPS (page 235); Show Me Editing (page 242); Digging into Editing (page 248)
Uses conventions of capitalization in written compositions	Capital Creations (page 225); The Color of CUPS (page 235); Show Me Editing (page 242); Digging into Editing (page 248)

Correlation to Standards (cont.)

McREL Standards (cont.)

Standard	Lesson
Uses conventions of punctuation in written compositions	Common Comma Conventions (page 231); The Color of CUPS (page 235); Dandy Dialogue (page 239); Show Me Editing (page 242); Digging into Editing (page 248)
Contributes to group discussions	All lessons
Responds to questions and comments	All lessons
Listens to classmates and adults	All lessons
Uses level-appropriate vocabulary in speech	All lessons
Listens for specific information in spoken texts	All lessons

Correlation to Standards (cont.)

Common Core State Standards

The purpose of the Common Core State Standards is to guarantee that all students are prepared for college and career literacy as they leave high school. These standards indicate that all students need the ability to write logical opinions and informational texts with sound reasoning to support their findings. *Getting to the Core of Writing* provides the fundamental writing skills to support students in their continued growth as writers, thus enabling them to enjoy continued success as the challenges presented by the curriculum become increasingly complex.

The structure of Writer's Workshop and the lessons in this book address the Common Core State Standards for **writing**. They also address **speaking and listening** standards, which are the building blocks of written language, through the Engage and Share components of the lesson. Due to the reciprocal nature of reading and writing, *Getting to the Core of Writing* naturally meets many of the Common Core State Standards for **reading** and for **language** as well. The standards below can also be found on the Teacher Resource CD (standards.pdf).

Standard	Lesson
Writing: Text Types and Purposes, W.4.1.	Don't You Agree? (page 158); It's Your Business (page 161)
Writing: Text Types and Purposes, W.4.2.	Powerful Paragraphs (page 142); How-To Writing (page 165); Composition Planner (page 168)
Writing: Text Types and Purposes, W.4.3.	Narrative Notes (page 145); Build-a-Character (page 148); Story Building Blocks (page 151); It's a Bear Beginning (page 154)
Writing: Production and Distribution of Writing, W.4.4.	All lessons in Ideas (pages 77–100); All lessons in Sentence Fluency (pages 103–136); All lessons in Organization (pages 139–174); All lessons in Word Choice (pages 177–205); All lessons in Voice (pages 209–221); All lessons in Conventions (pages 225–251)

Correlation to Standards *(cont.)*

Common Core State Standards *(cont.)*

Standard	Lesson
Writing: Production and Distribution of Writing, W.4.5.	All lessons in Ideas (pages 77–100); All lessons in Sentence Fluency (pages 103–136); All lessons in Organization (pages 139–174); All lessons in Word Choice (pages 177–205); All lessons in Voice (pages 209–221); All lessons in Conventions (pages 225–251)
Writing: Research to Build and Present Knowledge, W.4.7.	I Wonder List (page 98); Composition Planner (page 168)
Writing: Research to Build and Present Knowledge, W.4.9.	Build-a-Character (page 148); Story Building Blocks (page 151); Narrative Notes (page 165)
Writing: Range of Writing, W.4.10.	All lessons in Ideas (pages 77–100); All lessons in Sentence Fluency (pages 103–136); All lessons in Organization (pages 139–174); All lessons in Word Choice (pages 177–205); All lessons in Voice (pages 209–221); All lessons in Conventions (pages 225–251)
Speaking and Listening: Comprehension and Collaboration, SL.4.1.	All lessons
Speaking and Listening: Presentation of Knowledge and Ideas, SL.4.6.	All lessons

Correlation to Standards (cont.)

Common Core State Standards (cont.)

Standard	Lesson
Language: Conventions of Standard English, L.4.1.	Circle and Count (page 103); Subject + Predicate = Sentence (page 106); Sentence Search (page 110); Appositive Action (page 117); Compound Sentences (page 121); Writing Complex Sentences (page 126); Stepping Up Sentences (page 131); Building Triangle Sentences (page 134); Auspicious Adjectives (page 193); Be Explicitly Specific (page 196); Adverb Alert (page 199)
Language: Conventions of Standard English, L.4.2.	Capital Creations (page 225); Super Spellers (page 228); Common Comma Conventions (page 231); The Color of CUPS (page 235); Dandy Dialogue (page 239); Show Me Editing (page 242); Trait's Team Checklist (page 245); Digging into Editing (page 248)
Language: Knowledge of Language, L4.3.	All lessons
Language: Vocabulary Acquisition and Use, L.4.5.	Stupendous Similes (page 177); Alliteration Action (page 203)
Language: Vocabulary Acquisition and Use, L.4.6.	All lessons

Acknowledgments

We stand on the shoulders of national and world-renowned teachers of teachers-of-writing, such as our friend the late Donald Graves, Lucy Calkins, Ralph Fletcher, Donald Murry, Vicki Spandel, Ruth Culham, Katie Wood Ray, Carl Anderson, Charles Temple, Jean Gillet, Stephanie Harvey, Debbie Miller, Regie Routman, Marissa Moss, Steve Graham, and Connie Hebert to name a few, as well as educators at Northwest Regional Educational Laboratory. Thank you. We are also truly grateful to the faculty at Auckland University, workshop leaders, and experiences with the teachers in New Zealand some 20 years ago who got us started.

While writing this series and in the past, there were frequent chats about writing and words of wisdom from Dona Rice, Sara Johnson, Jean Mann, Lois Bridges, and Tim Rasinski. Scores of teachers who read our manuscripts, praised our work, gave us confidence, and adjusted our missteps. We could not have succeeded without two super editors, Dona and Sara, and the great staff at Teacher Created Materials/Shell Education.

We attribute much of what's good about our series to teachers who invited us into their classrooms. Over all the years that went into this project, there are too many people to list separately, but here's a sampling: Thank you to all the teachers and districts who allowed us to visit and model in your classrooms, try our materials, and listen to your insights as we refined our writing instruction. A special thank you to the teachers at Fayette, Logan, Mingo, Pocahontas, Upshur, Wood, Wirt, and Harrison County Schools. We owe special gratitude to French Creek Elementary, Mt. Hope Elementary, and Nutter Fort Elementary teachers. We can't forget the "Writing Teachers Club": Debbie Gaston, Tammy Musil, Judy McGinnis, Jenna Williams, Cheryl Bramble, Karen Vandergrift, Barb Compton, Whitney Fowler, and Jennifer Rome, who spent countless hours learning, questioning, and sharing ideas. "You really need to write a book," you said, and your words have made that happen. You and many others inspired us, including the WC Department of Teaching and Learning (especially Angel, Karen, Lesley, Marcia, Matt, M.C., and Wendy). We can't forget Jean Pearcy, Miles 744, the talented teachers of the West Clermont Schools, the 4 Bs (Bailey, Bergen, Blythe, and Brynne), Candy, Mrs. Hendel, the lab rats (Becky, Mary, Mike, Sally, Sharon, and Vera), and the littlest singers at CHPC. Last but not least, a special thank you to Rick and Ro Jensen, Bill McIntyre, and Carolyn Meigs for years of support, and to Dawna Vecchio, Loria Reid, Terry Morrison, Laura Trent, Jeanie Bennett, Millie Shelton, Therese E., and Kathy Snyder for listening, cheering, and celebrating!

Many thanks to administrators who provided opportunities, leadership, and support for teachers as they explored the implementation of writing workshop and applied new teaching strategies: superintendents Beverly Kingery, Susan Collins, director Kay Devono, principals Allen Gorrell, Frank Marino, Joann Gilbert, Pattae Kinney, Jody Decker, Vickie Luchuck, Jody Johnson, and Wilma Dale. We owe many thanks to WVDE Cadre for continuous professional development—you brought us together.

We owe immense gratitude for having been blessed with the company of children who have graced us with their writing, creativity, and wisdom. Thank you to hundreds of children who have shared marvelous writing and insight.

Finally, for never-ending patience, love and support we thank our families: Clint, Luke, and Lindsay; Lanty, Jamey, John, Charlie, Jacki, Jeffrey; and Bill. You all are the best!

About the Authors

Richard Gentry, Ph.D., is nationally recognized for his work in spelling, phase theory, beginning reading and writing, and teaching literacy in elementary school. A former university professor and elementary school teacher, his most recent book is *Raising Confident Readers: How to Teach Your Child to Read and Write—From Baby to Age 7*. Other books include topics such as beginning reading and writing, assessment, and spelling. He also blogs for *Psychology Today* magazine. Richard has spoken at state and national conferences and has provided teachers with inspiring strategies to use in their classroom.

Jan McNeel, M.A.Ed., is a forty-year veteran of education and leader of staff development throughout West Virginia and Maryland. Formerly a Reading First Cadre Member for the West Virginia Department of Education and Title I classroom and Reading Recovery teacher, Jan consults with schools and districts across the state. Jan's studies of literacy acquisition at the Auckland University in New Zealand serve as the foundation of her expertise in reading and writing. Her practical strategies and useful ideas are designed to make reading and writing connections that are teacher-friendly and easy to implement. She has won awards for her excellent work as a master teacher and has presented her work in early literacy at state, regional, and national conferences.

Vickie Wallace-Nesler, M.A.Ed., has been in education for 30 years as an itinerant, Title 1, and regular classroom teacher. Through her current work as a Literacy Coach for grades K–5, conference presenter, and literacy consultant, Vickie brings true insight into the "real world" of educators and their challenges. That experience, along with Master's degrees in both Elementary Education and Reading, National Board certification in Early and Middle Literacy for Reading and Language Arts, and studies at The Teachers College Reading and Writing Project at Columbia University, drive her passion for helping all teachers and students develop a love for learning.

Managing Writer's Workshop

Writer's Workshop begins on the first day of school and is taught every day thereafter. Establishing routines is critical to developing a successful, productive writing time. Therefore, Managing Writer's Workshop lessons should be focused on early in the year and revisited when necessary. The mini-lessons require time and repetition to develop automaticity during Writer's Workshop. A wide range of topics can be addressed during management mini-lessons. Repeat mini-lessons as needed, especially on the topics of guidelines for Writer's Workshop and having students share their writing with partners. These two particular lessons will be crucial to having Writer's Workshop run smoothly and successfully for the rest of the year. Ensure students are responding to those lessons in the ways you want them to, or spend additional time teaching and modeling. Observe your class to find the needs of your particular students. Lessons in this section include:

- Lesson 1: Components of Writer's Workshop (page 35)
- Lesson 2: Our Group Meeting (page 38)
- Lesson 3: The Writing Folder (page 41)
- Lesson 4: The Writer's Notebook (page 50)
- Lesson 5: Organizing the Writer's Notebook (page 52)
- Lesson 6: Sharing (page 58)
- Lesson 7: Turn and Talk (page 62)
- Lesson 8: Guidelines for Writer's Workshop (page 65)
- Lesson 9: Teacher and Peer Conferences (page 68)
- Lesson 10: The Five-Step Writing Process (page 71)

Components of Writer's Workshop

Standard

Understands the structure of Writer's Workshop

Materials

• Model writing folder

• Model Writer's Notebook

• *Components of Writer's Workshop Anchor Chart* (page 37; writersworkshop.pdf)

Mentor Texts

• *A Writer's Notebook* by Ralph Fletcher

• *Amelia's Notebook* by Marissa Moss

• See *Mentor Text List* in Appendix C for other suggestions.

Procedures

Note: Create a model writing folder and Writer's Notebook to share with students. After students create their own notebooks (Managing Writer's Workshop Lesson 4), review the Components of Writer's Workshop and have students add the notebook entry to the Organization section of their Writer's Notebook.

Think About Writing

1. Introduce the concept of Writer's Workshop to students. For example, "During this time, we will explore and practice becoming writers. We will meet together, practice writing, and share our writing with each other. This time will be called Writer's Workshop. We will follow procedures so everyone knows what is expected at each point during our Writer's Workshop time."

2. Read quotes from the mentor texts by Ralph Fletcher and Marissa Moss, if desired.

Teach

3. Tell students, "Today I will show you the schedule we will use during Writer's Workshop so you can use your writing time wisely."

4. Explain that there will always be three components to the writing schedule.

   • "We will have a daily group meeting where we pull together as a community of writers to get information. This is called a mini-lesson."

   • "You will have time to write quietly about an idea or an experience in your life. While you write, I will meet with you to talk about your writing projects."

   • "We will come back together to share our thoughts, ideas, successes, or concerns."

Components of Writer's Workshop *(cont.)*

5. Tell students that they will have a short homework assignment each night that requires them to think about writing, talk to their families about writing, or make observations.

Engage

6. Review the three components of Writer's Workshop by naming each part: mini-lesson, student writing time, and sharing. Then have students repeat each part in turn.

Apply

7. Display the *Components of Writer's Workshop Anchor Chart* (page 37). Remind students that the three components of Writer's Workshop will help them become accomplished writers. Practice making transitions by moving students to where they will be located for each component of Writer's Workshop. For example, students may be sitting on the rug during the mini-lesson, at their desks for writing, and meeting with a partner, triad, or quad for sharing.

8. Tell students that today will be a free-write day where the writing topic is their choice; however, they must be writing for the entire time.

Write/Conference

9. Provide time for students to write. Do not conference today. Practice moving students through the schedule to help them internalize your management system; then practice sustained writing time.

Spotlight Strategy

10. Spotlight students who know exactly how to move to each designated area without the loss of one moment of writing time. A suggestion is to use a small flashlight, which can be shined on students to spotlight them. Remember to provide lots of praise during these introductory days of Writer's Workshop.

Share

11. Ask students to meet with partners to name and explain the focus of the three components of Writer's Workshop. Provide approximately two minutes for students to share. Choose one or two students who clearly understood the idea and have them share with the whole group.

Homework

Ask students to write the three components of Writer's Workshop on a sheet of paper and share it with their parents.

Components of Writer's Workshop Anchor Chart

Writer's Workshop

Easy as 1-2-3

1 Mini-Lesson

We will learn the writing process and study the writing of other authors.

2 Writing Time

We will practice new ideas, tools, and strategies in our writing.

3 Sharing

We will talk about our writing with our peers.

Our Group Meeting

Standard
Understands the structure of Writer's Workshop

Materials
- *Sample Looks Like, Sounds Like, Feels Like Anchor Chart* (page 40; lookssoundsfeelschart.pdf)
- Chart paper
- Markers

Mentor Texts
- *A Writer's Notebook* by Ralph Fletcher
- *Amelia's Notebook* by Marissa Moss
- See *Mentor Text List* in Appendix C for other suggestions.

Procedures
Note: Decide on an area in your room that will serve as a meeting place. You will need to repeat this lesson until the procedure is in place. Build solid routines. To build excitement, share your Writer's Notebook and folder in preparation for future lessons.

Think About Writing
1. Explain to students that today they will begin building an understanding of what a community of writers looks like, sounds like, and feels like.

2. Share from mentor texts, if desired.

Teach
3. Tell students, "Today I will show you how to work in Writer's Workshop with minimal noise and no confusion."

4. Model where and how to sit during the mini-lesson component of Writer's Workshop. You may wish to begin at a student's desk to show students exactly what they will do when they get ready for a mini-lesson. Then have students emulate what you modeled. Practice moving students several times. Throughout modeling and practicing, provide plenty of praise to students. It is important to draw attention to expected behaviors through praise and recognition. Repeat this same procedure for the other components of Writer's Workshop on subsequent days.

5. Begin an anchor chart to record students' observations of what Writer's Workshop will look like, sound like, and feel like. Add to the anchor chart over the next several days as students become familiar with the routines. Use the *Sample Looks Like, Sounds Like, Feels Like Anchor Chart* (page 40) to help guide students as they add information to the chart your class creates.

Our Group Meeting *(cont.)*

Engage

6. Have students tell partners how to move to the community meeting area for mini-lessons.

Apply

7. Remind students that it is important to move quickly to the meeting area so that precious instructional time is not lost. Tell students that today will be a free-write day.

Write/Conference

8. Provide students with paper and have them write for seven minutes. As students work, observe and rotate among them to solve problems. Procedures must be solidly in place to get students moving toward independence in Writer's Workshop.

Spotlight Strategy

9. Spotlight students who move quickly and quietly to and from the meeting area and began to transition into free-writing. Remember to provide lots of praise during these early days of Writer's Workshop.

Share

10. Have students meet with partners and share what they wrote today. Provide approximately two minutes for students to share. Choose one or two students who clearly understand the idea and have them share with the whole group.

Homework

Ask students to think about how important it is to move quickly and quietly during Writer's Workshop. Have students write two reasons why having this routine in place will help them as they work.

Sample Looks Like, Sounds Like, Feels Like Anchor Chart

Our Writer's Workshop…

Looks Like	Sounds Like	Feels Like
• Pencils, all supplies ready	• Buzz, hum, beehive	• Comfortable, natural, happy
• Journals/folders/notebooks	• Two-inch voices	• Nonthreatening, risk taking
• Crayons/art paper	• Conversation/oral language	• Purposeful
• Word walls	• Quiet during thinking and teaching phase	• Successful
• Mentor texts available	• "Hum" when sharing w/ partners, triads, quads	• Confident
• Phonics charts/alphabet charts	• Busy	• Excited
• Labeled items in the room	• Children making decisions	• Relaxed
• Author's chair	• Learning is happening	• Proud
• Partners/small groups	• Questioning	• Comfortable sharing thoughts
• Smiling faces		• "I can" attitude
• Writing tool kits		
• Student engagement		
• Vocabulary list		
• Writing prompts		
• Turn and talk		
• Productive		
• Organized		
• Writing		
• Busy		

#50918—Getting to the Core of Writing—Level 4 © Shell Education

The Writing Folder

Standard

Understands the structure of Writer's Workshop

Materials

- Two-pocket folders with fasteners
- Red and green dot stickers
- *Student Mini-Lesson Log* (page 43; minilessonlog2.pdf)
- Reference inserts:

  Dolch Sight Word List (page 44; dolchwordlist.pdf)

  Fry Sight Word List (page 45; frywordlist.pdf)

  Short and Long Vowel Charts (pages 46–47; shortlongvowelcharts.pdf)

  Vowel Teams Chart (pages 48–49; vowelteamschart.pdf)
- Model writing folder
- Protective sleeves

Mentor Texts

- *A Writer's Notebook* by Ralph Fletcher
- *Amelia's Notebook* by Marissa Moss
- See *Mentor Text List* in Appendix C for other suggestions.

Procedures

Note: Implement this lesson over several days. It is important to model and explain how each reference insert can serve as a helpful tool for student writing projects. If not explicitly taught, students will not recognize the value and usefulness of these resources.

Think About Writing

1. Explain to students that they will organize a folder to hold their writing projects for this school year. Tell students that they will keep records of mini-lessons, and at the end of each month, they will clean their folders. Writing projects they want to save will go into their Showcase Writing Folder, and drafts not wanted will be stapled with the *Student Mini-Lesson Log* (page 43) and taken home for their personal records.

2. Review mentor texts, if desired.

Teach

3. Tell students, "Today I will show you how to organize your writing folder."

4. Distribute folders, red and green dot stickers, the *Student Mini-Lesson Log* (page 43), and the reference inserts (pages 44–49) to students. Use the following steps to help students set up their writing folders.

   - Have students place a green dot sticker on the inside, left pocket. Explain that this will hold writing projects that are still in progress. It will also hold the *Student Mini-Lesson Log* for keeping records of what they are learning. Have students record a short note about each mini-lesson on the mini-lesson log on all subsequent days.

   - Have students place a red dot sticker on the inside, right pocket. Explain that this pocket will hold all the writing pieces that are finished. These will be taken home or stored at school to show students' growth as writers.

The Writing Folder (cont.)

- Tell students that the reference inserts you have given them are important tools to help them in their writing. Show students how to put the reference inserts into protective sleeves and fasten them in the writing folders.

- Share what a completed writing folder looks like.

Engage

5. Have students explain to partners the different parts of the writing folder and what each is for. Provide approximately two minutes for students to share.

Apply

6. Review with students the importance of having a personalized and organized writing folder. Provide students time to decorate their writing folders. Tell students that when they are finished, they should take out a sheet of paper and free-write.

Write/Conference

7. Allow time for students to work on their writing folders, depending on the developmental levels of your students.

Spotlight Strategy

8. Spotlight students that are following directions, sustaining themselves, and practicing organizational strategies.

Share

9. No sharing time today.

Homework

Ask students to think about all of the things that happen in their lives that would make good stories. Have students make a list of three things they would like to write about. Tell students to be ready to start writing tomorrow.

Name:_____

Student Mini-Lesson Log

Date	I am learning to . . .	I can use this strategy in my writing.

Dolch Sight Word List

Aa	Cc (cont.)	Hh	Mm (cont.)	Ss	Uu
a	could	had	may	said	under
about	cut	has	me	saw	up
after	**Dd**	have	much	say	upon
again	did	he	must	see	us
all	do	help	my	seven	use
always	does	her	myself	shall	**Vv**
am	don't	here	**Nn**	she	very
an	done	him	never	sing	**Ww**
and	down	his	new	sit	walk
any	draw	hold	no	six	want
are	drink	hot	not	sleep	warm
around	**Ee**	how	now	slow	was
as	eat	hurt	**Oo**	small	wash
ask	eight	**Ii**	of	so	we
at	every	I	off	some	well
ate	**Ff**	if	old	soon	went
away	fall	in	on	start	were
Bb	far	into	once	stop	what
be	fast	is	one	**Tt**	when
because	find	it	only	take	where
been	first	its	open	tell	which
before	five	**Jj**	or	ten	white
best	fly	jump	our	thank	who
better	for	just	out	that	why
big	found	**Kk**	over	the	will
black	four	keep	own	their	wish
blue	from	kind	**Pp**	them	with
both	full	know	pick	then	work
bring	funny	**Ll**	play	there	would
brown	**Gg**	laugh	please	these	write
but	gave	let	pretty	they	**Yy**
buy	get	light	pull	think	yellow
by	give	like	put	this	yes
Cc	go	little	**Rr**	those	you
call	goes	live	ran	three	yours
came	going	long	read	to	
can	good	look	red	today	
carry	got	**Mm**	ride	together	
clean	green	made	right	too	
cold	grow	make	round	try	
come		many	run	two	

Fry Sight Word List

First 100

a	before	get	I	me	out	there	when
about	boy	give	if	much	put	they	which
after	but	go	in	my	said	this	who
again	by	good	is	new	see	three	will
all	can	had	it	no	she	to	with
an	come	has	just	not	so	two	work
and	day	have	know	of	some	up	would
any	did	he	like	old	take	us	you
are	do	her	little	on	that	very	your
as	down	here	long	one	the	was	
at	eat	him	make	or	there	we	
be	four	his	man	other	them	were	
been	from	how	many	our	then	what	

Second 100

also	box	five	leave	name	pretty	stand	use
am	bring	found	left	near	ran	such	want
another	call	four	let	never	read	sure	way
away	came	friend	live	next	red	tell	where
back	color	girl	look	night	right	than	while
ball	could	got	made	only	run	these	white
because	dear	hand	may	open	saw	thing	wish
best	each	high	men	over	say	think	why
better	ear	home	more	own	school	too	year
big	end	house	morning	people	seem	tree	
black	far	into	most	play	shall	under	
book	find	kind	mother	please	should	until	
both	first	last	must	present	soon	upon	

Third 100

along	clothes	eyes	green	letter	ride	small	walk
always	coat	face	grow	longer	round	start	warm
anything	cold	fall	hat	light	same	stop	wash
around	cut	fast	happy	love	sat	ten	water
ask	didn't	fat	hard	money	second	thank	woman
ate	does	fine	head	myself	set	third	write
bed	dog	fire	hear	now	seven	those	yellow
brown	don't	fly	help	o'clock	show	though	yes
buy	door	food	hold	off	sing	today	yesterday
car	dress	full	hope	once	sister	took	
carry	early	funny	hot	order	sit	town	
clean	eight	gave	jump	pair	six	try	
close	every	goes	keep	part	sleep	turn	

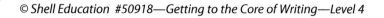

Short and Long Vowel Charts

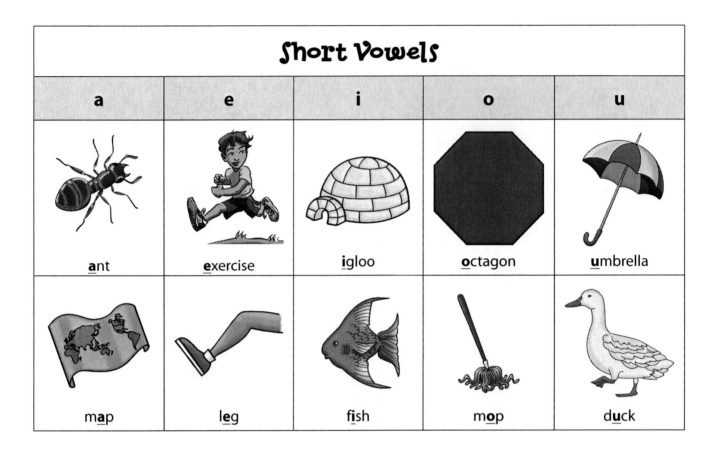

Short Vowels				
a	**e**	**i**	**o**	**u**
ant	exercise	igloo	octagon	umbrella
map	leg	fish	mop	duck

Short and Long Vowel Charts *(cont.)*

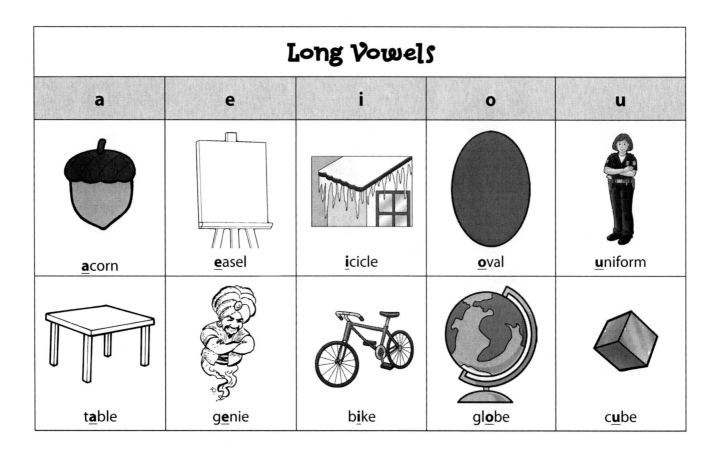

Long Vowels				
a	**e**	**i**	**o**	**u**
acorn	**e**asel	**i**cicle	**o**val	**u**niform
t**a**ble	g**e**nie	b**i**ke	gl**o**be	c**u**be

Vowel Teams Chart

CVCe	CVCe	CVCe	CVCe	ai
cave	kite	nose	mule	rain
ay	ea	ee	oa	oe
hay	eagle	cheese	boat	toe
ie	ue	au	aw	ew
tie	glue	sauce	hawk	news

#50918—*Getting to the Core of Writing—Level 4* © Shell Education

Vowel Teams Chart (cont.)

oi	oy	ou	ow	oo
o̲i̲l	t**oy**s	h**ou**se	c**ow**	m**oo**n
ar	ur	ir	or	er
guit**ar**	t**ur**tle	sk**ir**t	h**or**n	flow**er**

The Writer's Notebook

Standard

Understands the structure of Writer's Workshop

Materials

- Model Writer's Notebook
- Composition, spiral, or 3-ring notebooks
- Scissors
- Glue
- Materials and photos for decorating

Mentor Texts

- *A Writer's Notebook* by Ralph Fletcher
- *Amelia's Notebook* by Marissa Moss
- See *Mentor Text List* in Appendix C for other suggestions.

Procedures

Note: The notebook will be the foundation of the lessons that will follow. Give students the opportunity to decorate, love, and personalize their notebooks. Create a feeling of excitement and allow the time needed to send them on this exciting journey. Allow students the time to collect mementos from home or have magazines available for them to cut and paste to decorate their notebooks. Cover the notebooks with contact paper to help preserve them.

Think About Writing

1. Explain to students that today, they will be thinking and talking about how writers use a special Writer's Notebook. Tell them that just like Fletcher or Moss, the contents of their Writer's Notebooks is going to be unique.

2. Review mentor texts, if desired, and emphasize the use of a notebook. For example, in *Amelia's Notebook*, Amelia writes and draws her feelings about a number of her life experiences.

Teach

3. Tell students, "Today I will show you how to create your own Writer's Notebook." Share your model Writer's Notebook with students. Tell students why you selected the items on your cover, emphasizing how the items generate ideas for writing.

4. Explain to students that a Writer's Notebook is filled with special ideas and thoughts about an author's observations and experiences. Tell students that you will give them information to add to their notebooks that will help them as they write.

The Writer's Notebook *(cont.)*

Engage

5. Have students tell partners how they plan to personalize their Writer's Notebook. Listen in on conversations, making anecdotal notes. Select several students to share their thoughts and point out brilliant comments.

Apply

6. Distribute blank notebooks and materials to students. Review with students that their notebooks will be the place to keep ideas and strategies for writing. Explain that each notebook will be unique as they work to personalize them.

Write/Conference

7. Provide materials and time for students to personalize their Writer's Notebook. Be available to assist, problem solve, and observe.

Spotlight Strategy

8. Spotlight students who have begun personalizing their notebooks.

Share

9. Have students meet with someone new and share how their special Writer's Notebook is progressing. Through observations, select one or two students to share with the whole group.

Homework

Ask students to tell their parents about how they are personalizing their Writer's Notebook. Ask students to bring a few mementos or pictures to add to the covers of their notebooks.

Organizing the Writer's Notebook

Standard

Understands the structure of Writer's Workshop

Materials

- *Traits of Writing Notebook Entry* (page 54; traitswriting.pdf)
- Chart paper
- Markers
- Writer's Notebooks
- Glue
- *Traits Team Mini Posters* (pages 55–57; traitsteamposters.pdf)

Mentor Texts

- *A Writer's Notebook* by Ralph Fletcher
- *Amelia's Notebook* by Marissa Moss
- Books by favorite authors, such as Eve Bunting, Patricia Polacco, Cynthia Rylant, etc.
- See *Mentor Text List* in Appendix C for other suggestions.

Procedures

Note: Notebook entries are always glued on the left side of the notebook and skills are practiced on the right. The notebook is arranged into sections as described in Step 4 below.

Think About Writing

1. Remind students that the class has been establishing Writer's Workshop routines and creating personal Writer's Notebooks.

2. Review mentor texts, if desired. Authors often integrate all the writing traits in their stories.

Teach

3. Tell students, "Today I will show you each of the writing traits and how we will use them to organize our Writer's Notebooks." Explain that there are six very important keys to writing success, called the *traits of writing*. Display the *Traits of Writing Notebook Entry* (page 54). Briefly explain each trait to students: Ideas, Sentence Fluency, Organization, Word Choice, Voice, and Conventions.

4. Share how to organize the Writer's Notebook as you develop a classroom anchor chart on a sheet of chart paper with the following information:

> *Table of Contents*
>
> *Chapter 1: Managing Writer's Workshop* (10 pages)
>
> *Chapter 2: Ideas* (15 pages)
>
> *Chapter 3: Sentence Fluency* (15 pages)
>
> *Chapter 4: Organization* (15 pages)
>
> *Chapter 5: Word Choice* (15 pages)
>
> *Chapter 6: Voice* (5 pages)
>
> *Chapter 7: Conventions* (15 pages)
>
> *Chapter 8: Assessment* (5 pages)

Organizing the Writer's Notebook (cont.)

5. Have students copy the Table of Contents into the front of their notebooks.

6. Model how to glue the *Traits of Writing Notebook Entry* on the first page of the Managing Writer's Workshop section of the notebook. Show students how to count the appropriate number of blank pages in each section and glue the *Traits Team Mini Posters* (pages 55–57) on the first page of each section of the Writer's Notebook.

Engage

7. Have students talk with partners about the traits of writing and how they are essential in developing quality writing. Listen to conversations, making anecdotal notes. Have a few groups share out their thoughts. Point out brilliant comments and notice positive behaviors and knowledge.

Apply

8. Remind students that the traits of writing will help them be successful as they begin to develop their own stories. Tell students that today they will divide their Writer's Notebook into sections for each writing trait.

Write/Conference

9. Provide time for students to divide their Writer's Notebook into sections by gluing the *Traits Team Mini Posters* into the notebook. Remind students to use the anchor chart as a guide so they will have the appropriate number of blank pages in each section.

Spotlight Strategy

10. Spotlight the students who have organized their notebooks neatly and carefully.

Share

11. Have students meet with partners to share their Writer's Notebook. Choose one or two students who clearly understand the idea and have them share with the whole group.

Homework
Ask students to share what they learned about the traits of writing with their families. Challenge students to remember all six traits and to make a list.

Traits of Writing Notebook Entry

Traits of Writing

Ideas are the main topic and details that tell the writer's message. They are the heart ♥ of the story.

Sentence Fluency is the rhythm and flow of our words.

Organization includes the structure of the writing—beginning, middle, end, and more.

Word Choice is using just the right word in your writing.

Voice allows the reader to know the writer—it creates personality.

Conventions are needed to make our writing readable—CUPS!

Traits Team Mini Posters

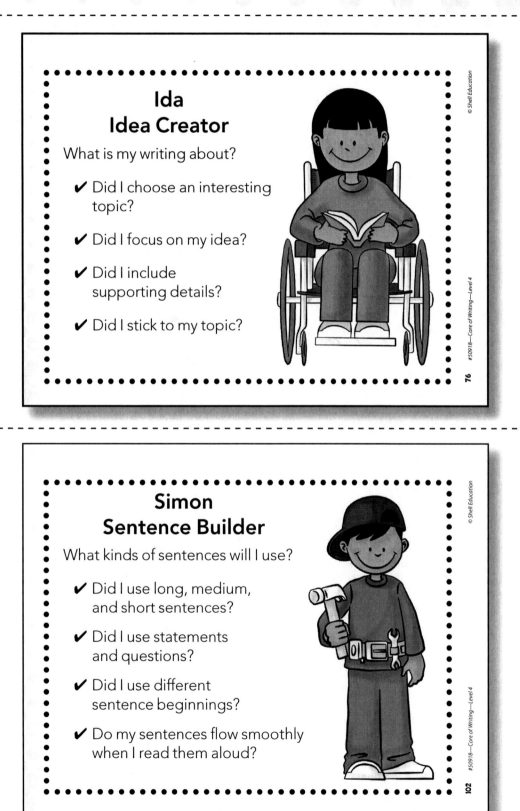

Ida
Idea Creator

What is my writing about?

✔ Did I choose an interesting topic?

✔ Did I focus on my idea?

✔ Did I include supporting details?

✔ Did I stick to my topic?

© Shell Education

#50918—Core of Writing—Level 4

76

Simon
Sentence Builder

What kinds of sentences will I use?

✔ Did I use long, medium, and short sentences?

✔ Did I use statements and questions?

✔ Did I use different sentence beginnings?

✔ Do my sentences flow smoothly when I read them aloud?

© Shell Education

#50918—Core of Writing—Level 4

102

Traits Team Mini Posters *(cont.)*

Owen Organization Conductor

How do I plan my writing?

✔ Did I sequence my thoughts?

✔ Did I have a beginning, middle, and end?

✔ Did I hook my reader?

✔ Did I include transition words?

© Shell Education

#50918—Core of Writing—Level 4

138

Wally Word Choice Detective

What words will paint a picture for my reader?

✔ Did I use some amazing words?

✔ Did I use sensory words?

✔ Did I use action words?

✔ Did I use a variety of words?

© Shell Education

#50918—Core of Writing—Level 4

176

Traits Team Mini Posters *(cont.)*

Val and Van
Voice

What is the purpose of my writing?

✔ Did I write to an audience?

✔ Did I share my feelings?

✔ Did I make my reader smile, cry, think?

✔ Does my writing sound like me?

© Shell Education

#50918—Core of Writing—Level 4

208

Callie
Super Conventions
Checker

How do I edit my paper?

✔ Did I check my capitalization?

✔ Did I check my punctuation?

✔ Did I check my spelling?

✔ Did I use good spacing?

✔ Did I read over my story?

© Shell Education

#50918—Core of Writing—Level 4

224

Sharing

Procedures

Note: You may need to repeat this lesson until procedures are consistent and automatic. Sharing can take place in the meeting area or at student desks, depending on the personalities in your class.

Think About Writing

1. Review with students that they have been learning the expected behaviors to manage themselves during Writer's Workshop.

2. Explain that another component of Writer's Workshop is sharing. Remind students that sharing is the last part of Writer's Workshop and will take place after students have had an opportunity to write.

Teach

3. Say, "Today I will show you how to meet with classmates to share." Tell students that sharing can take place in several different group situations. Remind them that they will need to use this time productively.

4. Explain to students that when you say, "Meet with a partner," they should each find a partner by the time you count to five on your fingers. Model this group formation. Then, ask students to practice. Use this procedure to practice forming other groups of three called *triads* and groups of four called *quads*.

5. Remind students that sharing time will be short and is not an opportunity to read an entire writing piece. Reinforce that students should share their best example on the topic of the mini-lesson that day.

Sharing (cont.)

6. Share the *Compliment and Comment Cards* (page 61) with students. Explicitly model how to use these cards to compliment and comment on students' work.

7. Revisit the anchor chart created in Managing Writer's Workshop Lesson 2 and add student insights about what Writer's Workshop looks like, sounds like, and feels like.

Engage

8. Have students meet with partners and share what they learned about sharing today. Then, ask students to move into quads and share in a larger group. Provide lots of praise as students work to form the various groups.

Apply

9. Remind students that sharing gives them opportunities to have conversations with others about their writing work. Provide students with copies of the *Sharing Notebook Entry* (page 60) and have them paste the entry into their Writer's Notebook. Distribute the *Compliment and Comment Cards* and have students store them in their writing folders.

10. Tell students that today they should either work on a piece of writing from their folders or begin a new piece.

Write/Conference

11. Provide time for students to write. All students write every day, even when mini-lessons are on managing Writer's Workshop. As students work, rotate among them to assist those who are having a difficult time getting started.

Spotlight Strategy

12. It will not be necessary to spotlight students until the end of Writer's Workshop, during the sharing component.

Share

13. Tell students that they will practice the procedures for sharing. Remind them to use the *Compliment and Comment Cards*. First, have students meet with partners. Allow students to share their writing for one minute.

14. Repeat Step 13, this time having students meet in quads. Finally, have students meet in triads. Provide praise for students who are moving to form groups and share quickly.

Homework
Ask students to think about how to meet with partners, triads, and quads. Have students tell their parents the kind of compliments they might give to a friend about his or her writing.

Sharing Notebook Entry

Compliments and Comments

Compliments

A **compliment** is something you like about your partner's writing.

- I like the way you…
- Your details made me feel…
- The order of your writing really…
- Your sentences have…
- You used words that…

Comments

A **comment** is a positive statement that will improve your partner's writing.

- Can you say more about…?
- I am confused about the order because…
- Your sentences are…
- You might use a variety of words, such as…

Compliment and Comment Cards

Directions: Cut out the cards to distribute to students. Have them use the sentence stems to compliment and make suggestions about their partner´s writing.

Compliment

Tell your partner what you like about his or her writing.

"I like the way you…"

"Your details make me…"

"Your sentences have…"

Compliment

Tell your partner what you like about his or her writing.

"I like the way you…"

"Your details make me…"

"Your sentences have…"

Comment

Make a suggestion that will help your partner improve his or her writing.

"Can you say more about…?"

"I am confused about the order because…"

"You might use a variety of words, such as…"

Comment

Make a suggestion that will help your partner improve his or her writing.

"Can you say more about…?"

"I am confused about the order because…"

"You might use a variety of words, such as…"

Turn and Talk

Procedures

Note: Teachers may assign writing partners that have been carefully selected based on language acquisition, or have students select their own partners. The collective personality of your class should guide your decision. You will need to repeat this lesson until the procedure is in place. Glue the notebook entry on the left side of the notebook. Students can reflect and write their thoughts on the right side.

Think About Writing

1. Tell students that they are getting the routines and procedures of Writer's Workshop in place. Remind students that it is important that they have a way to talk to others about mini-lessons and the writing that they do.

2. Review the mentor texts, if desired.

Teach

3. Tell students, "Today I will show you how to have conversations with partners." Explain to students that when you say, "Turn and Talk," that is a signal for them to immediately turn to the person who is nearby and quickly follow directions on the discussion topic. Tell students to use a "two-inch voice"—a quiet voice that can only be heard two inches away. Explicitly model for students what this will look like, then have students practice.

4. Tell students when you say, "Heads-up, Stand-up, Partner-up," that is a signal that they will immediately stand up, join a partner, and make eye contact with him or her. Then students must follow directions for the discussion topic. Model what *Heads-up, Stand-up, Partner-up* would look and sound like. Then provide time for students to practice with each other. Praise students for their efforts.

Turn and Talk *(cont.)*

5. Revisit the anchor chart created in Managing Writer's Workshop Lesson 2 to add student insights into what Writer's Workshop looks like, sounds like, and feels like.

Engage

6. Remind students that they practiced how to *Turn and Talk*. Ask students to talk with partners about how they will be expected to conduct themselves as they talk with other students.

Apply

7. Provide students with the *Turn and Talk Notebook Entry* (page 64) to add to their Writer's Notebook. Remind students to follow the guidelines established today when they talk with peers. Encourage students to work on a piece of writing from their folders or begin a new piece of writing as they work today.

Write/Conference

8. Provide time for students to write. Continue to have quick roving conferences until the management of Writer's Workshop is solid and successful. Provide praise to your student writers.

Spotlight Strategy

9. No spotlight strategy today. Celebrating is done through the sharing component instead.

Share

10. Have students meet with partners to share their writing. Provide students approximately two minutes to share what they think about the value of sharing time.

Homework

Ask students to think about how sharing with other students energizes their writing ideas. Also, have them think about how important it is to show respect for every writer in the room by using a two-inch voice during Writer's Workshop.

Turn and Talk Notebook Entry

Turn and Talk

Remember to...

find your partner quickly

use a soft, two-inch voice

make eye contact with your partner

stick to the writing topic

ask questions to clarify thinking

make sure each person has a turn to talk

give only compliments— no put-downs

give a compliment when needed

Guidelines for Writer's Workshop

Standard
Understands the structure of Writer's Workshop

Materials
- *Guidelines for Writer's Workshop Notebook Entry* (page 67; guidelineswritersws.pdf)
- Chart paper
- Markers
- Writer's Notebooks

Mentor Texts
- *A Writer's Notebook* by Ralph Fletcher
- *Amelia's Notebook* by Marissa Moss
- See *Mentor Text List* in Appendix C for other suggestions.

Procedures
Note: You will need to repeat this lesson many times until procedures are in place. Adjust the guidelines to meet the needs of your class.

Think About Writing
1. Explain to students that getting Writer's Workshop routines in place creates order and efficiency in the classroom.

2. Review mentor texts, if desired. You may also want to begin reading literature from your favorite authors to begin exploring mentor texts.

Teach
3. Tell students, "Today I will show you the guidelines for Writer's Workshop and what you need to be doing to make efficient use of the time scheduled for writing." Explain that after each daily mini-lesson, students will be expected to systematically follow some guidelines.

4. Model and explain the ideas listed on the *Guidelines for Writer's Workshop Notebook Entry* (page 67). Record each idea on a sheet of chart paper as it is discussed with students. Display the anchor chart in the room and refer to it often until students effortlessly follow the guidelines.

Engage
5. Have students turn to partners to review the guidelines for Writer's Workshop. Encourage students to use the anchor chart to guide their discussions.

Guidelines for Writer's Workshop *(cont.)*

Apply

6. Encourage students to think about how the guidelines for writing will help them spend their time more efficiently. Provide students with the *Guidelines for Writer's Workshop Notebook Entry* to add to their Writer's Notebook. Encourage students to work on a piece of writing from their folders or begin a new piece as they write today.

Write/Conference

7. Provide time for students to write. There should be no conferencing about writing until procedures are firmly in place. Begin to increase the amount of sustained writing time according to the developmental levels of your students.

Spotlight Strategy

8. Spotlight a student who immediately gets to work on his/her writing. For example, "Trevor did something brilliant. He went to his seat and immediately started to write in his Writer's Notebook."

Share

9. Have students meet with partners to share what they wrote today. Provide approximately two minutes for students to share. Choose one or two students, and have them share with the whole group.

10. Do a group reflection on how the guidelines will help students become better writers. Continue to add to the anchor chart created in Managing Writer's Workshop Lesson 1.

Homework

Ask students to think about the guidelines introduced today. Have students write two sentences to explain how knowing what is expected of them will make them more disciplined writers.

Guidelines for Writer's Workshop Notebook Entry

Guidelines for Writer's Workshop

- You must always be writing or sketching in your Writer's Notebook.

- Always include the date of your work.

- Keep your drafts in your writing folder.

- Work quietly so that everyone can do their best thinking.

- Write on every other line when drafting.

- Request a conference when you are ready for a final draft.

- Use a soft, two-inch voice.

- Use your best handwriting or the computer on a final draft.

- Place your final draft in the editor's basket.

- Record what you have learned as a writer when you have completed a project.

Remember...

A writer's work is never done!

Teacher and Peer Conferences

Standard

Understands the structure of Writer's Workshop

Materials

- *Peer Conference Notebook Entry* (page 70; peerconference.pdf)
- Chart paper
- Markers
- *Compliment and Comment Cards* (page 61; complicommentcards.pdf)
- Writing folder
- Writer's Notebooks

Mentor Texts

- *A Writer's Notebook* by Ralph Fletcher
- *Amelia's Notebook* by Marissa Moss
- See *Mentor Text List* in Appendix C for other suggestions.

Procedures

Note: You may assign writing partners or allow students to form partners on their own. The collective personality of your class should guide your decision. Repeat this lesson until the procedure is in place. Remind students that they should always glue the notebook entry pages on the left side of their notebook.

Think About Writing

1. Explain to students that it is important to build teacher and peer conferencing into Writer's Workshop. Tell students that meeting with another person to share their writing is how they will get compliments and comments for improving their writing.

2. Review mentor texts, if desired.

Teach

3. Tell students, "Today I will show you how to meet with a teacher or partner in an assigned place in the room to review your writing."

4. Explain that getting feedback from another person is a great way to improve writing. Show students a designated area of the room for peer conferences. Then, explicitly model for students how to sit shoulder-to-shoulder with a partner so that they can read each other's work. Review how to give compliments and comments on writing. (See Managing Writer's Workshop Lesson 6.)

5. Review the questions on the *Peer Conference Notebook Entry* (page 70). Add each question to a sheet of chart paper and discuss each one. Model what a teacher conference will look like with a student. Next have students practice peer conferencing. Revisit the anchor chart created in Managing Writer's Workshop Lesson 2 and add student insights about what Writer's Workshop looks like, sounds like, and feels like.

Teacher and Peer Conferences *(cont.)*

Engage

6. Have students meet with partners by the time you count to five with your fingers. Provide lots of praise for students who quickly meet with partners. Remind students to use the *Compliment and Comment Cards* (page 61) in their writing folders to help them make appropriate comments about writing work.

Apply

7. Encourage students to schedule weekly conferences with peers or with you in order to get feedback on their writing work. Provide students with the *Peer Conference Notebook Entry* to add to their Writer's Notebook. Tell students that today they can work on drafting a new piece of writing or continue with something from their folder.

Write/Conference

8. Provide time for students to write. Select two students to move to the designated peer conferencing area of your room and assist them in providing feedback to each other. Continue to select pairs of students to peer conference, paying close attention to the conferencing partners.

Spotlight Strategy

9. Spotlight a student who is revising his/her work based on a peer conference. For example, "Allison is doing something brilliant. She is working on one small detail that was suggested by her partner to improve the quality of her writing."

Share

10. Have students *Turn and Talk* with partners about how providing compliments and comments during conferences will support their writing.

Homework

Ask students to think about the procedures for meeting with a peer to conference. Have students write one compliment and one comment they could give to a partner about his or her writing.

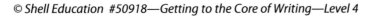

Peer Conference Notebook Entry

The Five-Step Writing Process

Standard

Understands the structure of Writer's Workshop

Materials

- *The Five-Step Writing Process Notebook Entry* (page 73; fivestepprocess.pdf)
- Chart paper
- Markers
- Writer's Notebooks
- Index cards
- Writing samples *(optional)*

Mentor Texts

- *Amelia's Notebook* by Marissa Moss
- *The Sloppy Copy Slip Up* by DyAnne DiSalvo
- *Look at My Book: How Kids Can Write and Illustrate Terrific Books* by Loreen Leedy
- See *Mentor Text List* in Appendix C for other suggestions.

Procedures

Note: Refer to the five-step writing process (prewriting, drafting, revising, editing, and publishing) as students work through the writing process on numerous projects throughout the year.

Think About Writing

1. Remind students that they have been developing their writing by using a variety of ideas and talking about how authors write. Explain that writing can be separated into simple steps that make the process more manageable. These simple steps will help them improve their finished writing.

2. Review mentor texts, if desired.

Teach

3. Tell students, "Today I will show you each step of the Five-Step Writing Process to help you become better writers."

4. Record each step from *The Five-Step Writing Process Notebook Entry* (page 73) onto a sheet of chart paper. Discuss each step with students as you write it. If possible, display student work samples that show each step of the process. For example, for prewriting, you could show a graphic organizer.

Engage

5. Have students talk with partners to name and briefly discuss the steps of the writing process. Encourage students to talk across their five fingers and name each of the five steps. Students may refer to the anchor chart, if necessary. Provide approximately two or three minutes of talk time.

The Five-Step Writing Process *(cont.)*

Apply

6. Remind students to use the steps of the writing process to make their writing the best it can be. Provide students with *The Five-Step Writing Process Notebook Entry* to add to their Writer's Notebook. Today, students can revise or edit an existing writing piece or begin with a new idea.

Write/Conference

7. Provide students time to write. Prepare index cards with the five steps of the writing process. Gather a small group at a table or the carpet to reteach the steps as needed. Explain and clarify each step. Use concrete samples to demonstrate. Allow four or five minutes to reteach. Then begin to rotate around the room and individually confer.

Spotlight Strategy

8. Spotlight a student who is using an idea from a draft in his/her writing. For example, "Writers, you rock! Notice how Daniel is capturing a moment from an experience in his draft." Echo your thinking from the mini-lesson strategy.

Share

9. Have students share their writing with partners. Provide approximately two minutes for students to talk.

> ### Homework
> Ask students to think about how the Five-Step Writing Process can help their writing.

#50918—Getting to the Core of Writing—Level 4 © Shell Education

The Five-Step Writing Process Notebook Entry

The Five-Step Writing Process

1 **Prewriting:**
Think about your topic:
brainstorm and plan

2 **Drafting:**
Write your thoughts on paper:
rough copy

3 **Revising:**
Reread, rethink, and refine:
check organization and add
details and interesting words

4 **Editing:**
Review and correct:
Capitalization
Usage
Punctuation
Spelling

5 **Publishing:**
Complete the final copy and
share your writing with others

#50918—Getting to the Core of Writing—Level 4 © Shell Education

Ideas

Thinking, Thinking, Thinking!

Ideas are the heart of writing. The purpose of this section is to help students generate ideas for writing. The lessons assist students in exploring the ideas of authors through mentor texts and in discovering unique writing ideas in their own lives. Through class-created anchor charts and individually created lists, students will collect plenty of ideas so that when they begin to write, they are not at a loss for topics. Students are encouraged to keep their ideas in their writing folders so the ideas are readily at hand. Lessons in this section include the following:

- Lesson 1: My Authority List (page 77)
- Lesson 2: Authors as Mentors (page 80)
- Lesson 3: Interesting Places (page 83)
- Lesson 4: The Best Times! The Worst Times! (page 86)
- Lesson 5: Brainstorming Boxes (page 89)
- Lesson 6: What Should We Write? (page 92)
- Lesson 7: Pocket of Picture Topics (page 95)
- Lesson 8: I Wonder List (page 98)

The *Ida, Idea Creator* poster (page 76) can be displayed in the room to provide a visual reminder for students that ideas is one of the traits of writing. You may wish to introduce this poster during the first lesson on ideas. Then, refer to the poster when teaching other lessons on ideas to refresh students' memories and provide them with questions to help hone their writing topics.

Ida
Idea Creator

What is my writing about?

❧ Did I choose an interesting topic?

❧ Did I focus on my idea?

❧ Did I include supporting details?

❧ Did I stick to my topic?

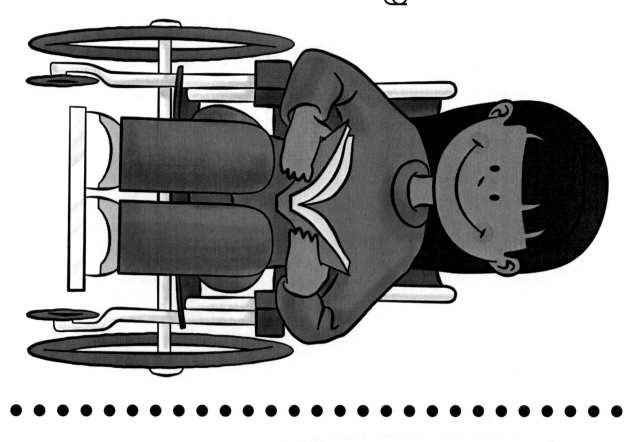

My Authority List

Standard

Uses prewriting strategies to plan written work

Materials

- Chart paper
- Markers
- Writer's Notebooks
- *My Authority List Notebook Entry* (page 79; myauthoritylist.pdf)

Mentor Texts

- *You Have to Write* by Janet Wong
- *Nothing Ever Happens on 90th Street* by Roni Schotter
- See *Mentor Text List* in Appendix C for other suggestions.

Procedures

Note: Add to this list throughout the year to increase student value of their own experiences as writing topics.

Think About Writing

1. Remind students of the procedures in place for Writer's Workshop. Explain that authors gather ideas for stories they may want to write. Tell students that they will also gather ideas for stories they want to write.

2. Review mentor texts, if desired, and emphasize the author's ideas for writing. For example, in *Nothing Ever Happens on 90th Street*, Eva is given the following writing assignment by her teacher: "Write about what you know!" As she sits on the stoop of her apartment Mr. Sims makes the following comment: "The whole world's a stage and each of us plays a part. Watch the stage, observe the players carefully, and don't neglect the details."

Teach

3. Tell students, "Today I will show you how to create an authority list, a list of things you are an expert on." Explain that students' lists will be based on their environments and experiences.

4. Label a sheet of chart paper with the title *My Authority List*. Model how to create your own list of ideas that may include special traditions, special hobbies, favorite books, etc.

5. Allow students to chime in with additions to the chart from their own backgrounds. Suggest some topics that may appeal to students, such as specific video games, a favorite movie, a unique character who lives in the neighborhood, or an irreplaceable treasure. Keep this chart displayed as an anchor chart.

My Authority List (cont.)

Engage

6. Have each student turn to a partner to discuss ideas for their own lists. Encourage students to use their background knowledge. As students talk, rotate around the room, listen in on conversations, and share your own ideas. Provide approximately two minutes for students to talk.

Apply

7. Remind students that their lives are full of details, suspense, and mystery. Provide students with the *My Authority List Notebook Entry* (page 79) to add to their Writer's Notebook. Have students work on the *Your Turn* section before proceeding to their writing folders.

Write/Conference

8. Provide time for students to work. Monitor students to see if any need assistance in getting started. Engage students who appear reluctant, and begin conversations to make them feel competent and successful. Keep notes to plan future instruction. You may need to revisit this lesson on several occasions.

Spotlight Strategy

9. Spotlight one or two writers who are focused and successful with the task. For example, "Remarkable work today! You must be so proud of your effort. Just listen to this list."

Share

10. Have students work with partners to share the lists they made. Tell students to share only a few items from their lists. Provide approximately two minutes for students to talk.

Homework

Ask students to have their parents help think of additional ideas that can be added to their authority lists. Have students add five more ideas for their authority lists.

My Authority List Notebook Entry

My Authority List

Your experiences are a reservoir full of delightful and mysterious ideas. Think! Think! Think! What have I seen or done that will inspire an opinion, essay, story, or composition? Here are some things to think about:

- A scary experience
- The worst day of my life
- A special memory
- The best present ever
- My favorite place to visit
- The funniest person in the world and why
- The saddest day of my life
- My best friend
- An animal of the wild
- A famous person
- The sport I like the best
- A hero is…
- I can…
- The most interesting book, movie, game

Your Turn:

Create your own authority list with at least five items on it.

Authors as Mentors

Standard

Uses prewriting strategies to plan written work

Materials

- Chart paper
- Markers
- Writer's Notebooks
- *Authors as Mentors Notebook Entry* (page 82; authorsmentors.pdf)

Mentor Texts

- *Everybody Needs a Rock* by Byrd Baylor
- *When I Was Young in the Mountains* by Cynthia Rylant
- *I'm in Charge of Celebrations* by Byrd Baylor
- *The Table Where Rich People Sit* by Byrd Baylor
- See *Mentor Text List* in Appendix C for other suggestions.

Procedures

Note: Throughout the year, review literature and study each author's style and craft of writing so that students can imitate it with your support. Create anchor charts indicating author style, for example, repetitive text or cumulative text. Start with simple books so that students will feel confident imitating the author's style of writing.

Think About Writing

1. Explain to students that each month they will study an author's craft to help shape their skills and opinions about writing.

2. Review mentor texts, if desired, and emphasize the author's craft. For example, Byrd Baylor, who writes about nature in the Southwest, utilizes a very unique style of writing. Her collection of books is written in columns, and the message is connected to relationships between people and the environment.

Teach

3. Tell students, "Today I will show you how to use an author's style of writing to improve the quality of your writing."

4. Select a mentor text, for example *Everybody Needs a Rock* by Byrd Baylor. Begin a list on chart paper of any noticeable attributes of author's text, for example: sentence variety (long sentences and short sentences), written in columns, opening paragraphs grab attention, makes up rules, has a message or ethical meaning.

5. Identify one attribute from the list to use as a springboard for generating ideas. For example, in *Everybody Needs a Rock*, Baylor develops a list of rules for finding a rock.

Authors as Mentors (cont.)

6. Follow the author's model, and have students think of possible writing ideas. Make a list of possible topics on chart paper. If students are developing ideas for making rules, they may think about rules for getting homework completed, playing with a friend, preparing for the school day, taking a walk, or making observations in nature.

Engage

7. Have students talk with partners about ideas for emulating the author of the mentor text. Allow approximately two minutes for students to talk.

Apply

8. Remind students that they can draw on the work of real authors to support their writing efforts. Provide students with *Authors as Mentors Notebook Entry* (page 82) to add to their Writer's Notebook. Have students work on the *Your Turn* section before proceeding to their writing folders.

Write/Conference

9. Provide time for students to work. Then, scan the room for students who may need assistance getting started. Gather a small group of students to do a guided writing mini-lesson or reteach the concept before sending them off to write. Make astute observations of writing behaviors so that you can plan your next instruction.

Spotlight Strategy

10. Do not interrupt to spotlight today. Let students develop deep understanding of the important work of studying the craft of a real author and internalize their various patterns.

Share

11. Select several students to sit in the Author's Chair. Focus on the importance of studying the craft of real authors so that students acquire a basic understanding of organizational structures.

Homework

Ask students to share with their family members how they are using a favorite author to improve the quality of their writing. Have students find one more example of an author they would like to emulate and bring it to school.

Authors as Mentors Notebook Entry

Authors as Mentors

As we study the craft and style of expert authors, we become better observers of quality writing. We might do these things:

1. **Gather ideas** from Patricia Pollacco, Byrd Baylor, and Seymour Simon

2. **Listen for voice** in the works of Eve Bunting and Cynthia Rylant

3. **Focus on sentence fluency** with Jane Yolen and Margie Palatini

4. **Explore the word choice** of William Stieg and Ralph Fletcher

5. **Study organization patterns in stories**, such as:

   - Listing patterns: list of rules
     Everybody Needs a Rock by Byrd Baylor
   - Alphabet: each page represents a letter
     The Ocean Alphabet Book by Jerry Palotta
   - Cumulative sequence: adds a word or phrase each time
     The Pot That Juan Built by Nancy Andrew-Goebel
   - Circular endings: endings and beginnings are similar
     Two Bad Ants by Chris Van Allsburg
   - Chronological sequence: follows a time sequence
     Alexander and the Terrible, Horrible, No Good, Very Bad Day by Judith Viorst
   - How-to: instructions or directions to complete a task
     How to Write Your Life Story by Ralph Fletcher

Your Turn:

Make a list of three authors or organization patterns you would like to emulate in your writing.

Interesting Places

Standard

Uses prewriting strategies to plan written work

Materials

- Chart paper
- Markers
- Writer's Notebooks
- *Interesting Places Notebook Entry* (pager 85; interestingplaces.pdf)
- Pictures of places

Mentor Texts

- *All the Places to Love* by Patricia MacLachlan
- *Owl Moon* by Jane Yolen
- Other CCSS literature
- See *Mentor Text List* in Appendix C for other suggestions.

Procedures

Note: When you notice students struggling with generating their own ideas, return to ideas generated in mini-lessons to create confident writers. Students should continue to add to their idea lists throughout the year.

Think About Writing

1. Remind students that they have been gathering ideas for writing. Explain that everyone creates lists, for example: grocery lists, things to do, and Christmas lists. Having lists of writing topics will allow them to always have ideas for writing.

2. Review mentor texts, if desired, and emphasize the author's use of observation. For example, in *Owl Moon*, Jane Yolen's characters observe tree shadows, train whistles, the meadow, a woolen scarf, and mittens. Patricia MacLachlan in *All the Places to Love* writes about a hilltop, a river, a barn, and a meadow.

Teach

3. Tell students, "Today I will show you how to create a list of interesting places." Explain that even ordinary places can be made interesting to the reader by using detailed descriptions to make the reader feel as if he or she is in that place.

4. Write the title *Interesting Places* on a sheet of chart paper. Model creating a list of places that are interesting to you, for example: an old log barn, a decrepit old house, and a chestnut tree with dying limbs. Add items to your list that are pertinent to your particular environment.

Interesting Places (cont.)

5. Allow students to chime in with ideas for places that are interesting to them. Add their ideas to the list.

Engage

6. Have students talk with partners about places that are interesting to them. Challenge students to count on their fingers to try to come up with ten places. Remind students to take turns with each other and be ready to share with the group. Provide approximately two minutes for students to talk. As they talk, listen in on conversations and add your own suggestions.

Apply

7. Encourage students to consider writing about an interesting place as a writing topic. Provide students with *Interesting Places Notebook Entry* (page 85) to add to their Writer's Notebook. Have students work on the *Your Turn* section before proceeding to their writing folders.

Write/Conference

8. Provide time for students to work. Support student efforts as they finish their lists and move to write pieces from their writing folders. Move around with your Conferring Notebook and make observations.

Spotlight Strategy

9. Spotlight students who have made a list of interesting places. For example, "Extraordinary list-making today. Just listen to this list of places to inspire Connie's writing."

Share

10. Have students work with partners to share five interesting places from each of their lists. Provide approximately two minutes for students to talk.

Homework

Ask students to look around for interesting places in their homes and communities. Have students make lists with at least three places they want to add to their lists at school.

Interesting Places Notebook Entry

Interesting Places

Special places you visit inspire ideas and can be connected to special stories, essays, poems, messages, and compositions. Always keep records so you can spring into action with writing.

You might use these places in your notebook or add some of your own:

- a bubbling brook in the mountains
- pine trees in the backyard
- a tent in the forest
- a grove of trees in the hills
- a treehouse in the yard
- an alley in the city
- a hiding place under the stairs
- on the creek bank
- grandma's kitchen
- the snake house at the zoo
- a sports stadium
- a concert hall
- a bike or hiking trail

Your Turn:

Make a list of places you find interesting or places that are special to you.

The Best Times! The Worst Times!

Standard

Uses prewriting strategies to plan written work

Materials

- Chart paper
- Markers
- Writer's Notebooks
- *The Best Times! The Worst Times! Notebook Entry* (page 88; bestworst.pdf)

Mentor Texts

- *The Best Part of Me* by Wendy Ewald
- *Amelia's Most Unforgettable Embarrassing Moments* by Marissa Moss
- *One of Those Days* by Amy Krouse Rosenthal
- See *Mentor Text List* in Appendix C for other suggestions.

Procedures

Note: Students may continue to build their lists throughout the year. The goal is that students use their lists to initiate topic ideas for other writing entries and projects.

Think About Writing

1. Remind students that they have been gathering ideas for writing in a variety of ways. Tell students that authors can turn any topic into an interesting piece of writing by starting with an idea and adding rich words and sophisticated sentences.

2. Review mentor texts, if desired, and emphasize the author's use of life experiences in the book.

Teach

3. Tell students, "Today I will show you how to make a list of the best things and worst things that you have experienced. You will be able to draw on ideas from the list for writing projects."

4. Draw a two-column table on chart paper. Label one side of the table *The Best Times*. Label the other side of the table *The Worst Times*.

5. Model how to add ideas to each side of the chart. Think aloud as you recall the best and worst events in your life. For example:

The Best Times	The Worst Times
Received a surprise visit from…	Fell on a patch of ice
Got the best grade ever on…	Had flat tire on my bike
Traveled to…	Fell out of bed and hit my head

The Best Times! The Worst Times! (cont.)

6. Solicit ideas from students to add to the chart. Post the chart on the wall for students to utilize as they create their own lists.

Engage

7. Have students talk with partners about their best and worst life experiences. Provide approximately two minutes for students to talk.

Apply

8. Remind students that every experience they have had can make wonderful writing projects. Provide students *The Best Times! The Worst Times! Notebook Entry* (page 88) to add to their Writer's Notebook. Have students work on the *Your Turn* section before proceeding to their writing folders.

Write/Conference

9. Provide time for students to write. Rotate around the room and talk with students about their work. Use your Conferring Notebook and jot down ideas of interest to add to the anchor chart. If students have difficulties, bring a small group to the carpet or a table and generate ideas with them.

Spotlight Strategy

10. Spotlight students who are writing about their life experiences. For example, "Listen to the ideas of Louis. He's made a list and has already moved into a writing project." Make sure your praise is authentic.

Share

11. Have students work with partners to share at least three writing ideas. Then, have students rotate to different partners and share again.

Homework

Ask students to talk with their families about the experiences they have shared together. Have students make lists of two best and two worst experiences they have shared with their families.

The Best Times! The Worst Times! Notebook Entry

The Best Times! The Worst Times!

Authors write about **special memories** and **events** in their own lives and sometimes the lives of their friends. Their stories might tell the **best** times or the **worst** times.

The Best Times	The Worst Times
With my family at the beach	A best friend got mad at me
Playing ball with Dad	I got sick at school
A visit from Grandma and Grandpa	Mom said, "No sleepover!"
Sleeping over at a friend's house	We lost the big game
Going to the park	I fell and had to get stitches

Your Turn:

Create a list of the best and worst events in your own life.

#50918—*Getting to the Core of Writing*—Level 4 © Shell Education

Brainstorming Boxes

Standard

Uses prewriting strategies to plan written work

Materials

- Chart paper
- Markers
- Writer's Notebooks
- *Brainstorming Boxes Notebook Entry* (page 91; brainstormbox.pdf)

Mentor Texts

- *Nothing Ever Happens on 90th Street* by Roni Schotter
- *Written Anything Good Lately?* by Susan Allen
- *Marshfield Dreams* and *A Writer's Notebook* by Ralph Fletcher
- See *Mentor Text List* in Appendix C for other suggestions.

Procedures

Note: This lesson may be used to generate ideas for topics for opinion, informative, and narrative writing. Also, additional brainstorming boxes can be created throughout the year with different stems in them, such as: *A time I will never forget* or *The craziest thing I ever saw…*

Think About Writing

1. Tell students that some days, authors know exactly what they want to write about, and other days, it is harder to find a topic. Explain that many authors, such as Susan Allen and Ralph Fletcher, keep a list or collection of topics for those days when they have a difficult time thinking about a topic.

2. Review mentor texts, if desired, and emphasize the author's ideas.

Teach

3. Tell students, "Today I will show you how to use brainstorming to help you gather writing ideas." Explain that brainstorming is capturing the thoughts and ideas in our heads and writing them down on paper. Brainstorming can be done alone, with partners, or with a group of friends.

4. Draw a table with three rows and three columns on a sheet of chart paper. Create large boxes with plenty of room for adding ideas. Write *Brainstorming Boxes* in the center box. Write the following topics from the notebook entry, one per box.

Things that make me happy	Things that make me sad	Foods I enjoy
Things or people I love	**Brainstorming Boxes**	Favorite sports
Things I like	Things I dislike	Favorite books

Brainstorming Boxes (cont.)

5. Model how to fill in ideas in each box that are related to the box topic. Think aloud as you add topics to each box. For example, for the box *Things That Make Me Happy*, you could add: singing, babies, being with my friends, etc.

Engage

6. Select a topic and have students talk with partners about ideas related to the topic. Then, select another topic, and have students talk with new partners about ideas for that topic. Continue with the rest of the boxes on the same day or on subsequent days.

Apply

7. Remind students that they are keeping collections of topics so they will always have something interesting to write about. Provide students with the *Brainstorming Boxes Notebook Entry* (page 91) to add to their Writer's Notebook. Have students work on the *Your Turn* section before proceeding to their writing folders.

Write/Conference

8. Provide time for students to write. Conduct conferences with students about their writing. Guide students as they select topics they know and care about that can be used in their writing.

Spotlight Strategy

9. Spotlight one or two students who have a clear understanding of generating topics and have them share their Brainstorming Boxes.

Share

10. Have students work with partners to share their ideas from their Brainstorming Boxes. Remind students to take turns and to share a few ideas and take a few ideas from their partners.

Homework

Ask students to listen and watch for new ideas to add to their Brainstorming Boxes. Have students make lists of three other topics.

Brainstorming Boxes Notebook Entry

Brainstorming Boxes

Things that make me happy	Things that make me sad	Foods I enjoy
Things or people I love	My Brainstorming Boxes	Favorite sports
Things I like	Things I dislike	Favorite books

Your Turn:

Complete the brainstorming boxes above with your own ideas.

What Should We Write?

Standard

Uses prewriting strategies to plan written work

Materials

- Chart paper
- Markers
- Writer's Notebooks
- *What Should We Write? Notebook Entry* (page 94; write.pdf)
- A variety of writing samples: menus, picture books, ABC books, newspaper and magazine articles, brochures, how-to manuals, letters, etc.

Mentor Texts

- *Written Anything Good Lately?* by Susan Allen
- Other CCSS literature
- See *Mentor Text List* in Appendix C for other suggestions.

Procedures

Note: Providing options for writing purposes and types promotes interest in reluctant writers. Creating travel brochures and alphabet books related to science or social studies themes incorporates writing across the curriculum. Build a bulletin board with types of writing to create enthusiasm and motivation.

Think About Writing

1. Explain that authors build writing stamina by sustaining writing for longer and longer periods of time. Remind students that they have been collecting ideas for their writing projects.

2. Review mentor texts, if desired, and emphasize the author's ideas.

Teach

3. Tell students, "Today I will show you a variety of writing types you may wish to use as you write." Explain to students that authors write for different purposes and in different formats. They may write a speech to *persuade* an audience to recycle, a travel brochure to *inform* readers of a summer camp, or perhaps a book of poetry for a reader's *entertainment*.

4. Create a three-column table on chart paper. Label the columns: *Persuade*, *Inform*, and *Entertain*. Share writing samples of various types, such as menus, newspapers, picture books, comic strips, or letters, and discuss the author's purpose in creating each type of text. Work together as a class to decide the author's purpose in creating the writing. List the type of text in the appropriate column.

5. Select a specific project and model for students how to create it. For example, create a travel brochure by folding a piece of paper into three columns. Then, sketch and write important information about a vacation destination.

What Should We Write? *(cont.)*

Engage

6. Make a variety of mentor texts and other text types available to students. Have students work in groups of four to look through the texts to find the author's purpose for each.

Apply

7. Encourage students to explore many different kinds of writing. Provide students with the *What Should We Write? Notebook Entry* (page 94) to add to their Writer's Notebook. Have students work on the *Your Turn* section before proceeding to their writing folders.

Write/Conference

8. Provide time for students to write. Scan to make certain that all students have a focus and have selected something to work on. Brainstorm other ideas with anyone who does not get started right away. Make notes on the success of this lesson or note a change in plans.

Spotlight Strategy

9. Spotlight students who have selected a clear purpose for writing. For example, "Look at all of Vanessa's amazing ideas! She has decided to…"

Share

10. Select one or two students who clearly understand the idea and have them share with the whole group.

Homework

Ask students to search for different kinds of writing in their homes and communities. Have students bring or make a list of three examples of each type of author's purpose.

What Should We Write? Notebook Entry

What Should We Write?

Authors write for different purposes and in different formats. They may write a speech to *persuade* an audience to recycle, a travel brochure to *inform* readers of a summer camp, or perhaps a book of poetry for a reader's *entertainment*. Just remember:

P.I.E.

Here are a few types of writing you may consider when creating your own writing projects.

Persuade	Inform	Entertain
advertisement	biography	comic strip
commercial	brochure	ghost story
letter to the editor	essay	greeting card
speech	how-to manual	personal letter
	interview	play
	newsletter	poetry
	newspaper article	song lyrics
	poster	
	speech	

Your Turn:

Think of other types of writing. Decide on the authors' purposes. Add and label three columns on your notebook page. As you discover purposes for your writing, add them to your list. Use these ideas when creating your own writing projects.

#50918—*Getting to the Core of Writing—Level 4* © Shell Education

Pocket of Picture Topics

Standard

Uses prewriting strategies to plan written work

Materials

- Sheet protectors or 6" × 9" manila envelopes
- 3" × 5" index cards
- Sticky notes
- Crayons or markers
- Writer's Notebooks
- *Pocket of Picture Topics Notebook Entry* (page 97; pocketpictures.pdf)
- Photographs, magazines, newspaper clippings, postcards, blank cards

Mentor Texts

- *Tuesday* and *Flotsam* by David Wiesner
- See *Mentor Text List* in Appendix C for other suggestions.

Procedures

Note: In your explanation, be certain to clarify that the pictures collected should stir up ideas and topics for writing. Photographs are a terrific resource for children struggling with their own ideas for writing.

Think About Writing

1. Tell students that authors are always thinking and gathering ideas for writing topics. Explain that all stories start with ideas. The more ideas we have, the more choices we have for writing topics.

2. Review mentor texts, if desired, and emphasize the author's idea for the book.

Teach

3. Tell students, "Today I will show you how to make a picture pocket to store your writing ideas." Explain that pockets store important things until we are ready to use them. A pocket for story ideas will be a safe place for ideas until they are needed for writing topics.

4. Discuss the quote, "A picture is worth a thousand words." Explain that pictures can be described to remind us about the event in the picture.

5. Use a blank index card to model drawing a picture of a family member, pet, or other personalized idea. Think aloud the decisions you are making as you include the details in your picture.

6. Place the picture in a sheet protector or a 6" × 9" manila envelope. The sheet protector can be stored in students' writing folders or the manila envelope can be glued into their Writer's Notebook.

Pocket of Picture Topics (cont.)

Engage

7. Have students talk with partners about ideas they may want to sketch and place in their Pocket of Picture Topics. Provide approximately two minutes for students to share. As students talk, move around to listen and talk with different groups. Write notes about student ideas on sticky notes. Then, gather students back together and share out a couple of ideas that you heard.

Apply

8. Encourage students to be on the lookout for ideas to add to their pockets. Provide students with the *Pocket of Picture Topics Notebook Entry* (page 97) to add to their Writer's Notebook. Have students work on the *Your Turn* section before proceeding to their writing folders. Place several blank index cards at student writing tables for them to draw pictures on. Provide pictures from magazines or other sources for students to add to their pockets or to get ideas from. Also, encourage them to bring photographs from home.

Write/Conference

9. Provide time for students to write. Begin conferencing with individual students when all students are at work.

Spotlight Strategy

10. Spotlight students who are adding ideas to their pockets. For example, "I'm noticing that Shreeva has already sketched and labeled three ideas and dropped them into her pocket. Smart writing work!"

Share

11. Have students share the ideas they drew with partners. Provide approximately two minutes for students to share.

Homework

Ask students to think about some ideas they may want to write about while they are doing homework, playing, or eating dinner. Have students draw three pictures to add to their pockets.

Pocket of Picture Topics Notebook Entry

Pocket of Picture Topics

Photographs and drawings are excellent resources for developing writing ideas.

You can draw your own pictures, collect family photos, or find pictures in magazines, newspapers, postcards, books, or on the Internet. With so many images, you will always have a topic for writing.

What kind of writing ideas do you get from these photos?

Your Turn:

Draw some pictures or add some photographs or pictures to your Pocket of Picture Topics.

I Wonder List

Standard

Uses prewriting strategies to plan written work

Materials

- Chart paper
- Markers
- Writer's Notebooks
- *I Wonder List Notebook Entry* (page 100; iwonder.pdf)

Mentor Texts

- *I Wonder Why Whales Sing: and Other Questions About Sea Life* by Caroline Harris
- See *Mentor Text List* in Appendix C for other suggestions.

Procedures

Note: Use this lesson to encourage students to wonder about the people and world around them. You may want students to publish an *I Wonder* series to promote accountability and motivation.

Think About Writing

1. Explain to students that one of the ways that authors get ideas for writing is by asking questions. Review with students that as readers we ask questions of ourselves to clarify an author's message and to better understand what we have read. Explain that authors often generate questions as the basis of a book.

2. Review mentor texts, if desired, and emphasize how the author generates a whole book around wondering about things.

Teach

3. Tell students, "Today I will show you how to take a text pattern and use that pattern to create your own writing."

4. Choose one of the examples from the notebook page, and write it on chart paper. Explain to students that the *I wonder* text pattern follows a structure: an *I wonder* statement followed by two questions. Tell students that this pattern can be used as the basis of ideas for writing topics.

5. Model how to create your own *I wonder* text using any topic you desire. Then, have students help create one together as a class.

I Wonder List (cont.)

Engage

6. Have students work with partners to think of an *I wonder* statement followed by two related questions. Suggested topics include parents, community, or a person you admire. Provide approximately two minutes for students to talk.

Apply

7. Encourage students to be curious about the world around them by asking questions to clarify their thinking, grow their knowledge, or improve their writing. Provide students with the *I Wonder List Notebook Entry* (page 100) to add to their Writer's Notebook. Have students work on the *Your Turn* section before proceeding to their writing folders.

Write/Conference

8. Provide time for students to write. Keep yourself available to roam and conference with individuals. Assist students who need guidance.

Spotlight Strategy

9. Spotlight students who have created strong *I wonder* statements for writing. For example, "Your questioning strategies are right on target. Just notice how Shabir is using the language of a writer. His writing sounds like a few *I Wonder* books might develop from this activity."

Share

10. Have students share their writing with partners. Ask students to read their questions to their partners and have the partners ask questions, such as: "Where did you get your ideas?" "Why are you curious about that topic?" Provide approximately two minutes for students to share.

Homework

Ask students to work with their parents to generate additional questions. Have students make lists of at least three *I wonder* statements they would like to add to their notebook at school.

I Wonder List Notebook Entry

I Wonder List

Authors are curious. They select topics to research and learn more about their interests. They use questions, such as *Who? What? Where? When? Why? How?* and *What if?*

Use these steps to create your own *I wonder* ideas for writing.

1. Select a topic and write an *I Wonder* statement.

2. Ask two questions.

Topic: Frogs

I wonder **how** frogs croak.

> Where is the croaker located in the frog's body?
>
> Why does the frog's throat wiggle when he croaks?

I wonder **why** frogs croak.

> Are they talking to other frogs?
>
> Is croaking a way to warn other frogs of danger?

I wonder **when** frogs croak.

> Is it in the morning when the sun has just peeked over the horizon?
>
> Is it at the end of the day in the late evening?

Your Turn:

Write an *I Wonder* statement and two related questions.

Sentence Fluency

Getting Started

Sentence fluency helps make writing interesting. It is a trait that allows writers to add interest to their writing. By changing the sentence length and where words are placed next to each other in the sentence, writers are able to help guide the reader though their work. Authors with good sentence fluency know the techniques needed to construct sentences that flow and have rhythm. The lessons assist students in exploring parts of sentences, ways sentences are built, and ways to expand sentences to develop more interesting ideas. Lessons in this section include the following:

- Lesson 1: Circle and Count (page 103)
- Lesson 2: Subject + Predicate = Sentence (page 106)
- Lesson 3: Sentence Search (page 110)
- Lesson 4: Appositive Action (page 117)
- Lesson 5: Compound Sentences (page 121)
- Lesson 6: Writing Complex Sentences (page 126)
- Lesson 7: Stepping Up Sentences (page 131)
- Lesson 8: Building Triangle Sentences (page 134)

The *Simon, Sentence Builder* poster (page 102) can be displayed in the room to provide a visual reminder for students that sentence fluency is one of the traits of writing. You may wish to introduce this poster during the first lesson on sentence fluency. Then, refer to the poster when teaching other lessons on sentence fluency to refresh students' memories and provide them with questions to help guide them as they create sentences.

Simon
Sentence Builder

What kinds of sentences will I use?

✔ Did I use long, medium, and short sentences?

✔ Did I use statements and questions?

✔ Did I use different sentence beginnings?

✔ Do my sentences flow smoothly when I read them aloud?

Circle and Count

Standards

- Uses a variety of sentence structures in writing
- Uses strategies to draft and revise written work

Materials

- Chart paper
- Markers
- Writer's Notebooks
- *Circle and Count Notebook Entry* (page 105; circlecount.pdf)
- Document camera *(optional)*
- Photocopies of a page of text from a mentor text

Mentor Texts

- *Owl Moon* by Jane Yolen
- *Bedhead* by Margie Palatini
- Other CCSS literature
- See *Mentor Text List* in Appendix C for other suggestions.

Procedures

Note: It is important to repeat this lesson using a variety of literature to build the concept of creating sentences with varied beginnings. Also, listen to the rhythm and flow that draws the reader's attention.

Think About Writing

1. Explain to students that authors observe their writing for sentence flow and rhythm. Using literature as mentor texts is a great way to see how experts craft sentences.

2. Review mentor texts, if desired, and emphasize the author's use of sentence variation. For example, in *Bedhead*, Margie Palatini keeps the reader on the edge of his or her seat with a variety of sentences that are well crafted.

Teach

3. Tell students, "Today I will show you how to use a strategy called *circle and count* in order to check your sentences for interest."

4. Display a copy of any mentor text, or use the following from *Bedhead*:

   "Baaaaddddddddd!" Wrong. It was that bad. "Yes, Sir, no doubt about it," said Dad, surveying the hairy situation from the sinkside. "Oliver, my boy, you're having one bad hair day." "Major," said Mom. "Total," agreed Emily. "Maybe if we just push it this way," Mom said, giving it a try.

   Either display the text on a document camera or write the text on chart paper. Use a pencil to circle the first word of every sentence. Discuss with students how the author keeps the text interesting by not beginning every sentence with the same word.

Circle and Count *(cont.)*

5. Point out to students how Margie Palatini keeps the text tight and interesting by varying sentence length and sentence beginnings, a must for providing sophistication in sentence construction. Count the number of words in each sentence and write the number off to the side of each sentence. Discuss with students how the author keeps the text interesting by varying the number of words in each sentence so they are not all the same length.

6. Provide students with a new text selection from their Core Reading Program, and have them work with partners to circle the beginning words and count the number of words in each sentence. Gather students back together to discuss the findings.

Engage

7. Have students talk with partners about how the strategy they practiced today will help improve the sophistication of their writing. Provide approximately two minutes for students to talk.

Apply

8. Remind students to imitate master authors to help them improve the rhythm and cleverness of their sentences. Provide students with the *Circle and Count Notebook Entry* (page 105) to add to their Writer's Notebook. Have students work on the *Your Turn* section before proceeding to their writing folders.

Write/Conference

9. Provide time for students to write. As they work, conference with individual students or work with a small group of students who are having the same difficulties. Keep notes on what you do during conferences each day.

Spotlight Strategy

10. Spotlight students who are adding sentence variety to their writing. For example, "Just notice the change in Camila's text. Writers, you truly rock! Keep working!"

Share

11. Have students work with partners to share any changes they made to improve their writing.

Homework

Ask students to look around their homes for evidence of sophisticated sentences. Have students copy three sentences they find and bring them to school to share tomorrow.

Circle and Count Notebook Entry

Circle and Count

Sentence variety makes your writing more interesting for your reader. Authors use different sentence lengths to add variety to their writing. They also vary sentence patterns, such as changing the beginning of a sentence.

Practice circle and count with the sentences below. Circle the first word in each sentence. Then, count the words to see if the author used sentence variety.

Sentence	Number of Words
I walked on through the woods.	
The tips of my fingers and the tip of my nose felt cold from the excruciating wind.	
The dog stopped and I stroked his head.	
We tiptoed on through the forest and I listened so hard I could hear my heart pounding in my ears.	
At last, I heard the exciting sound.	

Your Turn:

Now challenge yourself to write three brilliant sentences in your notebook. Be sure to vary the length and the beginning of each sentence.

Remember to practice circle and count in one of your current writing projects.

Subject + Predicate = Sentence

Standards

- Uses a variety of sentence structures in writing
- Uses strategies to draft and revise written work

Materials

- Chart paper
- Markers
- *Sentence Puzzle Pieces* (page 109; sentencepuzzle.pdf)
- Writer's Notebooks
- *Subject + Predicate = Sentence Notebook Entry* (page 108; subjpred.pdf)

Mentor Texts

- *Bedhead* by Margie Palatini
- *The Relatives Came* by Cynthia Rylant
- See *Mentor Text List* in Appendix C for other suggestions.

Procedures

Note: Teach grammar skills through the writing process. Repeat this lesson many times so that subject/verb agreement is mastered.

Think About Writing

1. Explain that authors use complete sentences with variety, rhythm, and flow to improve the quality of their writing.

2. Review mentor texts, if desired, and emphasize the author's sentence fluency.

Teach

3. Tell students, "Today I will show you how to develop a complete sentence containing a subject and a predicate." Explain that one part of a sentence is the naming part— a person, place, or thing. It is the *subject* and tells the reader whom or what the sentence is about. The other part of the sentence tells the reader the action that the naming part is doing. It is called the *predicate*.

4. Write the following sentence on chart paper.

   My cat chases her long tail.

   Work with students to identify the subject and predicate. You may want to underline or highlight the subject and predicate in different colors. Provide students with additional sentences to practice orally.

   - *The bumblebee flew into Justin's mouth.*
   - *That dog barked all night.*
   - *Many people ride the subway train each day.*

Subject + Predicate = Sentence *(cont.)*

Engage

5. Show students the subject *Sentence Puzzle Pieces* (page 109), and have them work with partners to think of predicates in order to create complete sentences. Then, show students the predicate *Sentence Puzzle Pieces,* and have students think of subjects in order to make complete sentences. Practice for approximately three minutes. Have students share their sentences with the group.

Apply

6. Remind students to write sentences that are complete with subjects and predicates. Provide students with the *Subject + Predicate = Sentence Notebook Entry* (page 108) to add to their Writer's Notebook. Have students work on the *Your Turn* section before proceeding to their writing folders.

Write/Conference

7. Provide time for students to write. Scan your classroom to make certain that all students are working. Begin to conference with individual students or in small groups. Create additional puzzle pieces with subjects and predicates as manipulatives for students to practice.

Spotlight Strategy

8. Spotlight students who have created new sentences. For example, "Look at all of your amazing sentences. Maria has used interesting subjects and predicates."

Share

9. Have students work with partners to share their writing. Remind students to provide a compliment and a comment. From teacher observations, choose one or two students to share with the whole group. Allow two to three minutes for sharing.

Homework

Ask students to play the sentence game with their families. Have students provide the subjects and the families provide the predicates. Have students write down three of the sentences they create.

Subject + Predicate = Sentence Notebook Entry

Subject + Predicate = Sentence

Sentences have two parts:

1.   The **subject** tells who or what the sentence is about.

2.   The **predicate** tells what the subject is doing.

My cat   chases her long tail.
subject   **predicate**

Your Turn:

Create sentences using these subject stems. Then, create sentences using these predicate stems. Check your writing for the two parts of a sentence. Add your new sentences to your notebook.

Subjects	Predicates
The barking dog…	…drank the milk.
The basketball team...	…jumped into the icy water.
Britney's mom…	…raced through the streets.
Snow covered trees…	…gazed at the sky.
The yellow taxi…	…sleeps.
A frog…	…smiles proudly.

#50918—Getting to the Core of Writing—Level 4 © Shell Education

Sentence Puzzle Pieces

Directions: Cut out the puzzle pieces. Show students the subject pieces and have them think of predicates to create complete sentences. Then, show students the predicate pieces and have them think of subjects to create complete sentences.

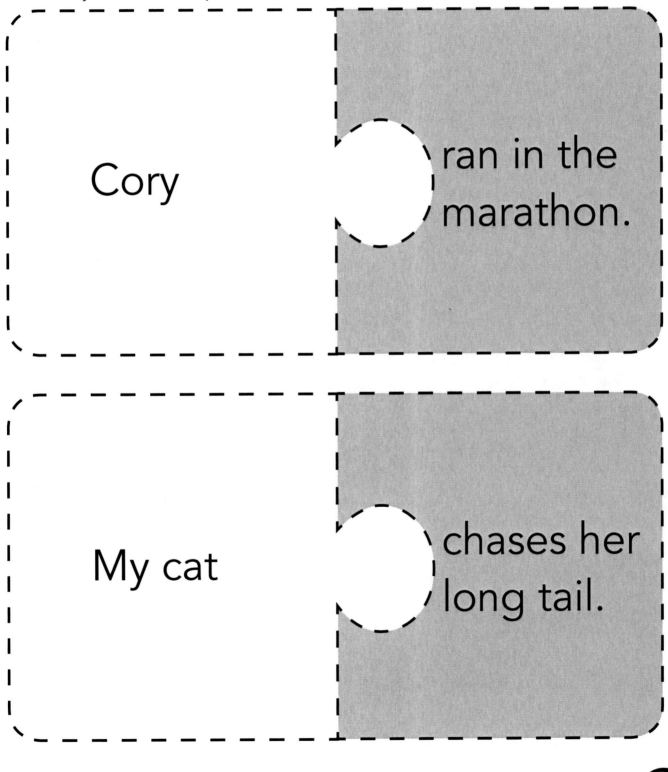

Sentence Search

Standards

- Uses a variety of sentence structures in writing
- Uses strategies to draft and revise written work

Materials

- *Sentence Type Posters* (pages 113–116; sentencetype.pdf)
- Chart paper
- Markers
- *Sentence Search Notebook Entry* (page 112; sentencesearch.pdf)
- A variety of picture books
- Writer's Notebooks

Mentor Texts

- *Thank You, Mr. Falker* by Patricia Polacco
- Literature from CCSS or Core Reading Program
- See *Mentor Text List* in Appendix C for other suggestions.

Procedures

Note: Repeat this lesson throughout the year. Use literature to identify different types of sentences and sentence structures to help students recognize the connection between reading and writing. Many writing assessments require application of the different kinds of sentences.

Think About Writing

1. Tell students that authors play with their sentences and include creative phrases and word order to make reading the sentence feel natural. Explain that sentences need to be varied to keep the reader's interest.

2. Review mentor texts, if desired, and emphasize the types of sentences the author uses and how the sentences flow from one to another.

Teach

3. Tell students, "Today I will show you four different kinds of sentences." Explain to students that when authors use different kinds of sentences, their writing automatically becomes more interesting!

4. Display the *Sentence Type Posters* (pages 113–116). Review the purpose of each sentence type and the corresponding punctuation. Display the posters in the room for students to reference as they write.

5. Write the sentences from the notebook entry on a sheet of chart paper. Challenge students to determine which type of sentence each one is. Use the posters displayed in the room as a reference. Provide additional sentences for modeling, if needed.

Sentence Search *(cont.)*

Engage

6. Have students work with partners to play Simon's Sentence Search. Provide each pair of students with a book. Tell students that you will give a direction and they will search in their texts for an example. For example, you can say, "Simon says, search for an interrogative sentence." Tell students to give thumbs up when they have found an example. Allow several students to share their examples out loud. Continue the game with other sentence types.

Apply

7. Remind students to use a variety of sentences to make their writing more interesting. Provide students with the *Sentence Search Notebook Entry* (page 112) to add to their Writer's Notebook. Have students work on the *Your Turn* section before proceeding to their writing folders.

Write/Conference

8. Provide time for students to write. Select two or three students who are having difficulty and work with them in a small group to provide additional support and practice, if needed. Support your own observations by making notes in your Conferring Notebook.

Spotlight Strategy

9. Spotlight students who are using different types of sentences. For example, "Jennifer did something brilliant. Listen to the rhythm and flow of her sentences. Exceptional sentence work today."

Share

10. Have students meet with partners to share their writing. Ask students to choose two of their best sentences to share. Then, ask the partners to meet with another partner group to create a quad to share their best sentences.

Homework

Ask students to listen for different types of sentences in the language that they hear. Have students write one of each type of sentence on a sheet of paper.

Sentence Search Notebook Entry

Sentence Search

Did you know that using different kinds of sentences automatically makes your writing more interesting? It's true!

A **declarative** sentence makes a statement and ends with a period.

>   Cole and Gina moved to Florida.

An **imperative** sentence gives a command or makes a request. Most imperative sentences end with a period. A strong command ends with an exclamation point.

>   Be very quiet. (command)

>   Please lock the door. (request)

>   Watch out! (strong command)

An **interrogative** sentence asks a question and ends with a question mark.

>   When will the concert begin?

An **exclamatory** sentence shows excitement or expresses strong feeling and ends with an explanation point.

>   Wow, you did a fantastic job!

Your Turn:

Search the writing in your notebook and add different kinds of sentences. Did you include a variety of sentences in your own writing? Remember the punctuation!

Sentence Type Posters

Declarative

Makes a statement and ends with a period.

●

Cole and Gina moved to Florida.

Sentence Type Posters

Interrogative

Asks a question and ends with a question mark.

When will the concert begin?

#50918—Getting to the Core of Writing—Level 4 © Shell Education

Sentence Type Posters

Imperative

Gives orders, commands, or instructions, and ends with a period or exclamation point.

!

Be very quiet.

Sentence Type Posters

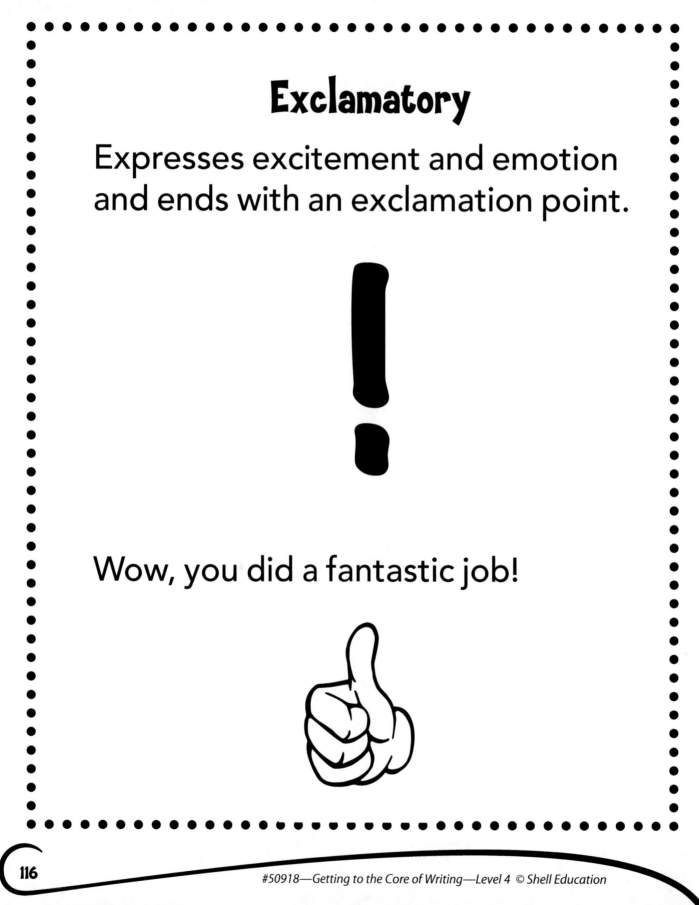

Exclamatory

Expresses excitement and emotion and ends with an exclamation point.

!

Wow, you did a fantastic job!

Appositive Action

Standards

- Uses a variety of sentence structures in writing
- Uses strategies to draft and revise written work

Materials

- *Appositive Action Puzzle Sentences* (page 120; appositivepuzzle.pdf)
- Chart paper
- Markers
- Writer's Notebooks
- *Appositive Action Notebook Entry* (page 119; appositiveaction.pdf)

Mentor Texts

- *Grandpa's Teeth* by Rod Clement
- *Thank You, Mr. Falker* by Patricia Polacco
- See Mentor Text List in Appendix C for other suggestions.

Procedures

Note: Revisit this lesson to provide repetitions necessary for students to fully understand the use of appositives in their writing work.

Think About Writing

1. Remind students that authors improve their sentences by using a variety of sentence development strategies. Sometimes authors add to a sentence, increasing interest, and improving specificity.

2. Review mentor texts, if desired, and emphasize the author's interesting sentences. For example, in *Grandpa's Teeth* when Grandpa was interviewed, he asked the reporter, Pearl White, if he could borrow her teeth. The author added *Pearl White* to give the reader a little more specific information.

Teach

3. Tell students, "Today I will show you how to add a simple appositive to your sentences that will add information, interest, and variety." Explain that an appositive adds more information about a noun and helps the reader understand who or what the sentence is about. Appositives add specificity, but an appositive can be removed from a sentence without changing the meaning of that sentence.

4. Use the *Appositive Action Puzzle Sentences* (page 120) to show how an appositive is separated by commas and is added to give the reader more information. Visually show students how the puzzle still fits together and maintains a complete sentence both with the appositive and without the appositive.

Appositive Action (cont.)

5. Divide a sheet of chart paper into three columns. Label the columns: *Noun*, *Appositive*, and *End of Sentence*. With students, create sentences using appositives and record them on the chart. After writing each sentence, cover the appositive to ensure that the sentence still works without it.

Engage

6. Write the following sentence on chart paper.

   Hayden ran down the lonely road.

   Ask students to work with partners to add an appositive to the sentence to tell more about Hayden. Provide approximately two or three minutes for students to work, and then have students share their sentences with the whole group.

Apply

7. Remind students to add appositives to sentences to add detail and variety to their writing. Provide students with the *Appositive Action Notebook Entry* (page 119) to add to their Writer's Notebook. Have students work on the *Your Turn* section before proceeding to their writing folders.

Write/Conference

8. Provide time for students to write. Scan your classroom to make certain that all students are working. Then, pull a small group to reteach. Remember to use your Conferring Notebook to make anecdotal notes.

Spotlight Strategy

9. Spotlight students who use appositives in their writing. For example, "Wow! Look how Daniel used an appositive in his writing. Your hard work in writing is paying off!" Give affirmations when students are attempting to apply the mini-lesson strategy.

Share

10. Have students meet with partners to share sentences they wrote today. Provide approximately two minutes for students to share. Observe and make notes as students share.

Homework

Ask students to search for nouns and create new sentences with appositives. Have students write two sentences that have appositives in them.

Appositive Action Notebook Entry

Appositive Action

An **appositive** is a noun or noun phrase that describes or explains another noun. Authors use appositives to provide details and add sentence variety in their writing.

1. **Sentence:**
   Mr. Gorrell retired after 35 years at the Primary Center.

2. **Identify noun:**
   Mr. Gorrell

3. **Add detail:**
   my principal

4. **Rewrite sentence with an appositive:**
   Mr. Gorrell, my principal, retired after 35 years at the Primary Center.

Another Example:

A cheetah, the fastest land mammal, can reach speeds up to 70 mph.

Your Turn:

Practice by using these phrases as appositives and create your own sentences.

- my best friend
- the 16th president
- my favorite book
- a fascinating animal
- our next-door neighbor
- an outstanding musician

Improve your sentence variety by moving into your own writing and adding some appositives.

Appositive Action Puzzle Sentences

Directions: Cut out the puzzle pieces. Model how to create complete sentences with and without appositives.

My friend | , Bobby, | has a black sports car.

The chef | , a personal friend, | made delicious cupcakes.

My car | , a small grey two door, | gets great gas mileage.

Compound Sentences

Standards

- Uses a variety of sentence structures in writing
- Uses strategies to draft and revise written work

Materials

- Chart paper
- Markers
- *Coordinating Conjunction Cards* (create 2 sets) (pages 124–125; conjunctioncards.pdf)
- Writer's Notebooks
- *Compound Sentences Notebook Entry* (page 123; compoundsentences.pdf)

Mentor Texts

- *Grandpa's Teeth* by Rod Clement
- See *Mentor Text List* in Appendix C for other suggestions.

Procedures

Note: Revisit and have students practice this strategy to build sentence variety.

Think About Writing

1. Remind students that authors build sentences in many different ways to gain and keep the reader's attention.

2. Review mentor texts, if desired, and emphasize the author's use of interesting sentences.

Teach

3. Tell students, "Today I will show you a way to remember the coordinating conjunctions and to use them to add additional information to your sentences." Explain that coordinating conjunctions are used to join words, phrases, and independent clauses.

4. Write *FANBOYS* vertically down a sheet of chart paper. Read the word *fanboys* to students. Tell students that this word can help them remember all the coordinating conjunctions.

5. Write each coordinating conjunction next to the appropriate letter and write the following sentences to illustrate the use of the conjunctions, or have students generate sentences.

   For   *Olivia had the best chance to be on the first team, **for** her granddad was the coach.*

   And   *No teeth had been found, **and** no clues had been uncovered.*

   Nor   *Jesse's younger brother is neither handsome, **nor** does he look like his dad.*

   But   *Lanty used his money wisely, **but** he gave away a great deal to his family.*

   Or   *You can pass your driving exam on the first attempt, **or** you can fail miserably.*

   Yet   *Jeff works hard at his job, **yet** he loves time off.*

Compound Sentences (cont.)

So   *The politicians are garnering huge crowds, **so** their electability is not in question.*

Engage

6. Distribute the *Coordinating Conjunction Cards* (pages 124–125) to pairs of students. Have students work with their partners to create compound sentences using the coordinating conjunction on their cards. Allow time for discussion and then have several groups share their sentences. Have students trade cards and practice with new coordinating conjunctions.

Apply

7. Remind students to use coordinating conjunctions to add variety to their sentence lengths and add details to show the reader information. Provide students with the *Compound Sentences Notebook Entry* (page 123) to add to their Writer's Notebook. Complete practice in the *Your Turn* section and then continue folder writing projects.

Write/Conference

8. Provide time for students to write. Use the *Coordinating Conjunction Cards* to give additional practice to a group that needs further explanation. Then, rotate around the room to conference with individual students. Remember to make wise decisions about your next instructional focus based on your observations of student work.

Spotlight Strategy

9. Spotlight students who are writing compound sentences. For example, "Writers, you rock! Amazing sentence construction work today. This is such an important piece of information to build your sentence length and sentence variety. Listen to this sentence!" Share a student's sentence.

Share

10. Have students meet with partners to share the best sentences they wrote today. Encourage them to look for conjunctions in their partner's writing. Remind students to give their partners comments so they will grow as writers.

Homework

Ask students to write the word FANBOYS vertically on a sheet of paper and try to remember each of the coordinating conjunctions. Then, have students choose two coordinating conjunctions and write sentences using the conjunctions.

Compound Sentences Notebook Entry

Compound Sentences

Authors use **coordinating conjunctions** to combine short, choppy sentences and to add rhythm and flow to their writing.

A coordinating conjunction links two or more simple sentences to create a compound sentence. A comma is placed before the coordinating conjunction. Here's the formula:

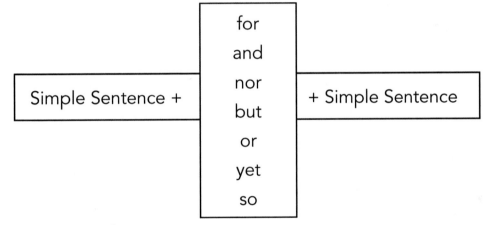

| Simple Sentence + | for
and
nor
but
or
yet
so | + Simple Sentence |

Here is an example:

> He was sick. He went to the doctor.
>
> He was sick, **so** he went to the doctor.

Your Turn:

Help these choppy sentences by using coordinating conjunctions to create compound sentences.

- Vinnie lives in Baltimore. He studies at Johns Hopkins.
- Bill is retired. Karen continues to teach.
- I could cook dinner. We could order a pizza.

Coordinating Conjunction Cards

Directions: Cut out the cards. Distribute a card to each pair of students and have each pair create compound sentences using the conjunction on their card.

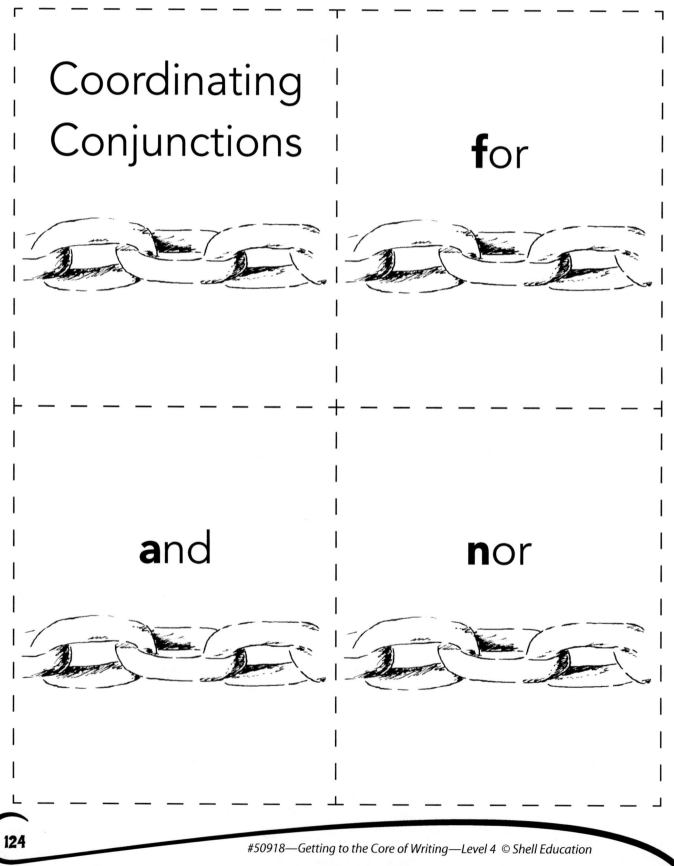

Coordinating Conjunctions

for

and

nor

Coordinating Conjunction Cards *(cont.)*

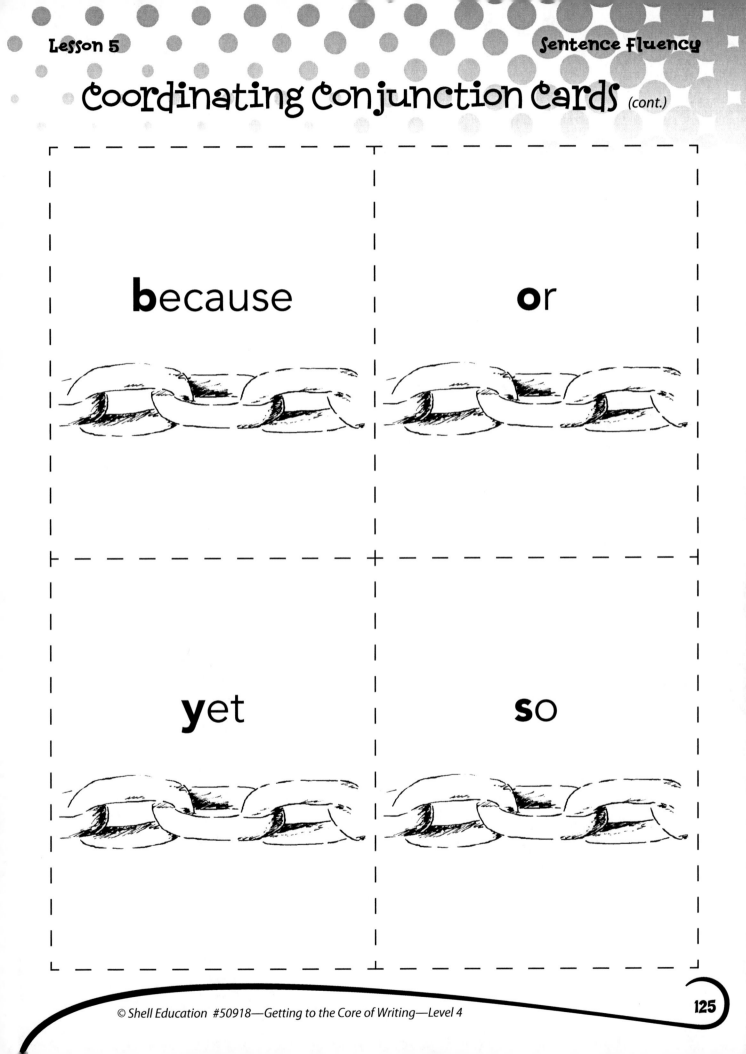

because

or

yet

so

Writing Complex Sentences

Standards

- Uses a variety of sentence structures in writing
- Uses strategies to draft and revise written work

Materials

- *Subordinating Conjunction Cards* (pages 129–130; subconjunctioncards.pdf)
- Chart paper
- Markers
- Writer's Notebooks
- *Writing Complex Sentences Notebook Entry* (page 128; writingcomplex.pdf)

Mentor Texts

- *Thank You, Mr. Falker* by Patricia Polacco
- Other CCSS literature
- See *Mentor Text List* in Appendix C for other suggestions.

Procedures

Note: Complex sentences and subordinating conjunctions work together. A subordinating conjunction works within a complex sentence to begin a dependent clause. Revisit this lesson many times and coordinate with a lesson on complex sentences to bring meaning to the process. Spread the lesson over several days using literature to demonstrate and model sentences using the conjunctions.

Think About Writing

1. Explain to students that one of our greatest resources is the work of authors we know and love. We can study their craft, sentences, and word choice to support our work as authors. Shaping our sentences to mimic theirs gives us confidence as we write.

2. Review mentor texts, if desired, and emphasize the author's use of sentence variation, including sentence length.

Teach

3. Tell students, "Today I will show you how to construct sentences using subordinating conjunctions." Explain to students that using subordinating conjunctions will help them increase the lengths of their sentences, helping them to have sentence variation.

4. Display the *Subordinating Conjunction Cards* (pages 129–130) on a chalk rail or in a pocket chart. Write the following sentences on a sheet of chart paper.

   - *After the rain stopped, a beautiful rainbow appeared in the Eastern sky.*
   - *Although I love sports, I'm too busy to attend any games.*
   - *Because he grew up in the country, he always returned to his beloved farm on the holidays.*

Writing Complex Sentences (cont.)

5. Identify the subordinating conjunctions in each sentence. Cover up the clause in several examples and read the sentences. Then, cover up the rest of the sentence and read the clause. Note with students that the clause is dependent on the rest of the sentence for meaning.

Engage

6. Have students work with partners to create sentences using *after*, *although*, and *because*. Remind students to take turns with their partners. Provide approximately three minutes for students to talk.

Apply

7. Remind students to construct meaningful sentences and have sentence variety by using conjunctions to stretch and enrich their sentences. Provide students with the *Writing Complex Sentences Notebook Entry* (page 128) to add to their Writer's Notebook. Have students work on the *Your Turn* section before proceeding to their writing folders.

Write/Conference

8. Provide time for students to write. Be prepared to reteach to a small group, if needed. Use the *Subordinating Conjunction Cards* to review literature with the group to demonstrate how conjunctions are used. Reteach with the group for three or four minutes, and then work with another small group or begin conferencing with individual students.

Spotlight Strategy

9. Spotlight students who are writing complex sentences. For example, "Extraordinary sentence work today. Just listen to this sentence." Share a sentence.

Share

10. Have students meet with partners to share the best sentences they wrote today. Remind students to give each other compliments.

Homework

Ask students to look around their homes to see if they can find any evidence of conjunctions. Have each student make a list of at least three conjunctions found in writing or speech.

Writing Complex Sentences Notebook Entry

Writing Complex Sentences

Authors use **complex sentences** to add fluency and variety in their writing.

A complex sentence contains one independent clause and one dependent clause, which includes a subordinating conjunction, such as *after, although, because, before, since, though, when,* or *where.*

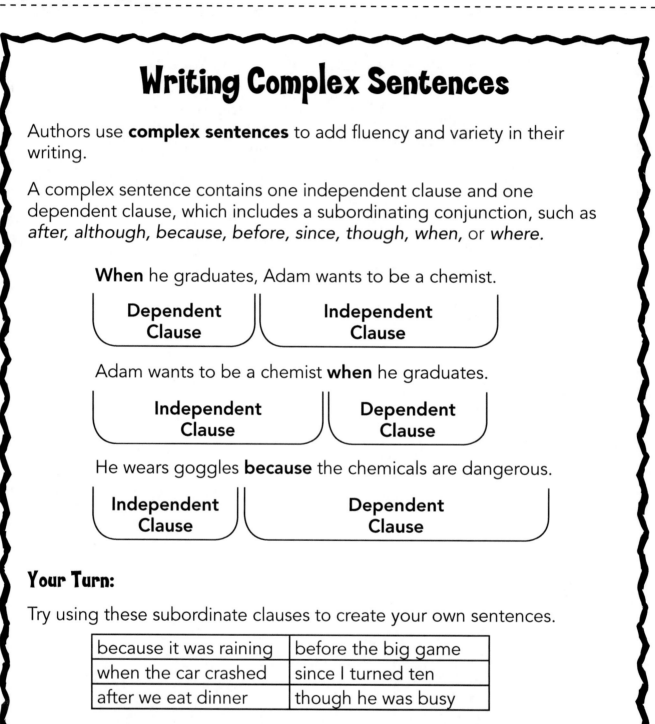

When he graduates, Adam wants to be a chemist.

| Dependent Clause | Independent Clause |

Adam wants to be a chemist **when** he graduates.

| Independent Clause | Dependent Clause |

He wears goggles **because** the chemicals are dangerous.

| Independent Clause | Dependent Clause |

Your Turn:

Try using these subordinate clauses to create your own sentences.

because it was raining	before the big game
when the car crashed	since I turned ten
after we eat dinner	though he was busy

Revise your writing by including complex sentences to add variety and interest for your reader.

#50918—Getting to the Core of Writing—Level 4 © Shell Education

Subordinating Conjunction Cards

Directions: Cut out the cards. Use the cards to demonstrate how the conjunctions are used as you review literature.

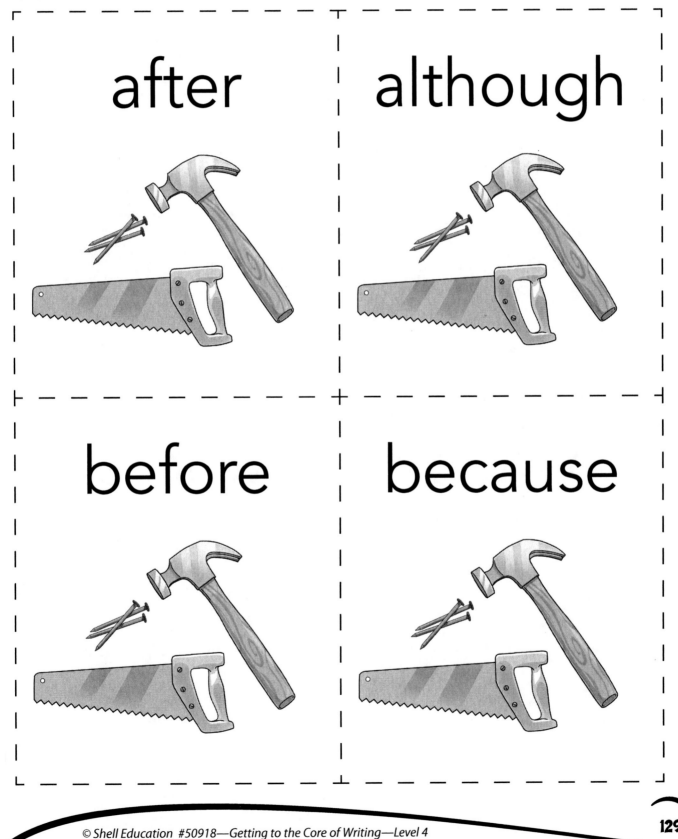

after

although

before

because

Subordinating Conjunctions Cards (cont.)

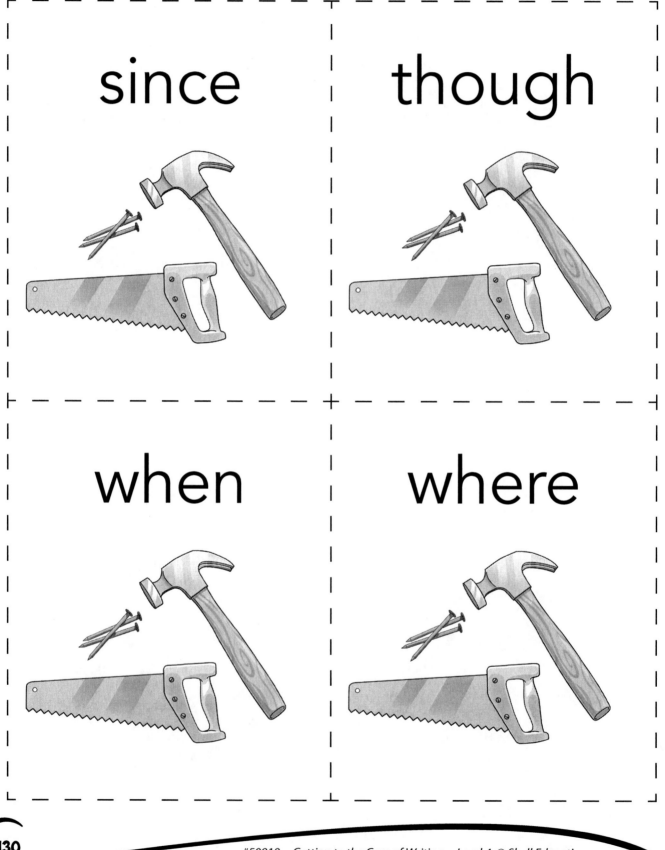

Stepping Up Sentences

Standards

- Uses a variety of sentence structures in writing
- Uses strategies to draft and revise written work

Materials

- Chart paper or 8.5" × 11" drawing paper
- Markers
- Writer's Notebooks
- *Stepping Up Sentences Notebook Entry* (page 133; steppingup.pdf)

Mentor Texts

- *Owl Moon* by Jane Yolen
- *Thank You, Mr. Falker* by Patricia Polacco
- See *Mentor Text List* in Appendix C for other suggestions.

Procedures

Note: Repeat this mini-lesson often, as it will help students improve their sentence lengths, rhythm, and understanding of sentence variety.

Think About Writing

1. Explain that good authors create sentences that are rhythmic and flow smoothly on to the next sentence. To make that happen, authors work on their sentences, sometimes rewriting them over and over in order to get them just right.

2. Review mentor texts, if desired, and emphasize the author's use of sentence variation.

Teach

3. Tell students, "Today I will show you an easy way to build sentences that will improve your sentence fluency and word choice."

4. Demonstrate the strategy on chart paper by drawing a table with four columns, or take a piece of 8.5" × 11" paper and fold it in half and then in half again so that when you open it, there are four columns for demonstration.

5. Number the columns as shown below:

Step 3: Adjective	Step 1: Noun	Step 2: Verb/Adverb	Step 4: Prepositional Phrase
Describe it.	What is your sentence about?	What does it do? How?	Tell where or when?
lanky	giraffe	loped/ listlessly	across the plains

Stepping Up Sentences *(cont.)*

6. Fold the two outside columns to the back, so only column 1 and 2 are visible. Complete the questions in column 1 and 2. Next, fold out Column 3 and answer the question; fold out Column 4 and answer the question. Use this information to create sentences. Use sentence samples from the notebook entry or create your own.

Engage

7. Have students work with partners to create interesting sentences using the numbered columns. Encourage students to use the questions listed in each column to guide their sentence building. Provide approximately two or three minutes for students to build sentences.

Apply

8. Remind students to practice sentence fluency and variety to energize their writing. Provide students with the *Stepping Up Sentences Notebook Entry* (page 133) to add to their Writer's Notebook. Have students work on the *Your Turn* section before proceeding to their writing folders.

Write/Conference

9. Provide time for students to write. Then, scan the room for any students having difficulties getting started. If necessary, pull a small group to reteach and practice. Remember to make many observations to plan your next day's instruction. Record everything you observe in your Conferring Notebook.

Spotlight Strategy

10. Spotlight students who are writing sentences with strong detail. For example, "Trevor has a brilliant sentence."

Share

11. Have students meet with partners to share interesting sentences they have written. Allow approximately two minutes for students to share. As students share, rotate around the room and make observations to share at the end of the share time. Call attention to students' work that is a good model of great sentences.

Homework

Ask students to share this strategy for sentence writing with their parents. Have students write three sentences at home and bring them back to school to share with the class.

Stepping Up Sentences Notebook Entry

Stepping Up Sentences

Authors add details to their sentences to paint a picture for their readers.

Try these easy steps to expand your sentences:

1. What is your sentence about? (*noun*)

2. What does it do? (*verb*) How? (*adverb*)

3. Describe it. (*adjective*)

4. Tell where or when. (*prepositional phrase*)

Step 3: Adjective	Step 1: Noun	Step 2: Verb/Adverb	Step 4: Prepositional Phrase
Describe it.	What is your sentence about?	What does it do? How?	Where or when?
curious	child	read/quietly	in the grass
The curious child read quietly in the grass.			

Your Turn:

Practice writing sentences with details that will inform and interest your readers. Work with a partner or by yourself to develop some splendid sentences.

Building Triangle Sentences

Standards

- Uses a variety of sentence structures in writing
- Uses strategies to draft and revise written work

Materials

- Chart paper
- Markers
- Writer's Notebooks
- *Building Triangle Sentences Notebook Entry* (page 136; trianglesentences.pdf)

Mentor Texts

- *Thank You, Mr. Falker* by Patricia Polacco
- *Shrek!* by William Steig
- See *Mentor Text List* in Appendix C for other suggestions.

Procedures

Note: Use this lesson to develop an anchor chart to keep up as a reminder of parts of speech used to create sentence interest.

Think About Writing

1. Explain to students that authors work to ensure that their sentences flow. They also use many details to show their story instead of just telling a tale.

2. Review mentor texts, if desired, and emphasize the author's use of interesting and detailed sentences. For example, author William Steig creates sentences with rich details in his book *Shrek!*

Teach

3. Tell students, "Today I will show you how to add descriptive details to make your writing interesting and help the reader become part of the story." Explain that knowing the parts of speech and using them in writing will support their sentence writing.

4. Draw the triangle diagram from the *Building Triangle Sentences Notebook Entry* (page 136) on a sheet of chart paper. Use the notebook entry as a guide as you draw. Write the parts of speech down the side of the triangle.

5. Model how to build a triangle sentence by writing words for each part of speech in the corresponding section inside the triangle. You may wish to use a different colored marker for each line. Remember to think aloud throughout the process so students have an explicit model of how to assemble a triangle sentence. Keep the chart paper up as a resource for students.

Building Triangle Sentences (cont.)

Engage

6. Write the words *tree*, *puppy*, and *teacher* at the bottom of the chart paper. Have students work with partners to create triangle sentences using those nouns. Remind students to praise their partners' attempts and to give feedback.

Apply

7. Remind students to use descriptive details in their sentences so the reader becomes a part of the story and wants to read more. Provide students with the *Building Triangle Sentences Notebook Entry* to add to their Writer's Notebook. Have students work on the *Your Turn* section and move into their writing folders to revise sentences or begin a new writing project.

Write/Conference

8. Provide time for students to write. Scan the classroom to make certain that all students are working. Then, rotate around the room to conference with students individually or in small groups. Remember to use your Conferring Notebook to make anecdotal notes. Ask questions, such as, "What will you do next in writing?"

Spotlight Strategy

9. Spotlight students who are creating Triangle Sentences. For example, "Look at your amazing sentence work. Allison created an exceptional Triangle Sentence."

Share

10. Have students work with partners to share their new sentences. Remind students to give a compliment and a comment. Provide approximately two minutes for students to share. From your teacher observations, choose one or two students and have them share with the whole group.

Homework

Ask students to notice details in things they read. Have them check newspaper and magazine articles for sentences with details that make the writing more interesting. Ask students to write down or bring in two examples of interesting, detailed sentences.

Building Triangle Sentences Notebook Entry

Building Triangle Sentences

Authors use details to show us stories, not just tell us tales.

Build triangle sentences to add details to your sentences.

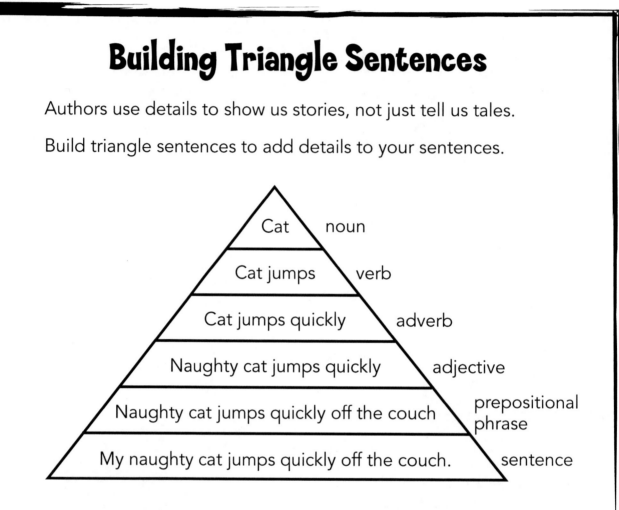

Your Turn:

Use these nouns to practice building triangle sentences. Then, search for sentences in your writing that may need more interesting details.

- boy
- biker
- tiger
- teacher

- baby
- tree
- turtle
- storm

- puppy
- deer
- music
- sun

#50918—Getting to the Core of Writing—Level 4 © Shell Education

Organization
Linking the Pieces Together

Organization provides the structure of writing. It helps readers make connections from one idea to the next. Organization provides the skeletal support for the overall meaning of writing. The lessons assist students to explore different types of writing and the ways they are organized. Lessons in this section include the following:

- Lesson 1: Creating Cinquains (page 139)
- Lesson 2: Powerful Paragraphs (page 142)
- Lesson 3: Narrative Notes (page 145)
- Lesson 4: Build-a-Character (page 148)
- Lesson 5: Story Building Blocks (page 151)
- Lesson 6: It's a Bear Beginning (page 154)
- Lesson 7: Don't You Agree? (page 158)
- Lesson 8: It's Your Business (page 161)
- Lesson 9: How-To Writing (page 165)
- Lesson 10: Composition Planner (page 168)
- Lesson 11: A Cache of Poetry (page 172)

The *Owen, Organization Conductor* poster (page 138) can be displayed in the room to provide a visual reminder for students that organization is one of the traits of writing. You may wish to introduce this poster during the first lesson on organization. Then, refer to the poster when teaching other lessons on organization to refresh students' memories and provide them with questions in order to guide them as they organize their writing.

Owen
Organization
Conductor

How do I plan my writing?

✔ Did I sequence my thoughts?

✔ Did I have a beginning, middle, and end?

✔ Did I hook my reader?

✔ Did I include transition words?

Creating Cinquains

Standards

- Uses strategies to draft and revise written work
- Writes narrative accounts, such as poems and stories

Materials

- Chart paper
- Markers
- Writer's Notebooks
- *Creating Cinquains Notebook Entry* (page 141; cinquains.pdf)

Mentor Texts

- *A Kick in the Head: An Everyday Guide to Poetic Forms* by Paul Janeczko
- *Pizza, Pigs, and Poetry: How to Write a Poem* by Jack Prelutsky
- See *Mentor Text List* in Appendix C for other suggestions.

Procedures

Note: Use the lesson plan idea to complete several different formats of poetry patterns. Keep patterns displayed as anchor charts to be used throughout the year. At the beginning of the year, you may wish to have students create cinquain poems that describe them to personalize their notebook.

Think About Writing

1. Remind students that they are getting Writer's Workshop structures organized and are collecting ideas for writing. Tell students that poetry can be a fun writing project. Explain that there are many different kinds of poetry. Poems can be funny and silly or romantic and serious.

2. Review mentor texts, if desired, and emphasize the various forms of poetry.

Teach

3. Tell students, "Today I will show you a fun and easy poetry pattern called a *cinquain*." Explain that a *cinquain* is a five-line poem that can be used for many different topics including science, social studies, and math.

4. Write the cinquain poetry pattern on chart paper and review it with students.

   Line 1:   *one noun*

   Line 2:   *two adjectives*

   Line 3:   *three verbs ending with –ing*

   Line 4:   *four-word phrase*

   Line 5:   *one word synonym for the noun*

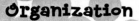
Creating Cinquains (cont.)

5. Model how to create a cinquain poem of your own or use the example below:

> *Space*
> *Vast, empty*
> *Piercing, chilling, freezing*
> *Changing beauty into barren*
> *Cosmos*

6. Create a list on chart paper of possible poem topics, such as family, friends, school, sports, objects, or any subject, including content area topics.

Engage

7. Remind students to decide on their topics, and then experiment with words and phrases using the pattern on the chart. Have students talk with partners for approximately two or three minutes about possible topics for their poems.

Apply

8. Encourage students to have a multitude of ideas so that choices will always be an option in writing projects. Provide students with the *Creating Cinquains Notebook Entry* (page 141) to add to their Writer's Notebook. Have students create several drafts from the *Your Turn* section and select one to publish.

Write/Conference

9. Provide time for students to write. Keep your Conferring Notebook in your hand as a reminder to students that you are unavailable when working with individual students. They can seek help from their peers and get your attention between conferences. Keep notes on individual students and the success of the lesson.

Spotlight Strategy

10. Spotlight students who have written interesting cinquains. For example, "Wow! You really rock, writers! Just listen to the cinquain that Charles has completed. I'm spotlighting these incredible words, phrases, and non-traditional sentences."

Share

11. Have students meet with partners to share their writing. Then, have students meet in quads. Remind students that everyone should have a chance to share. Encourage students to give compliments.

Homework

Ask students to tell their parents the pattern for writing a cinquain poem. Have students work with their parents to write one together.

Creating Cinquains Notebook Entry

Creating Cinquains

Pattern One:

Lines	Word Cinquain
1 noun	Space
2 adjectives	Vast, empty
3 verbs/-ing	Piercing, chilling, freezing
4-word phrase	Changing beauty into barren
1 word synonym for noun	Cosmos

Pattern Two:

Lines	Syllable Cinquain
2 syllables	Dragon
4 syllables	Lived long ago
6 syllables	In lands of enchantment
8 syllables	Glittering scales, fiery breath
2 syllables	Fearsome

Your Turn:

Use the topics below or create your own to create cinquain poetry in your notebook.

- weather
- space
- holidays
- animals
- family
- friends
- geology
- food
- sports
- characters
- teachers
- nature

Powerful Paragraphs

Standards

- Uses strategies to draft and revise written work
- Uses paragraph form in writing

Materials

- Chart paper
- Markers (black, green, yellow, and red)
- *Powerful Paragraphs Notebook Entry* (page 144; powerful.pdf)
- Writer's Notebooks
- Green, yellow, and red manipulatives, such as magnetic buttons or snap cubes

Mentor Texts

- *Owls* by Gail Gibbons
- See *Mentor Text List* in Appendix C for other suggestions.

Procedures

Note: Use this lesson plan to introduce students to the organizational structure of paragraphs. Review different types of paragraphs with students: Narrative—entertains and tells a story; Information—informs and gives facts about a topic; Opinion—persuades and gives a point of view. Images store learning in long-term memory, so be certain to use manipulatives again and again.

Think About Writing

1. Remind students that authors organize their ideas so they will be easy for the reader to follow. Explain that there are many ways to organize writing and that good writers use many different kinds of organizational tools.

2. Review mentor texts, if desired, and emphasize the way the writing is organized.

Teach

3. Tell students, "Today I will show you how to write a paragraph with a main idea sentence, a body, and a concluding sentence."

4. Create an anchor chart on chart paper with the three parts of a paragraph. Use the wording from the *Powerful Paragraphs Notebook Entry* (page 144). Use a magnetic board with one green, three yellow, and one red button to show the three parts of a paragraph. (If magnetic boards and buttons are not available use snap cubes to snap together, or draw dots with colored markers.)

   - Green represents *go*—The first sentence in a paragraph is the topic, or main idea, sentence and tells the reader what the paragraph is about.

   - Yellow represents *slow down*—The next several sentences form the body of the paragraph and should support or tell more about the topic.

   - Red represents *stop*—The concluding sentence tells the reader the paragraph is over.

Powerful Paragraphs *(cont.)*

5. Model how to write a paragraph. Write about your own topic or use the paragraph about trees from the notebook entry. As you write, think aloud to explain each part of the paragraph and why you are writing what you are writing. Write the paragraph using a black marker, but underline each sentence using a green, yellow, or red marker to show the paragraph parts.

Engage

6. Have students think of topics they might want to investigate. Brainstorm ideas together as a class and record students' ideas on a sheet of chart paper.

Apply

7. Remind students to group their ideas into a three-part paragraph. Provide students with the *Powerful Paragraphs Notebook Entry* to add to their Writer's Notebook. Remind students to return to the ideas section of their notebooks to choose a topic and write powerful paragraphs.

Write/Conference

8. Provide time for students to write. Observe students for difficulty and support their efforts in developing the three parts of the paragraph. Begin to conference with individuals or small groups using your Conferring Notebook for recordkeeping.

Spotlight Strategy

9. Identify a student who clearly understands the three parts of the paragraph and call attention to their brilliant ideas. Keep a small flashlight in your pocket or close by to spotlight students with a main idea sentence, body, and a concluding statement.

Share

10. Have students meet with partners to share their writing. Remind students to give each other feedback by giving a compliment and a comment. From your observations, choose one or two students who clearly understand the idea and have them share with the whole group.

Homework

Ask students to write down the parts of a paragraph and to use colored markers or pencils to color code each section of the paragraph.

Powerful Paragraphs Notebook Entry

Powerful Paragraphs

Paragraphs help to organize writing by grouping related ideas together. A paragraph has three parts: topic sentence, body, and closing sentence.

Topic Sentence: States the main idea

Body: All ideas are connected to the topic sentence and help the reader understand the main idea

Concluding Sentence: Sums up the paragraph's message

For example:

Trees are important to life on Earth. (*topic sentence*) They add beauty to the mountains and provide shelter for wildlife. Trees provide wood, paper, food, medicine, and other useful products. Humans need oxygen, and trees produce oxygen to help people breathe. (*body*) We need to remember the importance of trees and take action to protect them. (*concluding sentence*)

Your Turn:

Create your own three-part paragraph. Remember to include a topic sentence, a body, and a closing sentence.

Narrative Notes

Standards

- Uses strategies to draft and revise written work
- Writes narrative accounts, such as poems and stories

Materials

- Chart paper
- Markers
- Writer's Notebooks
- *Narrative Notes Notebook Entry* (page 147; narrativenotes.pdf)

Mentor Texts

- *Shortcut* by Donald Crews
- *Red Riding Hood* by James Marshall
- *Lon Po Po: A Red Riding Hood Story from China* by Ed Young
- *Pecos Bill* by Steven Kellogg
- *The Bunyans* by Audrey Wood
- *Once Upon a Time, The End* by Geoffrey Kloske
- See *Mentor Text List* in Appendix C for other suggestions.

Procedures

Note: Taking the time to explore samples of narrative writing will support young writers as they begin to go deeper into developing more details and events in their own writing. This lesson will be taught over several days.

Think About Writing

1. Remind students that authors write for three basic purposes: to persuade, to inform, and to entertain. Tell students that today they will explore how to entertain their readers.

Teach

2. Tell students, "Today I will show you the characteristics of narrative writing." Explain that in narrative writing, an author tells a story that may be factual, imaginary, or a mixture of both.

3. Begin a list of the many types of narrative writing, such as folk tales, fables, fairy tales, fantasies, mysteries, science fiction, realistic fiction, short stories, personal experiences. Keep the list posted in the classroom. As you read books aloud to students over the next several weeks, have students help identify which type of narrative writing the books are.

4. Tell students that most narrative writing shares some characteristics. Create a list and discuss each of the following characteristics of narrative writing.

    Characters: the people in the story

    Setting: where and when the story takes place

    Conflict: the problem or main purpose

    Plot: the sequence of events

    Theme: the author's message

Narrative Notes *(cont.)*

5. Share a mentor text with students and take narrative notes as shown in the *Narrative Notes Notebook Entry* (page 147). Record evidence from the text of the characteristics of a narrative.

6. Tell students that by completing narrative notes before they begin writing their stories, they will have many ideas to draw from in order to bring their stories to life.

Engage

7. Have students work with partners to analyze a narrative story and create their own narrative notes to share with the class. This may take a bit of time based on how familiar the students are with the text provided. Provide students with paper or chart paper and markers or pencils. As students work, listen in to partners' conversations and provide guidance. Have partners share their results in quads.

Apply

8. Remind students to create narrative notes as a way to organize their narrative writing before they begin to write sentences. Provide students with the *Narrative Notes Notebook Entry* to add to their Writer's Notebook. Have students work on the *Your Turn* section before proceeding to their writing folders.

Write/Conference

9. Provide time for students to write. Observe your group for any confusion. Gather a small group of students needing additional support and develop a story as a group.

Spotlight Strategy

10. Spotlight students who have created interesting narratives. For example, "Writers, Mila is developing characteristics for a very interesting narrative. Listen to her plot. Terrific planning!"

Share

11. Have students meet with partners to share the narrative notes for their next stories. Encourage students to listen closely to their partner's information. Remind students that compliments and comments help each other grow as writers. Allow approximately two minutes for sharing.

Homework
Ask students to work with their parents to read a storybook and create narrative notes about the book.

Narrative Notes Notebook Entry

Narrative Notes

Narrative writing may be factual, imaginary, or a mixture of both. Types of narrative writing include:

- fairy tales
- mysteries
- realistic fiction
- fantasies
- adventures
- folktales

Use this format to take narrative notes on a story.

Cinderella

Characteristic	Narrative Notes
Characters: Who is in the story?	Cinderella, wicked stepmother and sisters, fairy godmother, prince
Setting: Where and when does the story take place?	medieval times, house in the countryside, castle
Conflict: What is the problem in the story? What does the character need or want?	Cinderella is being treated unkindly and dreams of a better life.
Plot: The sequence of events or actions in your story. What is going to happen?	Cinderella's family is very unkind. They attend the king's ball but forbid her to go. Fairy godmother helps her. She has a great time, but time runs out! She loses her shoe. The prince finds her and the shoe fits! They get married.
Theme: What is the author's message or lesson learned by the character?	Those with a kind and giving heart deserve and eventually get kindness in return.

Your Turn:

Create your own story. Make narrative notes of your story's characteristics.

Build-a-Character

Standards

- Uses strategies to draft and revise written work
- Writes narrative accounts, such as poems and stories

Materials

- Chart paper
- Markers
- *Build-a-Character Notebook Entry* (page 150; buildcharacter.pdf)
- Writer's Notebooks

Mentor Texts

- *The Twits* by Ronald Dahl
- *John Henry* by Julius Lester
- *My Great Aunt Arizona* by Gloria Houston
- *Wilma Unlimited* by David Diaz
- *Shrek!* by William Steig
- *Charlotte's Web* by E. B. White
- See *Mentor Text List* in Appendix C for other suggestions.

Procedures

Note: This lesson may span across several writing sessions based on the prior knowledge of your students.

Think About Writing

1. Remind students that they have been learning about the many different types of narrative writing. Explain that one characteristic that is consistent in all the stories is interesting, well-developed characters.

Teach

2. Tell students, "Today I will show you how to build a character for a story." Remind students that *characters* are the people or animals in stories; they are the heart of narrative writing. The stories revolve around characters' attitudes and personalities.

3. Create a two-column table on chart paper.

Build-a-Character	
Appearance	
Personality	
Likes/Dislikes	
Relationship to others	

Explain to students that this chart will help them create traits that will bring their characters to life. A character's traits are best revealed to the reader through actions, words, thoughts, attitudes, and feelings.

4. Use a mentor text to complete the Build-a-Character chart. Think aloud as you complete the chart so students have an explicit model of how you decide which words to write in each section. Use the example in the *Build-a-Character Notebook Entry* (page 150) as a guide.

Build-a-Character *(cont.)*

5. Tell students that by completing a chart, such as the Build-a-Character chart, before they begin writing their stories, they will have many ideas to draw from in order to bring their characters to life.

Engage

6. Have students work with partners to analyze a character from a favorite text. Allow time for the activity based on how familiar the students are with the characters in the text provided. You might assign specific characters from current texts or provide a selection of characters. Provide students with paper or chart paper and markers or pencils. As students work, listen in on conversations and provide guidance. Have partners share their results in quads.

Apply

7. Encourage students to create a character that is believable to the reader. Provide students with the *Build-a-Character Notebook Entry* to add to their Writer's Notebook. Have students work on the *Your Turn* section before proceeding to their writing folders.

Write/Conference

8. Provide time for students to write. Make observations and identify any students who are confused. When finished, move into individual conferences, keeping anecdotal observations to plan the next steps.

Spotlight Strategy

9. Spotlight students who are creating interesting characters. For example, "You must be proud of your work! Just listen to the interesting features of this character! Notice how Karen's writing is building a memorable character."

Share

10. Have students meet with partners to share their characters and one or two traits that make them memorable. Allow approximately two minutes to share.

Homework

Ask students to think of a favorite character from a book, TV show, or movie. Have students work with their parents to complete a Build-a-Character chart based on the character they choose.

Build-a-Character Notebook Entry

Build-a-Character

Memorable characters are those that the reader gets to know well. They have traits that are believable and invite the reader into the story.

Character: Templeton the Rat from *Charlotte's Web*	
Appearance: a chubby rat, long tail, sharp teeth for gnawing, claws for clutching food	**Revealed by:** After his night at the fair he has swollen double his size. Later, he agrees to trade for food so he can become fatter and bigger than all the other rats.
Personality: sneaky, thoughtless, unkind, ill-tempered	**Revealed by:** He creeps up to the goslings, close to the wall. He snickers when Wilbur falls, takes his food, and bites his tail.
Likes/Dislikes: Likes being alone, food Dislikes being bothered	**Revealed by:** When Wilbur wants him to play, Templeton says, "…I never do those things if I can avoid them…I prefer to spend my time eating, gnawing, spying and hiding. I am a glutton not a merry-maker."
Relationship to others: He can do without them, but they continue to ask him for help even though they have to bribe him with food.	**Revealed by:** Each time he is asked to retrieve words for Charlotte, he ends up with something in return.

Your Turn:

Create and illustrate your character, then write a description of your character that includes the four character traits listed in this notebook entry. Just for fun, create a character cinquain!

Story Building Blocks

Standards

- Uses strategies to draft and revise written work
- Writes narrative accounts, such as poems and stories

Materials

- Chart paper
- Markers
- Writer's Notebooks
- *Story Building Blocks Notebook Entry* (page 153; storyblocks.pdf)

Mentor Texts

- *The Paperboy* by Dav Pilkey
- *Shortcut* by Donald Crews
- *Marshfield Dreams* by Ralph Fletcher
- *Saturdays and Teacakes* by Lester Laminack
- See *Mentor Text List* in Appendix C for other suggestions.

Procedures

Note: Writers need multiple opportunities to build their writing skills. This lesson is designed to explore literature and use mentor texts to support independent writing.

Think About Writing

1. Review with students that they have been developing an understanding of narrative writing and developing memorable characters for stories. Remind students that they have learned how important characters are to the success of writing. Explain that another critical feature of narrative writing is a well-developed plot—the order and manner events happen in the story.

Teach

2. Tell students, "Today I will show you how to use story building blocks to map out your narrative story plot." Explain that the plot must be a logically sequenced set of events that are linked together, each one affecting the next. Ask students to think about the events as cause and effect: If this happens, then it will cause this to happen next. For example, the prince found Cinderella's shoe, so he set out to search for her.

3. Display the *Story Building Blocks Notebook Entry* (page 153) or create your own on chart paper. Choose a mentor text that students are familiar with and model how to chart out the events.

4. Tell students that completing a chart, such as a story building blocks chart, before they begin writing their stories will help them create the events of the story and the sequence they will take place in.

Story Building Blocks *(cont.)*

Engage

5. Have students work in quads to select a mentor text and then identify the story building blocks from the story. Allow time for students to work and then have teams share their findings with the whole class.

Apply

6. Remind students to organize their writing in a logical, well-developed sequence of linked events. Provide students with the *Story Building Blocks Notebook Entry* to add to their Writer's Notebook. Have students begin a narrative story using the notebook entry for support and guidance.

Write/Conference

7. Provide time for students to write. Developing a narrative plan may be difficult for struggling students. Gather students who need additional assistance, and begin completing a story building blocks chart together based on a familiar story. When you are finished, rotate among the other students and conduct individual conferences. Make notes in your Conferring Notebook.

Spotlight Strategy

8. Spotlight students who are building strong narrative plots. For example, "Wow! Outstanding effort! Writers, you're right on target with your narrative plots. Listen to Armando's series of events. I feel in the moment of this story."

Share

9. Select two or three students to share their writing in the Author's Chair. Remind students to give praise to the authors who share.

Homework

Ask students to think of other topics they would like to write about. Have students ask their parents or other family members to help provide ideas. Ask students to write down three new topics to add to their notebook.

Story Building Blocks Notebook Entry

Story Building Blocks

The **plot** of a narrative story is a logical sequence of events a character(s) encounters. The events are linked together, each one affecting the next.

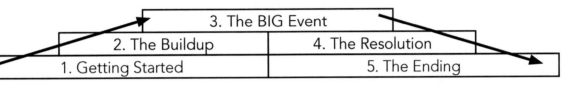

	3. The BIG Event	
2. The Buildup		4. The Resolution
1. Getting Started		5. The Ending

1. **Getting Started:**
   - Introduce character(s)
   - Setting/when & where
   - Create mood
   - Hint about what is to come

2. **The Buildup:**
   - "Get the story going" event (What is the character's problem and what event starts the adventure?)
   - Other linked events; who do they meet, obstacles along the way

3. **The BIG Event:**
   - The problem
   - Most exciting part of the story
   - Use short sentences for emphasis
   - Use powerful verbs

4. **Resolution:**
   - Events to solve the problem

5. **The Ending:**
   - Wrap it up
   - What has been learned?
   - How have characters changed?

Your Turn:

Use what you have learned about narrative writing, building characters, and using story building blocks to create your own story. Remember to revisit favorite authors to explore features of narrative writing.

It's a Bear Beginning

Standards

- Uses strategies to draft and revise written work
- Writes narrative accounts, such as poems and stories

Materials

- Chart paper
- Markers
- *Three Bears Hook Cards* (page 157; 3bearscards.pdf)
- *It's a Bear Beginning Notebook Entry* (page 156; bearbeginning.pdf)
- Writer's Notebooks

Mentor Texts

- *Goldilocks and the Three Bears* by Jan Brett
- Other familiar fairy tales
- See *Mentor Text List* in Appendix C for other suggestions.

Procedures

Note: Expose students to a variety of literature genres to learn how authors create hooks, leads, and grabbers.

Think About Writing

1. Review with students that authors use interesting openings to begin narrative, opinion, and informative writing. Explain that the goal is to hook the reader from the very first page. As readers and writers, we can examine, explore, and experiment with hooks and grabbers used by our favorite authors to lift the quality of our writing projects.

2. Review the opening lines of mentor texts, if desired, and emphasize the author's use of hooks.

Teach

3. Tell students, "Today I will show you several types of hooks and an entertaining way to practice writing hooks." Read aloud these opening lines for *Goldilocks and the Three Bears*: "Once upon a time, there were three bears. They all lived together in a house in a forest." Explain that this opening is just fine for primary writers and fairy tales. However, authors challenge themselves to write in a more scholarly way.

4. Copy the sentences from the *Action* section of the notebook entry on chart paper. Read aloud with students. Circle or highlight the action words in the sentences. Discuss why this is a more interesting beginning than, "Once upon a time…" and how the action grabs the reader.

5. Continue to add to the chart, discussing the action, opinion, sound, and dialogue hooks. Identify key words and the purpose of each hook so students gain a clear picture of how the hook is used.

It's a Bear Beginning (cont.)

Engage

6. Tell students that in addition to the four hooks the class discussed, there are three additional types of hooks. Write the following types of hooks on a sheet of chart paper: *Question*, *Fascinating Facts*, and *Character*. Distribute the *Three Bear Hook Cards* (page 157) to students. Have students work with partners to identify which category on the chart paper describes the hooks on their card. Partners should write the category on their card. Ask students to share with the class which key words helped them identify the type of hook each is.

Apply

7. Remind students to write sophisticated hooks that bring the reader quickly into the story action. Provide students with the *It's a Bear Beginning Notebook Entry* (page 156) to add to their Writer's Notebook. Have students practice hooks, leads, and grabbers in their notebooks.

Write/Conference

8. Provide time for students to write. Keep yourself free to roam the classroom in order to observe and support students. Revisit the topic again on the next writing day, if needed.

Spotlight Strategy

9. Spotlight students who are creating strong hooks. For example, "Smart writing work today! Spotlighting Jana for practicing an opinion hook."

Share

10. Have students meet with partners to share something they learned today that will improve their writing. Provide approximately two minutes for students to share.

Homework

Ask students to search through several books at their homes for hooks. Have students write down the opening lines of three books and identify what types of hooks were used.

It's a Bear Beginning Notebook Entry

It's a Bear Beginning

Authors use interesting openings to hook their readers right away.

Action

Papa, Momma, and I searched the house for the stranger who had eaten our food, broken our chairs and ruffled our beds. I noticed a lump in my covers and pulled my blanket…

Opinion

The way I see it, if the door's open, it says, "Come on in." Right?

Sound

Crrrack! went the tiny chair as it fell to the floor.

"Ahh!" I screamed in great surprise.

Question

"Whose porridge is all gone? Whose chair is broken? Whose bed is a mess? MINE! That's right! Me—Baby Bear!"

Fascinating Facts

Did you know that Goldilocks has exactly 36 curls on her golden head, and the three bears have 42 teeth in their porridge-eating mouths?

Character

Her mother had always warned her about being so curious, but little Goldilocks was too stubborn to listen. No one ever thought that this tiny little girl would get herself into so much mischief.

Your Turn:

Use the hook patterns above to practice and create grabbers of your own.

Three Bears Hook Cards

Directions: Cut out the cards. Have students work in pairs and provide each pair with one card. Have each pair identify the type of hook the card represents.

Papa, Momma, and I searched the house for the stranger who had eaten our food, broken our chairs and ruffled our beds. I noticed a lump in my covers and pulled my blanket…

The way I see it, if the door's open, it says, "Come on in." Right?

Crrrack! went the tiny chair as it fell to the floor. "Ahh!" I screamed in great surprise.

Did you know that Goldilocks has exactly 36 curls on her golden head, and the three bears have 42 teeth in their porridge-eating mouths?

"Whose porridge is all gone? Whose chair is broken? Whose bed is a mess? MINE! That's right! Me—Baby Bear!"

Her mother had always warned her about being so curious, but little Goldilocks was too stubborn to listen. No one ever thought that this tiny little girl would get herself into so much mischief.

Don't You Agree?

Standards

- Uses strategies to draft and revise written work
- Writes opinion compositions

Materials

- Chart paper
- Markers
- Writer's Notebooks
- *Don't You Agree? Notebook Entry* (page 160; dontyouagree.pdf)

Mentor Texts

- *50 American Heroes Every Kid Should Meet* by Dennis Denenberg
- *Should We Have Pets?* by Sylvia Lollis
- *The Salamander Room* by Steve Johnson
- *The Great Kapok Tree* by Lynne Cherry
- See *Mentor Text List* in Appendix C for other suggestions.

Procedures

Note: Share and model several examples of persuasive texts with students before independent work is requested. Finding a topic that students are passionate about will bring authenticity to the activity. Give ample opportunities for students to express their opinions, argue their views, and find information to support their thinking. Inquiry-based approaches develop higher-order thinking.

Think About Writing

1. Review with students that there are many opinions about topics, such as the environment, friends, eating healthy, bullying, celebrities, and special heroes. Explain that for others to understand our opinions, we must offer facts, reasons, examples, and details that provide evidence to support our beliefs.

2. Review mentor texts, if desired, and emphasize the author's use of opinion.

Teach

3. Tell students, "Today I will show you how to develop an opinion essay using a graphic organizer to gather information that supports your view." Explain that the letters in the word *REF* will remind them to have **R**easons, **E**xamples, and **F**acts to support their views.

4. Model completing a graphic organizer for an opinion piece on chart paper. Write on your own topic or use the notebook entry as a guide.

   - What is the point of view I want others to know about? (goal/argument)

   - What are some reasons that might convince someone to agree with me? (main reasons) and what are some facts and examples that would support my view? (facts/examples)

   - The conclusion should summarize the most important details and state one more time why the reader should support my view.

Don't You Agree? *(cont.)*

5. Explicitly model how to complete the graphic organizer. Then on another day, model how to use the information from the graphic organizer to complete an opinion project.

Engage

6. Have students talk with partners about bullying or other interesting topics. Tell them to state an opinion and then develop their argument and Reasons, Examples, and Facts (**REF**) to support their view. Allow time for discussion and sharing.

Apply

7. Remind students of the importance of point of view and opinion on topics of their choosing. Provide students with the *Don't You Agree? Notebook Entry* (page 160) to add to their Writer's Notebooks. Have students work on the *Your Turn* section before proceeding to their writing folders.

Write/Conference

8. Provide time for students to write. Students tend to struggle with writing opinion papers. Be available to support students as they develop facts and examples to argue their points. Provide opportunities for group work. This provides security and a safety net.

Spotlight Strategy

9. Spotlight students whose facts support their opinions. For example, "London clearly understands that an opinion essay convinces someone of our views. His writing has facts to support his thoughts. Brilliant thinking!"

Share

10. Have students meet with partners to share their writing. Remind students to give a compliment and a comment to their partners. As students share, move around and talk with partners. Then, share out observations you make.

Homework

Ask students to look for places opinions are offered. Have students make a list of three opinions they find.

Don't You Agree? Notebook Entry

Don't You Agree?

Opinion writing can be used to influence the thoughts or actions of another person.

Opinion writing can include 3 basic steps:

1. State your view and grab your reader's attention.

2. Call the **REF**: Give **r**easons supported by **e**xamples and **f**acts.

3. Conclude with a summary and last plea to win your reader's support.

Beginning Step 1	**Opinion:** I believe exposure to violence contributes to risk factors for bullying. **Hook:** A 2010 study from the Josephson Institute of Ethics, half admit to bullying **Summary of Reasons:** 1. video games 2. lack of supervision	
Middle Step 2	**Reason #1:** violent video games	• <u>Example/Fact</u>: too many hours playing makes it seem unreal/won't hurt anyone • <u>Example/Fact</u>: violent video games make kids less sensitive
	Reason #2: improper supervision	• <u>Example/Fact</u>: unsupervised watching of violent TV programs and movies • <u>Example/Fact</u>: not monitored, easily engage in cyber bullying
End Step 3	**Restate Opinion:** You can see that exposure to violence increases the odds that bullying will continue to occur in our schools. **Last Plea-End on a Positive Note:** Your decision/take charge	

Your Turn:

Use what you have learned about opinion writing to create your own graphic organizer in your notebook. Then, develop your ideas into an essay or letter.

It's Your Business

Standards

- Uses strategies to draft and revise written work
- Writes personal letters

Materials

- Chart paper
- Markers (black and red)
- Writer's Notebooks
- *It's Your Business Notebook Entry* (page 163; itsyourbusiness.pdf)
- Examples of business letters *(optional)*
- *Dear Pen Pal Notebook Entry* (page 164; dearpenpal.pdf) *(optional)*

Mentor Texts

- *Sincerely Yours: Writing Your Own Letter* by Nancy Loewen
- See *Mentor Text List* in Appendix C for other suggestions.

Procedures

Note: When ready to begin a short unit on letter writing, build a display on a bulletin board and have available appropriate letterhead, envelopes, and stamps. Make it authentic. As a lesson extension, review friendly letters. A *Dear Pen Pal Notebook Entry* is provided on page 164.

Think About Writing

1. Explain to students that many years ago, written messages were the only ways to communicate with each other. Although texting and phone messages are now faster ways to connect, business and professional letters are still necessary and used to obtain information as well as to solve problems. People still write business letters for credit reports, to banks, to get information, to make complaints, and for a variety of other reasons.

2. Share several examples of types of business letters if desired, and emphasize the format of the letters.

Teach

3. Tell students, "Today I will show you the parts of a business letter and how to write and mail a letter to a community member." Explain that business letters are a necessary part of life.

4. Chart the pattern of a business letter and discuss each section with students.

   - *heading—includes your address and date*
   - *inside address—the name of the person receiving the letter and his or her address*
   - *greeting—a polite hello that usually begins, "Dear…"*
   - *body—contains the important information you are trying to convey*
   - *closing—a polite good-bye*
   - *signature line—the sender's signature*

It's Your Business (cont.)

5. Use chart paper to model how to write a business letter to a member of the community, such as your local Board of Education, to invite them for Career Day, or to banks to set up savings accounts. Discuss each part of the letter as you write it. Label each part with a red marker and display the anchor chart in the classroom for students to reference.

6. Explain that students will write letters to a community member and the letters will actually be sent in the mail. Make this activity authentic—follow through and mail students' letters. Remember to edit the letters for accuracy.

Engage

7. Have students work with partners to brainstorm reasons they might need to write business letters. Allow two minutes for students to talk, and then gather everyone together to share aloud with the whole class.

Apply

8. Remind students that writing letters is something they will have to do in real-life situations. Provide students with the *It's Your Business Notebook Entry* (page 163) to add to their Writer's Notebook. Have students work on the *Your Turn* section before proceeding to their writing folders.

Write/Conference

9. Provide time for students to write. If students have very little background knowledge on letter writing, have many samples available and pull a small group of students for extra support.

Spotlight Strategy

10. Spotlight students who are writing correctly formatted business letters. For example, "Wow! We might have some executive secretaries or high-powered CEO's in our room. Remarkable work on business letters."

Share

11. Have students meet with partners to discuss how they might extend this activity and write letters for other reasons. Provide approximately two minutes for discussion.

Homework
Ask students to work with their parents to practice writing business letters.

It's Your Business Notebook Entry

It's Your Business

A **business letter** may be written to request or share information, or tell someone about a problem. We may write business letters to persuade or convince someone to consider our ideas, our opinion about a topic, or maybe to request donations for a project. The six parts of a business letter include the heading, inside address, greeting, body, closing, and signature.

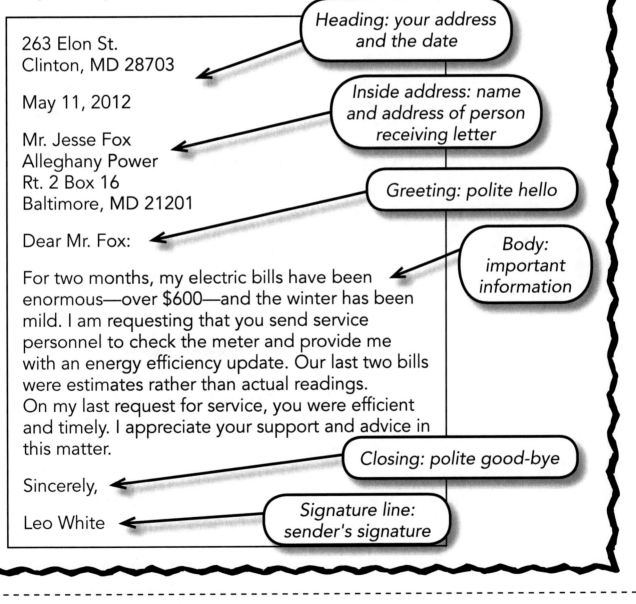

263 Elon St.
Clinton, MD 28703

May 11, 2012

Mr. Jesse Fox
Alleghany Power
Rt. 2 Box 16
Baltimore, MD 21201

Dear Mr. Fox:

For two months, my electric bills have been enormous—over $600—and the winter has been mild. I am requesting that you send service personnel to check the meter and provide me with an energy efficiency update. Our last two bills were estimates rather than actual readings.
On my last request for service, you were efficient and timely. I appreciate your support and advice in this matter.

Sincerely,

Leo White

Heading: your address and the date

Inside address: name and address of person receiving letter

Greeting: polite hello

Body: important information

Closing: polite good-bye

Signature line: sender's signature

Dear Pen Pal Notebook Entry

Dear Pen Pal

A **friendly letter** is written to someone you know well, such as a grandparent, cousin, or friend. Friendly letters are written to share an experience, give information, thank someone, offer an invitation, or share words of kindness. The five parts of a friendly letter include the date, greeting, body, closing, and signature.

Date

Greeting

Body

March 24, 2012

Dear Bobby,

Hello! I was so happy to get your letter yesterday. It is great that you won the spelling bee at your school. Will you get to go to the district spelling bee? I won second place in the science fair. My project was about "Keeping the Earth Green." My friend, Tommy, won. He had an exploding volcano.

Don't forget to write back soon.

Your friend,

Sam

Closing

Signature

Your Turn:

Write a friendly letter to someone you know well. Be sure to include all five parts.

How-To Writing

Standards

- Uses strategies to draft and revise written work
- Writes expository compositions

Materials

- Chart paper
- Markers
- Writer's Notebooks
- *How-To Writing Notebook Entry* (page 167; howtowriting.pdf)
- Examples of how-to writing (e.g., instruction guides, recipes, board game directions)

Mentor Texts

- *Show Me How: 500 Things You Should Know* by Derek Fagerstrom and Lauren Smith
- *Origami Fun Kit for Beginners* by Dover Publications
- *The Klutz Yo-Yo Book* by John Cassidy
- *Kid's Paper Airplanes* by Ken Blackburn
- See *Mentor Text List* in Appendix C for other suggestions.

Procedures

Note: How-to writing helps students problem solve everyday difficulties. The mentor texts that are suggested use simple illustrations to help students unravel simple as well as more difficult tasks (e.g., how to hang a tire swing, how to decorate an egg), life skills needed outside the classroom.

Think About Writing

1. Remind students that there are many different kinds of writing. Explain that another important genre of writing helps us to learn and do new things; how-to writing is frequently used in our everyday lives.

Teach

2. Tell students, "Today I will show you how to organize your thinking into how-to writing." Explain that how-to writing shows the steps for completing a task and must be very specific so the reader can complete the task correctly.

3. Distribute examples of how-to writing to students and allow them time to explore the materials. Ask students to spend time with partners exploring the materials, noting some of the characteristics of how-to writing.

4. Record students' observations on a class chart. Use the *How-To Writing Notebook Entry* (page 167) as a guide to ensure students have identified the key characteristics of this type of writing.

5. Model how to create a how-to writing. Use the graphic organizer as a guide for organizing your thoughts and then explicitly model how to use the information in the organizer in your writing. You may wish to do this on a subsequent day.

How-To Writing (cont.)

Engage

6. Remind students to consider the audience when they begin a how-to writing piece. Allow partners time to orally rehearse a plan for a how-to guide. A fun activity is for students to write directions for getting to the music room or other location at school; one team creates the directions, another team follows them.

Apply

7. Remind students to organize their thinking when writing a how-to piece. Provide students with the *How-To Writing Notebook Entry* to add to their Writer's Notebook. Have students work on the *Your Turn* section before proceeding to their writing folders.

Write/Conference

8. Provide time for students to write. Scan to make certain that all students are working. Then, provide small group instruction based on needs.

Spotlight Strategy

9. Spotlight students who are creating strong how-to writing pieces. For example, "Look at the brilliant way you are organizing your thinking. You can be proud that your reader will know exactly what to do when they read your how-to writing."

Share

10. Have students meet with partners to share their writing. Encourage students to *TAG*: **T**ell a compliment. **A**sk a question. **G**ive a suggestion.

Homework
Ask students to search for how-to writing at their homes. Have students make a list of three places they found how-to writing or better yet, bring them to class to share.

How-To Writing Notebook Entry

How-To Writing
1, 2, 3

How-to writing explains a process or how to do something new. It is important that all the steps are complete, clear, and in the right order. Each section leads clearly to the next with the use of time order words such as *first*, *next*, *then*, *finally*, and *last*.

Title: How to _____

Materials/Equipment needed: _____

Sequence Ladder:

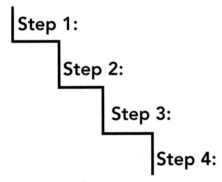

Step 1:

Step 2:

Step 3:

Step 4:

Final thoughts and tips for the reader: _____

Your Turn:

Create your own how-to writing. Use the graphic organizer to plan, and then write directions to show or teach something you have learned. You might consider writing about how to:

- make a paper airplane
- make a friendship bracelet
- bake chocolate chip cookies
- do a science experiment
- walk your dog
- make smores

Composition Planner

Standards

- Uses strategies to draft and revise written work
- Writes expository compositions

Materials

- Chart paper
- 8.5" × 11" paper
- Markers
- *All About Owls Writing Sample* (page 171; allaboutowls.pdf)
- Writer's Notebooks
- *Composition Planner Notebook Entry* (page 170; compplanner.pdf)

Mentor Text

- See *Mentor Text List* in Appendix C for other suggestions.

Procedures

Note: This planner works well for informative and opinion writing. Use this lesson again and again to prepare students for writing assessments, informative, and opinion persuasive pieces.

Think About Writing

1. Explain that graphic organizers help plan and sequence writing in a clear, logical way. Explain that writing teacher Ruth Culham says, "Think of organization as an animal's skeleton or the framework of a building under construction."

2. Review mentor texts, if desired, and emphasize the author's use of organization.

Teach

3. Tell students, "Today I will show you how to draw a simple graphic organizer that will help you organize your ideas for an introductory paragraph, a body, and a conclusion."

4. Model how to create the Composition Planner graphic organizer shown below on a piece of 8.5" × 11" paper.

   - Draw the lines at the top and bottom of the paper for the introduction and conclusion sentences first.

   - Create three columns in the middle section by drawing two vertical lines.

   - Divide the columns in the middle of the paper into four horizontal sections by drawing a line to divide the section in half and then lines to divide each of those sections in half.

   - Label each section.

Composition Planner (cont.)

Introduction		
Main Idea #1	Main Idea #2	Main Idea #3
Detail #1	Detail #1	Detail #1
Detail #2	Detail #2	Detail #2
Detail #3	Detail #3	Detail#3
Conclusion		

5. Have students practice drawing the organizer several times so that it becomes automatic.

6. Model how to complete a Composition Planner to help organize ideas for writing. Then, on a subsequent day, model how to transfer the information from the Composition Planner to a writing piece. Use *All About Owls Writing Sample* (page 171) as a guide if desired.

Engage

7. Have students talk with partners to share topics they might explore using the Composition Planner. You may wish to create a class list of possible topics for an informative essay or report.

Apply

8. Encourage students to use a graphic organizer to help them group similar ideas together. Provide students with the *Composition Planner Notebook Entry* (page 170) to add to their Writer's Notebook. Have students work on the *Your Turn* section before proceeding to their writing folders.

Write/Conference

9. Provide time for students to write. Scan the room to make certain that all students have understood. Allow yourself at least one or two minutes to observe. Then, move into an individual or a small group conference. Question students for understanding of the mini-lesson, for example, "How will this help to improve your writing?"

Spotlight Strategy

10. Spotlight students who are using the composition planner. For example, "Jack glued his entry into his notebook and completed a paper fold to try this in writing. Writers use their time wisely, exactly the way Jack used his time. Smart thinking!"

Share

11. Have students meet with partners to discuss how their folded papers organize and support their writing efforts.

Homework
Ask students to practice folding a piece of paper at home. Have them select a topic and complete each section of the organizer.

Composition Planner Notebook Entry

Composition Planner

Authors use planners to organize their ideas. Informative writing includes specific vocabulary and uses researched facts.

Introduction		
• Lead: Catch the reader's interest about the topic. • State your topic sentence and a hint of what's to come.		
Main Idea #1 appearance	**Main Idea #2** food	**Main Idea #3** owl babies
Detail #1 eyes	**Detail #1** nocturnal	**Detail #1** called owlets
Detail #2 rotating head	**Detail #2** pellet	**Detail #2** egg tooth
Detail #3 feathers	**Detail #3** ripe/rotten food	**Detail#3** practice flying
Conclusion Summarize, restate your main idea, and add a conclusion.		

Your Turn:

Use this planner to write an informative essay. Select a topic and gather and organize information. You might like to:

- Create a newspaper article or web page with information about healthy snacks, exercise, or recycling.
- Write the biography of a historical figure, celebrity, or family member.
- Write a book or movie review.

#50918—Getting to the Core of Writing—Level 4 © Shell Education

All About Owls Writing Sample

All About Owls

A large, feathery creature swooped across the road, just in front of our windshield! That happened in the middle of the night, and I determined it must have been a barn owl, searching for dinner. Owls are a special group of birds that have a rather unusual appearance. They search for their food just before a crack opens between night and day (after dusk and before dawn). Baby owls, called *owlets*, wait at home in their comfy nests, while the parents are out searching for food.

Clearly, owls are very different from other birds. Their big eyes face forward, unlike other birds whose eyes are on the sides of their head. Did you know owls cannot move their eyes in their sockets? So, in order to look around, they have to move their entire head. The feathers on the tops of their heads are not really ears, but part of their camouflage. The feathers encircling their eyes give them a wide-eyed, alert, one might even say, startled appearance.

Equally unusual is the process owls use for digesting their food. As stated earlier, owls are nocturnal and search for their food at night. An owl's food is swallowed whole and broken into small pieces in its stomach. After the food has been digested, the owl spits out a pellet, which contains all of the food that cannot be digested, such as bones, fur, and feathers. Ripe, rotten food can be digested quickly and does not require the owl's digestive system to separate it into smaller pieces.

Owl babies are weak and clumsy at birth. The baby owl, called an *owlet*, breaks out of the shell using a special egg tooth that disappears as the owlet matures. Before flying off to catch their own food, they must practice flapping their wings to make them strong enough to fly. Remember, they sleep during the day and search for food at night.

As you can see, owls are interesting birds. Their appearance and digestive system is unique to the bird family. Why don't you take the time to learn more about baby owlets, their parents, and their extraordinary habits? They live on every continent of the world except Antarctica. Their bodies are camouflaged like the surrounding environment!" Do you have an animal that you are curious about?

A Cache of Poetry

Standards

- Uses strategies to draft and revise written work
- Writes narrative accounts, such as poems and stories

Materials

- Chart paper
- Markers
- Writer's Notebooks
- *A Cache of Poetry Notebook Entry* (page 174; cachepoetry.pdf)

Mentor Texts

- *Pizza, Pigs, and Poetry: How to Write a Poem* by Jack Prelutsky
- *Kids' Poems: Teaching Third & Fourth Graders to Love Writing Poetry* by Regie Routman
- See *Mentor Text List* in Appendix C for other suggestions.

Procedures

Note: Poetry patterns can be used throughout the year, but are especially appropriate for holidays. Creating a poetry anthology or keeping a poetry notebook builds student writing confidence. Free verse poetry relieves the pressure associated with traditional prose and encourages choice. Collecting students' poems into an anthology of poetry or having an author's tea and having students present the poems to their families and friends is a great way to publish and end the year.

Think About Writing

1. Remind students of the many types of writing they have done this year; for example, essays, stories, compositions, and poetry. Explain that they will end the year by learning new types of poetry patterns.

2. Review mentor texts, if desired, and emphasize the various poetry styles the author uses.

Teach

3. Tell students, "Today I will show you how to write poems using several poetry patterns." Explain that students will have the opportunity to try several different types of poetry patterns.

4. Choose a poetry pattern from the *A Cache of Poetry Notebook Entry* (page 174). Model how to create a poem using the poetry pattern. Record the poem pattern on chart paper and create a poem following the pattern. Display the chart paper in the classroom for students to view. You may wish to model one type of poetry each day for several days.

   - Couplet: 2 rhyming lines
   - Limerick: nonsense poem with 5 lines—1st, 2nd, 5th lines rhyme
   - Five W's: each line answers a question—*who, what, where, when, why*

A Cache of Poetry (cont.)

- Triante: 5 lines, each line represents a sense

- Cinquain: 5 lines, 22 syllables 2–4–6–8–2

Engage

5. Have students describe the poetry pattern you reviewed and name the various parts of the poem. Then, have students share ideas for poetry topics.

Apply

6. Remind students to brainstorm topics, words, and phrases for possible use in poems. Provide students with the *A Cache of Poetry Notebook Entry* to add to their Writer's Notebook. Have students create poetry using the notebook entry as a model. Create a poetry anthology for an end-of-year celebration.

Write/Conference

7. Provide time for students to write. Today, keep yourself free to rove and confer. Make suggestions on topics, words, and phrases. Make observations in your Conferring Notebook to determine who and what to reteach, and plan future small group instruction.

Spotlight Strategy

8. Spotlight students who are writing interesting poetry. For example, "Hannah and Yui are working together, helping each other create poems."

Share

9. Have students meet with partners to share their writing. From teacher observations, select a couple of poems to share with the group.

Homework

Ask students to share the poetry pattern modeled each day with their parents. Have students and their parents brainstorm other topics that could be added to their notebook.

A Cache of Poetry Notebook Entry

A Cache of Poetry

There are many forms of poetry.

Couplet Two rhyming lines of verse	In the wintertime we <u>go</u> Walking through the fields of <u>snow</u>
Limerick Nonsense poem with 5 lines 1st, 2nd, and 5th lines rhyme	There once was a cow on the <u>moon</u>, Who traveled in the month of <u>June</u>. He mooed all night, And looked such a sight, As he continued to moo his <u>tune</u>.
Five W's Poetry Line 1: Who? Line 2: What? Line 3: Where? Line 4: When? Line 5: Why?	I Love to watch football In Mountaineer Stadium, During home games, Because excitement makes me happy.
Triante (Triangle Poem) Line 1: title, 1 word Line 2: smell, 2 words Line 3: touch/taste, 3 words Line 4: sight, 4 words Line 5: sound/action, 5 words	Ocean Clean, Fresh Salty, Wet, Cool Green, Murky, Wide, Deep Swell, Roll, Crash, Pound, Splash

Your Turn:

Chose one form of poetry from above, and write a poem.

Word Choice

Showing Your Story

The use of rich, descriptive words by the writer can show the reader a mental image. By studying word choice, students will learn how to use vivid, colorful, and dynamic words to enrich their writing and make it as precise as possible. The use of amazing words is encouraged; however, everyday words used correctly are also celebrated. The lessons assist students to explore different types of words and the ways they can be used to create interesting writing pieces. Lessons in this section include the following:

- Lesson 1: Stupendous Similes (page 177)
- Lesson 2: Be a Word Wizard (page 180)
- Lesson 3: Connecting Ideas (page 183)
- Lesson 4: Put "Said" to Bed (page 187)
- Lesson 5: COW to WOW (page 190)
- Lesson 6: Auspicious Adjectives (page 193)
- Lesson 7: Be Explicitly Specific (page 196)
- Lesson 8: Adverb Alert (page 199)
- Lesson 9: Alliteration Action (page 203)

The *Wally, Word Choice Detective* poster (page 176) can be displayed in the room to provide a visual reminder for students that word choice is one of the traits of writing. You may wish to introduce this poster during the first lesson on word choice. Then, refer to the poster when teaching other lessons on word choice to refresh students' memories and provide them with questions to help guide them as they make choices for words they use in their writing.

Wally
Word Choice Detective

What words will paint a picture for my reader?

- ✔ Did I use some amazing words?

- ✔ Did I use sensory words?

- ✔ Did I use action words?

- ✔ Did I use a variety of words?

Stupendous Similes

Standard

Uses descriptive and precise language that clarifies and enhances ideas

Materials

- Chart paper
- Markers
- Writer's Notebooks
- *Stupendous Similes Notebook Entry* (page 179; similes.pdf)

Mentor Texts

- *Stubborn as a Mule and Other Silly Similes* by Nancy Loewen
- *My Dog Is as Smelly as Dirty Socks* by Hanoch Piven
- *Duke Ellington: The Piano Prince and his Orchestra* by Andrea Pinkney
- See *Mentor Text List* in Appendix C for other suggestions.

Procedures

Note: Identifying similes while reading quality literature encourages students to explore figurative language in their own writing. Chart and display quality examples from read alouds for student support.

Think About Writing

1. Explain that authors practice clarity and preciseness when writing sentences. Authors can also successfully use some figurative language. Explain that similes are an example of figurative language.

2. Review mentor texts, if desired, and emphasize the author's use of similes.

Teach

3. Tell students, "Today I will show you how to use similes to add colorful details to your writing." Explain that a simile compares things using the words *like* or *as*.

4. Write the following sentence on chart paper: *Richard is as busy as a bee.* Have students identify the two things being compared (Richard and a bee). Discuss the meaning of the sentence. (It means he is always working, like a bee.)

5. Share, discuss, and record a few more similes, such as:

   - *old as the hills*
   - *wise as an owl*
   - *eats like a pig*
   - *sings like a bird*
   - *light as a feather*

   Review other familiar similes from literature or from your experience.

Stupendous Similes (cont.)

Engage

6. Have students work with partners to create sentences with similes. Assign each group one simile. Provide time for partners to talk. Then, have each pair share their sentences with the whole group.

   - *bright as the sun*
   - *cold as ice*
   - *mad as a hornet*
   - *pale as a ghost*
   - *sleeps like a log*
   - *shines like the stars*

Apply

7. Remind students to use descriptive similes to create vivid images for their readers. Caution students not to overuse similes in their writing. Provide students with the *Stupendous Similes Notebook Entry* (page 179) to add to their Writer's Notebook. Have students create and illustrate sentences using similes from the *Your Turn* section before proceeding to their writing folders.

Write/Conference

8. Provide time for students to write. Scan for a few seconds to see that all have started. For those who may need additional support, do a quick reteach with a few new similes.

Spotlight Strategy

9. Spotlight students who are using similes. For example, "Do you know what I just saw you do? I saw you use an interesting simile in your writing. Writers, your work is just like (name a known author)." Comparing student work to a known author provides identity.

Share

10. Have students select their best examples of similes and be ready to share out with the whole group. Allow several students to share. Add a few of the best selections to the anchor chart.

Homework

Ask students to listen to the language around their homes and on television or radio to see if they can hear any similes. Have students make a list of at least three similes.

Stupendous Similes Notebook Entry

Stupendous Similes

Authors use **similes** to provide vivid details and to create fun language for their readers.

A simile is used as a figure of speech that compares two things and contains the words *like* or *as*.

Sentence with Similes	Meaning
Richard is <u>as</u> busy <u>as</u> a bee.	Richard is compared to a bee. He is always working on something.
Kelly floats <u>like</u> a butterfly!	Kelly is compared to a butterfly. She seems to float when she moves.

Your Turn:

Use similes from the list below or use similes you know to create colorful, fun sentences in your notebook.

- as blind as a bat
- gentle as a lamb
- white as the snow
- sweet as honey
- hungry as a bear
- quiet as a mouse
- flat as a pancake
- hard as a rock

- swims like a fish
- works like a dog
- eats like a bird
- fight like cats and dogs
- hair like silk
- plays like a pro
- slept like a log
- works like a charm

Be a Word Wizard

Procedures

Note: There is clear evidence that vocabulary is associated with socioeconomic status. Children can acquire and retain two or three words a day. Do this lesson often with a variety of vocabulary strategies. Use this carousel activity for synonyms and antonyms.

Think About Writing

1. Explain to students that authors use just the right words to paint pictures for the reader. Tell students that since they are authors too, they need to be constantly on the lookout for words that can be used in their writing.

2. Review mentor texts, if desired, and emphasize the word choices the author makes.

Teach

3. Tell students, "Today I will show you how to begin a collection of various words that can be stored in your Writer's Notebook and called upon when searching for just the right image as you write." Explain that writers are word wizards as they work to conjure up images in the readers' minds.

4. Create a table with four boxes on chart paper. Label the boxes as shown below:

Words or phrases that show happy	Words or phrases that show sad
Words or phrases that show sounds (onomatopoeia)	Words or phrases that show action

5. Gather words that fit in each category. Provide a few examples from the notebook entry to get students started. Continue to build the chart by looking for examples in literature that you read over the coming weeks.

Be a Word Wizard *(cont.)*

Engage

6. Write the caption from each box on a separate sheet of chart paper and post the charts around the room. Divide students into groups and assign each group a different chart. Provide approximately four minutes for students to add their ideas to the chart. Rotate the groups and have students add words to the new chart. Continue rotating the charts until each group has worked on all the charts. Display the charts in the room for students to reference as they write.

Apply

7. Encourage students to increase their word knowledge by collecting and studying words. Provide students with the *Be a Word Wizard Notebook Entry* (page 182) to add to their Writer's Notebook. Have students write words from the chart activity in their notebook, then proceed to their writing folders.

Write/Conference

8. Provide time for students to write, if time allows. No conferring today. You will need to monitor student groups as they work on adding their ideas to the charts. Notice collaboration, cooperation, and work ethic and make notes in your Conferring Notebook.

Spotlight Strategy

9. Spotlight groups that have created interesting lists. For example, "This group has successfully collected a whole list of words that paint pictures. I want to add a few of those words to my Writer's Notebook. Smart work today, writers."

Share

10. Have several students share out to the whole group. Allow students to write down ideas in their Writer's Notebook that they want to remember.

Homework

Ask students to be word wizards in their homes tonight. Have students make lists of five wonderful words to add to their Writer's Notebook.

Be a Word Wizard Notebook Entry

Be a Word Wizard

Authors write memorable stories by creating images that capture the reader's attention.

Be a Word Wizard and conjure up words that paint a picture!

Words or phrases that show happy	Words or phrases that show sad
giggle	whined
joyous	gloomy
tickled pink	blue
Words or phrases that show sounds (onomatopoeia)	**Words or phrases that show action**
bang	swirling
slurp	racing
click-clack	wobbling

Your Turn:

Add words in your notebook that you can stir into your writing. Create additional boxes for word groups, such as *sensory words*, *colorful words*, and *character trait words*.

#50918—Getting to the Core of Writing—Level 4 © Shell Education

Connecting Ideas

Standards

- Links ideas using connecting words
- Uses descriptive and precise language that clarifies and enhances ideas

Materials

- Chart paper
- Markers
- Writer's Notebooks
- *Connecting Ideas Notebook Entry* (page 185; connectideas.pdf)
- *Transition Words Practice Paragraph* (page 186; transitionwords.pdf)

Mentor Texts

- *Meanwhile, Back at the Ranch* by Trinka Noble
- *Chicken Sunday* by Patricia Polacco
- *The Knight and the Dragon* by Tomie dePaola
- *Owl Moon* by Jane Yolen
- See *Mentor Text List* in Appendix C for other suggestions.

Procedures

Note: Using transition words to move smoothly from sentence to sentence or paragraph to paragraph allows the reader to understand the writer's message. Repeat this lesson, focusing on different transition words for different genres of writing.

Think About Writing

1. Tell students that writers use transition words and phrases that support movement from one idea to another. Explain that transition words are used in all types of writing: narrative, opinion, and informative.

Teach

2. Tell students, "Today I will show you how to organize your writing by adding signal words." Explain that these signal words are called *transition words* and that they are like bridges that help the reader travel from one part of your writing to the next.

3. Select a section from a mentor text that contains several transition words. List the transition words on a sheet of chart paper. Ask students to listen carefully for those words as you read the text aloud. Discuss how the transition words help connect ideas.

4. Display the *Connecting Ideas Notebook Entry* (page 185). Point out how the transition words in the notebook entry are separated into words that may be used in the beginning, middle, or end of their writing. You may want to use simple words in the beginning of the year and move to more rigorous words throughout the year.

Connecting Ideas (cont.)

Engage

5. Provide students with the *Transition Words Practice Paragraph* (page 186). Have them work in quads to add transition words to the paragraph. Display or provide students with the *Connecting Ideas Notebook Entry*. Explain that the goal is to select transition words that sound smooth and bring meaning to the writing. Have several groups share their newly written paragraphs.

Apply

6. Remind students to develop writing projects with descriptive details and transition words that bridge the story together for the reader. Provide students with the *Connecting Ideas Notebook Entry* to add to their Writer's Notebook. Have students work on the *Your Turn* section before proceeding to their writing folders.

Write/Conference

7. Provide time for students to write. Scan the classroom for students who need assistance getting started. Then, rotate among students to conference with individual students. Record your observations in your Conferring Notebook. If small groups of students are having difficulties, reteach the lesson as a guided writing.

Spotlight Strategy

8. Spotlight students who are using transition words. For example, "Listen to how Tiana tried a transition word in this part of her writing. Smart writing work! I love the way you are challenging yourself to try all of these strategies in your work."

Share

9. Have students meet in quads to share how they used transition words in their writing. Encourage students to share if it added fluency to their writing.

Homework

Ask students to listen for transition words in conversations. Have students make a list of five transition words they hear tonight.

Connecting Ideas Notebook Entry

Connecting Ideas

Authors use **transition words** to connect ideas and to create sentences and paragraphs that flow together smoothly.

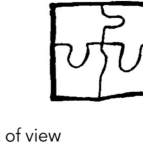

Beginning

- One reason
- In the first place
- It began
- It all started when

- To begin with
- First of all
- It is my belief
- From my point of view

Middle

- In addition
- Suddenly
- Meanwhile
- Later that same day
- Before long

- It is my belief
- From my point of view
- Let me explain
- A major reason
- In other words

End

- Finally
- In conclusion
- Now you see
- Always remember

- As you can see
- You can see why
- To summarize
- Let me remind you

Your Turn:

Choose a beginning, middle, and ending transition word and add them to one of your pieces of writing.

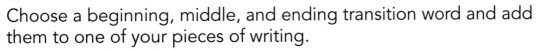

Name: _____ Date: _____

Transition Words Practice Paragraph

Directions: Arrange the sentences in the paragraph below in a good sequence. Add transition words so the ideas flow from one idea to the next.

He sprinted straight for his favorite, the swings.

It was time to head to our favorite ice cream shop.

I followed right behind him so I could push and he could fly into the sky.

Bobby and I went to the Veteran's Park.

_____

_____

_____

_____

_____

_____

_____

_____

_____

_____

_____

_____

_____

_____

_____

Put "Said" to Bed

Standard

Uses descriptive and precise language that clarifies and enhances ideas

Materials

- Chart paper
- Markers
- Children's literature
- Writer's Notebooks
- *Put "Said" to Bed Notebook Entry* (page 189; saidtobed.pdf)

Mentor Texts

- *Stellaluna* by Janell Cannon
- *Bedhead* by Margie Palatini
- *Chicken Little* by Steven Kellogg
- *The Odious Ogre* by Norton Juster
- See *Mentor Text List* in Appendix C for other suggestions.

Procedures

Note: Have students add words to their notebook as they discover synonyms for *said*. Repeat this lesson several times to remind students to challenge their thinking and vary their vocabulary.

Think About Writing

1. Remind students that authors make careful word choices in order to keep the reader interested in the story.

Teach

2. Tell students, "Today I will show you how to make your writing more interesting by using other words instead of *said.*" Explain that *said* is often overused and writing can be improved by choosing a word that shows the way a character speaks.

3. Read the following sentences adapted from *Bedhead*. Tell students to count how many times they hear the word *said*.

   "Oliver! Oliver!" said Mom, Dad and Emily…

   "Total," said Emily.

   "Been there. Done that," said Oliver.

   "I could curl it!" said Emily.

   "So spray already!" said Oliver.

   "Definitely stuck," said Dad.

   "A done deal," said Emily.

4. Write on chart paper or display the original sentences from *Bedhead*.

   "Oliver! Oliver!" <u>shouted</u> Mom, Dad and Emily…

   "Total," <u>agreed</u> Emily.

   "Been there. Done that," <u>groaned</u> Oliver.

   "I could curl it!" <u>offered</u> Emily.

   "So spray already!" <u>sputtered</u> Oliver.

   "Definitely stuck," <u>decided</u> Dad.

   "A done deal," <u>declared</u> Emily.

Put "Said" to Bed *(cont.)*

5. Underline the words that are used instead of the word *said*. Discuss how these words make the writing more interesting and help show how the characters spoke the words.

6. Tell students, "Today we will put *said* to bed." Write the word *said* in the center of a circle chart. Have students identify the words from *Bedhead* that were great substitutions for the word *said*. Record these words on the chart. See the notebook entry for an example of this chart.

Engage

7. Divide students into groups and place them around the room. Create several circle charts with the word *said* written in the middle. Give each group a chart and several examples of children's literature. Have students search through the literature for other words that can be used instead of *said*. Ask students to record their findings on the circle chart. Allow students to rotate to other charts in order to explore other literature. Display the charts in the room for students to use as resources when they write.

Apply

8. Remind students that *said* is a worn out word and they can jazz up their writing projects with word substitutions, such as those on the charts. Provide students with the *Put "Said" to Bed Notebook Entry* (page 189) to add to their Writer's Notebook. Have students work on the *Your Turn* section before proceeding to their writing folders.

Write/Conference

9. Provide time for students to write. Work with a small group at a table, if needed. Write sentences with the word *said* in them on the whiteboard. Work with students to rewrite the sentences using other words in place of *said*. Then, rotate among students to conference with individual students. If time permits, pull in an enrichment group to raise their levels of word awareness.

Spotlight Strategy

10. Spotlight students who are using interesting replacements for *said*. For example, "Scholarly words! You continually amaze me. Remember you may use books to find words and add them to your growing list." Spotlight a couple of students who have gone beyond expectations.

Share

11. Have students move around the room to form partnerships. Students should give a word, get a word, and then move on to find a new partner and repeat. Remind students to use a two-inch voice as they work.

Homework

Ask students to be word detectives and listen for words that are great substitutes for *said*. Have students make lists of at least five words. Add students' words to the classroom chart the next day.

Put "Said" to Bed Notebook Entry

Put "Said" to Bed

Authors use different words for *said* to emphasize the way the character is speaking.

cheered

blabbered   mumbled

whispered   **said**   commanded

declared   chuckled

groaned

Your Turn:

Make a circle chart in your notebook for the word *said*. Listen for other words that can be used in place of *said*. Add them to your circle chart. Try adding dialogue to one of your writing projects. Be sure to use words that show your reader how your character feels.

COW to WOW

Standard

Uses descriptive and precise language that clarifies and enhances ideas

Materials

- Chart paper
- Markers
- Index cards
- Toy barn *(optional)*
- Writer's Notebooks
- *COW to WOW Notebook Entry* (page 192; cowtowow.pdf)

Mentor Texts

- *Bedhead* by Margie Palatini
- Literature from CCSS or Core Reading Program
- See *Mentor Text List* in Appendix C for other suggestions.

Procedures

Note: Create a *COW to WOW* word chart or board. Add WOW as students discover them during reading, listening, speaking, or technology activities.

Think about Writing

1. Explain to students that authors use vibrant, colorful words to hold their readers' attention.

2. Review mentor texts, if desired, and emphasize the author's use of wonderful words. For example, read the following sentences from *Bedhead*.

   Oliver's scream shook. It rattled. It rolled all the way down the stairs and into the kitchen where Fruit Loops went flying. Milk was spilled, spit, and sputtered.

   Tell students that Margie Palatini could have written, *Oliver yelled!* Ask students if that would have been as interesting. Point out the words: *rattled*, *spilled*, *spit*, and *sputtered* to students.

Teach

3. Tell students, "Today I will show you how to make a list of commonly overused words that need to be WOWed." Explain to students that *COW* stands for **C**ommonly **O**verused **W**ords—words that are used a lot. In order to make writing more sophisticated, authors substitute those words for *WOW* words—**W**onderful **O**utstanding **W**ords.

4. Discuss reasons for commonly overused words. Ideas for some commonly overused words are listed on the *COW to WOW Notebook Entry* (page 192). Write the words you discuss on index cards. Discuss the meaning of *putting a cow out to pasture*. Tell students that they are going to put the overused words out to pasture, too. Children love it if you have a toy barn and place the index cards into the barn.

COW to WOW (cont.)

5. Write the following sentence on chart paper.

   Josh had a <u>nice</u> time at the movies.

   Discuss the word *nice* as a COW word. Identify a WOW word that can be used in the place of *nice*. Brainstorm several and then settle on one to use as you rewrite the sentence.

Engage

6. Select one COW word and write it on chart paper. Have students talk with partners to decide some WOW words that can be used in its place. Provide time for students to talk. Have students share out their WOW words and record them on the chart paper. Display the chart paper in the classroom for students to reference as they write. COW words to explore include *nice*, *come*, *good*, and *fast*.

Apply

7. Remind students to use the charts in the classroom both as a reminder of COW words to avoid and WOW words to include in their writing. Provide students with the *COW to WOW Notebook Entry* to add to their Writer's Notebook. Have students work on the *Your Turn* section before proceeding to their writing folders.

Write/Conference

8. Provide time for students to write. Scan your group for confusions that need to be clarified then begin to conference with individual students or work with a small group to quickly reteach or provide additional practice. Record your observations in your Conferring Notebook.

Spotlight Strategy

9. Spotlight students who are using WOW words. For example, "Look at all of your brilliant sentences. You have challenged yourself and must be proud of the way you're making important changes in word choice."

Share

10. Have students meet with partners. Have students *TAG*—**T**ell a compliment. **A**sk a question. **G**ive a suggestion. Provide approximately two minutes of talk time.

Homework

Ask students to tell their parents some of the COW words they learned. Have students work with their parents to name three WOW words that can be used in their place.

COW to WOW Notebook Entry

COW to WOW

Authors use strong, descriptive words that grab their readers' attention. Show, don't tell!

You can revise your writing by finding words from the list below that need to be "sent out to pasture." Replace them with strong, descriptive words that will grab your reader's attention.

COW ☹	WOW! ☺
pretty	adorable, gorgeous, lovely
a lot	several, multiple, scads of
kind	sweet, thoughtful
bad	atrocious, dreadful, obnoxious
very	greatly, positively, tremendously
large	massive, enormous, sizeable, king-size
good	excellent, satisfactory, exceptional
went	disappeared, escaped, headed
happy	joyous, elated, cheerful, pleased

Your Turn:

Create new sentences by replacing the **COW** (**C**ommonly **O**verused **W**ords) with **WOW** (**W**onderful **O**utstanding **W**ords) in each of these sentences:

- Jasmine is so <u>pretty</u>.
- I got a <u>good</u> grade on my spelling test.
- Lucas <u>went</u> to the game with AJ.
- Her little sister is <u>very</u> funny.

Auspicious Adjectives

Standards

- Uses descriptive and precise language that clarifies and enhances ideas
- Uses adjectives in written compositions

Materials

- Chart paper
- Markers
- Writer's Notebooks
- *Auspicious Adjectives Notebook Entry* (page 195; auspicious.pdf)

Mentor Texts

- *Bedhead* by Margie Palatini
- *The Odious Ogre* by Norton Juster
- *Many Luscious Lollipops* by Ruth Heller
- See *Mentor Text List* in Appendix C for other suggestions.

Procedures

Note: Adjectives should be used sparingly but sprinkled in to add flavor and energy. Repeat this lesson as often as necessary using a variety of literature, pointing out examples of adjectives.

Think About Writing

1. Explain to students that adjectives create pictures in the reader's mind. They help the reader to see what is happening in the story more clearly.

2. Review mentor texts, if desired, and emphasize the author's use of adjectives. For example, in *Bedhead*, Margie Palatini got right to work in the first paragraph with mighty images. Point out the following words used to get the reader interested: *faithful*, *old*, *battered*, *baseball cap*, *lumpy-looking head*, and *slick gelhead*.

Teach

3. Tell students, "Today I will show you how to use adjectives to create images with words." Explain that adjectives are describing words that, if used effectively, allow a reader to get a clearer picture about what is written.

4. On chart paper, write a sentence using each noun listed below. Then, rewrite the sentence using an adjective to describe the noun. Discuss with students how the adjective helps make a clearer picture for the reader.

Noun Only	Adjective and Noun
The kitten meowed.	The playful kitten meowed.
The boy helped his friend.	The brave boy helped his friend.
We watched a ballgame.	We watched an exciting ballgame.
Todd wore pants.	Todd wore baggy pants.
The class ate a snack.	The class ate a nutritious snack.

Auspicious Adjectives *(cont.)*

Engage

5. Have students work with partners to create sentences using the following adjectives and nouns:

   - terrifying troll
   - worn-out sneakers
   - fragile butterfly
   - muddy shoes
   - ice-cold milk
   - reckless driver

   Allow approximately two minutes for students to talk.

Apply

6. Remind students to sprinkle adjectives into their stories, essays, compositions, and poetry. Provide students with the *Auspicious Adjectives Notebook Entry* (page 195) to add to their Writer's Notebook. Practice sentences from the *Your Turn* section before proceeding to their writing folders.

Write/Conference

7. Allow students time to write. Meet with a small group to reteach, review, and add a few new adjectives. Then, bring an enrichment group to your table to improve and enhance their knowledge. Allow approximately four minutes with each group. Finally, walk through the classroom to conference with individual students with the remaining time.

Spotlight Strategy

8. Spotlight students who are using adjectives. For example, "Excellent word work today. Notice the use of auspicious adjectives in this piece of writing." Spotlight one or two to build echoes of thinking across the lesson.

Share

9. Have students "carousel" around the room. Tell students to share a sentence with a partner, move to a new partner, share, and move to another new partner. Provide time for students to share with at least three partners.

Homework

Ask students to tune in to TV to listen for the use of adjectives. Have students make a list of eight adjectives they hear used tonight. Add students' adjectives to a class chart the next day.

Auspicious Adjectives Notebook Entry

Auspicious Adjectives

Authors add **adjectives** to give the reader a perfect picture of what is written.

Try to visualize these examples:

- wiggly tooth
- venomous snake
- barren desert
- sleepy baby
- chocolate chip cookie

- shaggy dog
- strong wind
- sharp claws
- scary movie
- favorite book

Your Turn:

Use these adjective and noun examples to create sentences with a partner. Then, write five sentences in your notebook to practice using adjectives.

- angry teacher
- spoiled child
- disappointed mom

Be Explicitly Specific

Standards

- Uses descriptive and precise language that clarifies and enhances ideas
- Uses nouns in written compositions
- Uses adjectives in written compositions

Materials

- Chart paper
- Markers
- Writer's Notebooks
- *Be Explicitly Specific Notebook Entry* (page 198; bespecific.pdf)

Mentor Texts

- *An Angel for Solomon Singer* by Cynthia Rylant
- *All the Places to Love* by Patricia MacLachlan
- See *Mentor Text List* in Appendix C for other suggestions.

Procedures

Note: Teaching students about parts of speech as a portion of the writing process allows them to apply words strategically in stories, essays, and compositions.

Think About Writing

1. Review with students that authors construct effective sentences by using effective words. Explain that a sentence should contain no unnecessary words. The words that are in the sentence should be concise, crisp, and clear.

2. Review mentor texts, if desired, and emphasize the author's use of word choice that creates a mental image in the mind of the reader.

Teach

3. Tell students, "Today I will show you how to create a mental image for your reader by providing explicit details." Explain that you will show two strategies.

4. Tell students that common nouns that do not name a specific person, place, or thing can be expanded into proper nouns that do. Write the following sentence on chart paper: *We walked to the park.* Circle the word *park* and explain that by changing this common noun to a proper noun, the reader gets a better picture of the park. Rewrite the sentence with the name of a local, familiar park's name: *We walked to Heritage Park.* Review with students that a proper noun names a specific person, place, or thing and is capitalized.

5. Explain that another way to create a mental image for the reader is to be specific about the description of the person, place, or thing. Write the following sentence on chart paper: *We walked to the park.* Circle the word *park* and explain that by adding more description to the word, we can help the reader better visualize the park. Rewrite the sentence with more descriptive words, for example: *We walked to the secluded park.*

Be Explicitly Specific *(cont.)*

6. Model for students how to combine both strategies into one sentence: *We walked to the secluded Heritage Park.*

Engage

7. Remind students that using proper nouns will increase the power of their sentences. Write the following sentence on chart paper: *The boy got a lot of stuff for his birthday.* Have students work with partners to orally create more specific sentences. Allow several groups to share their sentences with the whole group.

Apply

8. Remind students to be explicit in their writing. Provide students with the *Be Explicitly Specific Notebook Entry* (page 198) to add to their Writer's Notebook. Have students work on the *Your Turn* section before proceeding to their writing folders.

Write/Conference

9. Provide time for students to write. Scan the room for students who may need assistance getting started. Always fill writing time by conferencing with individuals or working with small groups. Record your observations in your Conferring Notebook.

Spotlight Strategy

10. Spotlight students who are using explicit details in their writing. For example, "Darrell has truly used his memory to write explicit words that create a mental picture for his reader. Such clever, skillful writing!"

Share

11. Have students meet in triads to share their detailed sentences. Provide approximately two minutes for students to share.

Homework

Ask students to pay close attention to the details around them. Have students make lists of ten adjective and noun pairs.

Be Explicitly Specific Notebook Entry

Be Explicitly Specific

Authors use explicit words to create a sharp, crisp picture in the reader's mind. They do this by making changes from **common nouns** to **proper nouns**.

Common nouns are general names for people, places, and things while proper nouns are specific names of individual people, places, and things. Proper nouns are always capitalized.

Weak sentence: We go to the park on the holidays.

Common Noun	Proper Noun	Descriptive Words
park	Watoga State Park	green, secluded
holiday	4th of July	exciting, noisy

Strong sentence: Watoga State Park, a lush, green, secluded park in Pocahontas County, is a wonderful getaway on an exciting, noisy 4th of July.

Your Turn:

Be explicitly specific with these words. Then, use them to create and add new sentences to your notebook. Remember to capitalize your proper nouns!

Common Noun	Proper Noun	Descriptive Words
team		
magazine		
book		
man		
street		

#50918—Getting to the Core of Writing—Level 4 © Shell Education

Adverb Alert

Standards

- Uses descriptive and precise language that clarifies and enhances ideas
- Uses adverbs in written compositions

Materials

- Chart paper
- Markers
- Index cards *(optional)*
- *Adverb Cards* (page 202; adverbcards.pdf)
- Writer's Notebooks
- *Adverb Alert Notebook Entry* (page 201; adverbalert.pdf)

Mentor Texts

- *Suddenly Alligator: Adventures in Adverbs* by Rick Walton
- *The Bunyans* by Audrey Wood
- See *Mentor Text List* in Appendix C for other suggestions.

Procedures

Note: Well-chosen adverbs add life and color to action. Add additional adverbs to an anchor chart as they are discovered in literature and speech.

Think About Writing

1. Explain that as authors compose messages, stories, and compositions, they refine their skills and become better writers.

2. Review mentor texts, if desired, and emphasize the author's use of adverbs.

Teach

3. Tell students, "Today I will show you how to use adverbs to tell more about verbs and create a clearer mental image for your readers." Explain that adverbs tell *how*, *when*, *where*, or *to what degree* the action happens, and many adverbs end with *-ly*, such as *gently* and *slowly*.

4. Write the following sentences on chart paper. Ask students to name the verb used in each sentence. Then, help students identify and underline the adverb or adverbial phrase in each sentence and use the *Adverb Cards* (page 202) to identify the question it answers.

   My puppy ran <u>quickly</u>. (How?)

   My puppy ran <u>after the kitten</u>. (Where?)

   My puppy <u>often</u> ran <u>outside</u>. (When? Where?)

   My puppy ran <u>extremely fast</u>. (How? To what extent?)

Adverb Alert *(cont.)*

Engage

5. Write the following sentence stem on chart paper.

> *The cat meowed.*

Show students one of the *Adverb Cards*. Have students work with partners to strengthen the sentence by adding an adverb that answers the question on the card. Show other cards and have students create new sentences. Then, try the same activity with other sentence stems, such as: *"A baby cried." and "Eddie walked."* Play the game again on the same day or on subsequent days.

Apply

6. Remind students that adverbs add more detail to their writing. Provide students with the *Adverb Alert Notebook Entry* (page 201) to add to their Writer's Notebook. Have students work on the *Your Turn* section before proceeding to their writing folders.

Write/Conference

7. Provide time for students to write. Select students who may need additional support and provide a reteach lesson. Write several adverbs on index cards. Have students select a card and create a sentence using the adverb. Allow approximately five minutes for reteaching and then begin conferencing with individual students.

Spotlight Strategy

8. Spotlight students who are working diligently on their writing. For example, "Way to go writers! You are discovering the joy that comes with successful writing attempts. What a pleasure!"

Share

9. Have students meet with partners to share their best sentences. Remind students to give their partners praise. Provide approximately two minutes for students to share.

Homework

Ask students to listen to conversations in their homes for adverbs. Have students make a list of at least five adverbs they hear tonight.

Adverb Alert Notebook Entry

Adverb Alert

Adverbs add specific details to stories, essays, compositions, and poetry.

An adverb can tell the reader *how*, *where*, *when*, or *to what degree*. Many adverbs end with *–ly*. Often prepositional phrases act as adverbs in our writing.

- My puppy ran <u>quickly</u>. (how)
- My puppy ran <u>after the kitten</u>. (where)
- My puppy <u>often</u> ran outside. (when)
- My puppy ran <u>extremely fast</u>. (to what extent)

How?		When?	
quietly	slowly	finally	eventually
quickly	sadly	yesterday	later
bravely	skillfully	today	often
playfully	furiously	early	never
Where?		**To What Extent?**	
here	everywhere	extremely	almost
upstairs	in the house	too	very
there	at the game	barely	hardly
between	home	totally	quite

Your Turn:

Practice using adverbs by creating descriptive sentences in your notebook. Use the list above or choose your own. Reread and revise using adverbs to add emphasis and details in your writing.

Adverb Cards

Directions: Cut out the cards. Using the sentence stem you wrote on chart paper, have students work with partners to build the sentence as you display the cards.

Alliteration Action

Standard

Uses descriptive and precise language that clarifies and enhances ideas

Materials

- Chart paper
- Markers
- Writer's Notebooks
- *Alliteration Action Notebook Entry* (page 205; alliteration.pdf)

Mentor Texts

- *Some Smug Lug* by Pamela Edwards
- *Chicken Little* by Steve Kellogg
- *Shrek!* by William Steig
- See *Mentor Text List* in Appendix C for other suggestions.

Procedures

Note: Students enjoy creating and publishing ABC books of alliteration action. Explore poetry for examples of alliteration.

Think About Writing

1. Review with students some of the writing strategies they have been working on recently. Explain that writers are constantly learning new strategies to improve their writing.

2. Review mentor texts, if desired, and emphasize the author's use of alliteration.

Teach

3. Tell students, "Today I will show you a new strategy that will support your poetry writing—alliteration!" Explain that alliteration is when all words start with the same beginning sound. Alliteration is used in poetry, advertising, and to just play with words. It is a stylistic device that livens up writing.

4. Model the following procedure and example on chart paper, or consider creating your own examples using your students' names.

Step 1:	Think of a noun.
	Dog
Step 2:	Name some adjectives, words that describe, that begin with the same sound as the noun
	dirty, disobedient, droopy-eared
Step 3:	Think of some verbs that begin with the same sound. What does the dog do?
	digs, destroys, disappears
Step 4:	Choose some adverbs that begin with the same sound. How did the dog do it?
	deviously, daringly, destructively

Alliteration Action *(cont.)*

Step 5:   Write some prepositional phrases that include words that begin with the same sound and tell where the action takes place.

in the daffodils, in the dirt, out the door, in the dark

Step 6:   Alliteration action! Select from your list and create your own sentences. Pick and choose what you want to include

My disobedient dog daringly disappeared out the door.

David's droopy-eared dog daringly destroyed the daffodils in the dirt.

Here are a few more examples:

- Auntie Ann actually ate all the apples in Adam's attic.
- Margaret watched the mischevious monkey swinging from tree to tree.
- Cool, calm, creative cousins can collect cats, cougars, and camels.

Engage

5. Have students work with partners to create sentences using beginning letters you provide. Allow a few giggles, and remind students they can use humor, but their sentences should make sense. Provide approximately three minutes for students to talk. Have partners share their sentences out loud to the whole group.

Apply

6. Remind students to play with letters and sounds in their heads to create alliteration. Encourage them to publish an alphabet book or a poem. Provide students with the *Alliteration Action Notebook Entry* (page 205) to add to their Writer's Notebook. Have students work on the *Your Turn* section before proceeding to their writing folders.

Write/Conference

7. Provide time for students to write. Stay available to rotate and keep your Conferring Notebook handy to make observations about student learning. Spend additional time practicing this literary device if needed.

Spotlight Strategy

8. Spotlight students who are using alliteration. For example, "Spotlight! Jamil's alliteration gave me the shivers. Astonishing alliterations today. You are an amazing group of writers."

Share

9. Have students take one minute to read over their work. Then, have students meet with partners to share alliteration. Give students time to talk to at least three people to give and get examples of alliteration.

Homework

Ask students to create alliteration sentences with their parents. Have students select a letter of the alphabet and write a sentence with alliteration using that letter.

Alliteration Action Notebook Entry

Alliteration Action

Alliteration is the repetition of the initial sound in words. Authors use alliteration because it's fun to say and enjoyable to hear.

Peter **P**iper **p**icked a **p**eck of **p**ickled **p**eppers.

Try these steps to write your own alliteration action. Begin with the same sound as the noun you select for Step 1.

Step 1: Think of a noun.	dog
Step 2: Name some adjectives.	dirty, disobedient, droopy-eared
Step 3: Think of some verbs.	digs, destroys, disappeared
Step 4: Choose some adverbs.	deviously, daringly, destructively
Step 5: Write some prepositional phrases.	in the daffodils, in the dirt, out the door, in the dark
Step 6: Alliteration action! Select from your list and create your own sentences. Pick and choose what you want to include.	

My disobedient dog daringly disappeared out the door.

Your Turn:

Try using the following nouns to create sentences with alliteration.

- snake

- cat

- book

#50918—Getting to the Core of Writing—Level 4 © Shell Education

Voice

Expressing Yourself

Voice is the most elusive of the traits of quality writing. It is uniquely the passion, experiences, and creativity that are brought to the reader's attention through the writer's exceptional ability to convey his or her own observations gleaned from experiences. Voice grows as the writer grows! Donald Murray in *Write to Learn* (2004) describes voice as "the person in the writing." Donald Graves in his early work, *Writing: Teachers and Children at Work* (2003) writes a detailed explanation of how to listen for voice in student writing. When students are able to put their speech in writing, the fingerprint of their personality shines through.

Voice is evident in the stories and literature we share with our students every day. It is in those books that we can barely tear ourselves away from, the ones we want to keep reading and can hardly wait to turn the page. Think about the texts you pull out to read to your students again and again. You want to share them because the author's voice connects in some way to you personally. To call attention to voice, collect examples on anchor charts and help students recognize and value its purpose through your read alouds and student writing. As you model writing, use conventions to show emotions and transfer passion from speech to print.

Voice is what makes writing come alive. It is the personality of the writer coming through in the writing. Although sometimes difficult to teach, it is recognizable in writing through the personal tone and feeling of the writing piece. This section contains lessons that focus on how students can connect with their readers to compel them to continue reading. Lessons in this section include the following:

- Lesson 1: Show Me Your Voice (page 209)
- Lesson 2: What's My Voice? *(page 215)*
- Lesson 3: The Voices on the Bus (page 217)
- Lesson 4: Various Voices (page 220)

The *Val and Van, Voice* poster (page 210) can be displayed in the room to provide a visual reminder for students that voice is one of the traits of writing. You may wish to introduce this poster during the first lesson on voice. Then, refer to the poster when teaching other lessons on voice to refresh students' memories and provide them with questions to help guide them as they make an effort to show voice in their writing.

Val and Van
Voice

What is the purpose of my writing?

✔ Did I write to an audience?

✔ Did I share my feelings?

✔ Did I make my reader smile, cry, think?

✔ Does my writing sound like me?

Show Me Your Voice

Standard

Writes expressive compositions

Materials

- *Emotion Cards* (pages 212–214; emotioncards.pdf)
- Chart paper
- Markers
- Writer's Notebooks
- *Show Me Your Voice Notebook Entry* (page 211; showme.pdf)

Mentor Texts

- *The True Story of the Three Little Pigs* by Jon Scieszka
- *Sweet Tooth* by Margie Palatini
- *Amelia's Notebook* by Marissa Moss
- *Fly Away Home* by Eve Bunting
- *Walter, the Farting Dog* by William Kotzwinkle
- See *Mentor Text List* in Appendix C for other suggestions.

Procedures

Note: Explore voice through literature throughout the year. Give students small whiteboards and erasable markers for read aloud time. At important points in the story, stop reading and have students write or draw the emotion they are feeling from the texts, then hold up their whiteboards.

Think About Writing

1. Explain that authors add specific details to show the reader their story; they also add a special touch of themselves called *voice*.

2. Review mentor texts, if desired, and emphasize the author's use of voice in the story. For example, the voice in many of Margie Palatini's books is silly or funny.

Teach

3. Tell students, "Today I will show you how to use voice in your stories." Explain that voice is often shown through the emotion that authors share in their writing.

4. Select several *Emotion Cards* (pages 212–214) to display. Be sure to include the cards for the emotions you will discuss. Read aloud small sections from selected literature to give students clear examples of voice that show strong emotions. Discuss with students which *Emotion Card* best matches the emotions of the characters or how the reader feels as the story is read.

5. Discuss with students how emotions can change throughout a story. Also notice the various ways an author shows emotion without actually naming the emotion. Ask questions such as, "How do we know?" or "What made you feel that way?"

Show Me Your Voice (cont.)

Engage

6. Continue to share small sections from literature with strong examples of voice. Have students work with partners to identify the voice. Call on several students to share their responses. Encourage them to share the thinking they did that led to their decisions.

Apply

7. Remind students that showing voice is the way authors make the reader feel about the story. Encourage students to think about the voice they want to show in their writing. Provide students with the *Show Me Your Voice Notebook Entry* (page 211) to add to their Writer's Notebook. Have students write sentences from the *Your Turn* section before continuing their work in their writing folders.

Write/Conference

8. Provide time for students to write. Check and scan briefly, then move into conference sessions with students who need further support with the trait of voice. Record your observations in your Conferring Notebook.

Spotlight Strategy

9. Spotlight students who are using voice in their writing. For example, "Paul, you have clearly used voice in your writing. Listen and guess the emotion Paul is using in his story."

Share

10. Have students write the emotion they are trying to convey in their writing on the back of their papers. Then have students share their writing with partners. Have partners try to guess the emotions.

Homework

Ask students to listen for voice in the stories they read in books or see on TV. Have students write down the emotions that they felt.

Show Me Your Voice Notebook Entry

Show Me Your Voice

Authors show **voice** by sharing the emotions of their characters. They might plan for their readers to feel lonely, excited, or frightened.

Be on the lookout for voice in the stories you read, movies you watch, and even the music you hear. Write down sentences in your notebook that make you feel an emotion, such as, "The youngster quickly ran behind his father and peeked around to see what might be happening."

Here are some other emotions you could use to show voice in your writing:

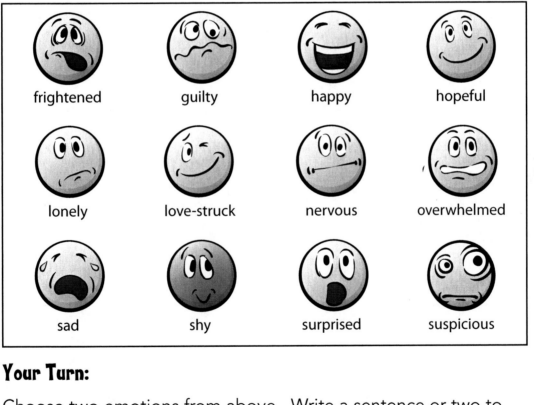

frightened	guilty	happy	hopeful
lonely	love-struck	nervous	overwhelmed
sad	shy	surprised	suspicious

Your Turn:

Choose two emotions from above. Write a sentence or two to show the emotion without naming it.

Emotion Cards

Directions: Cut out the cards. As you read excerpts from mentor texts, display the cards and discuss with students which emotion best matches the emotions of the characters.

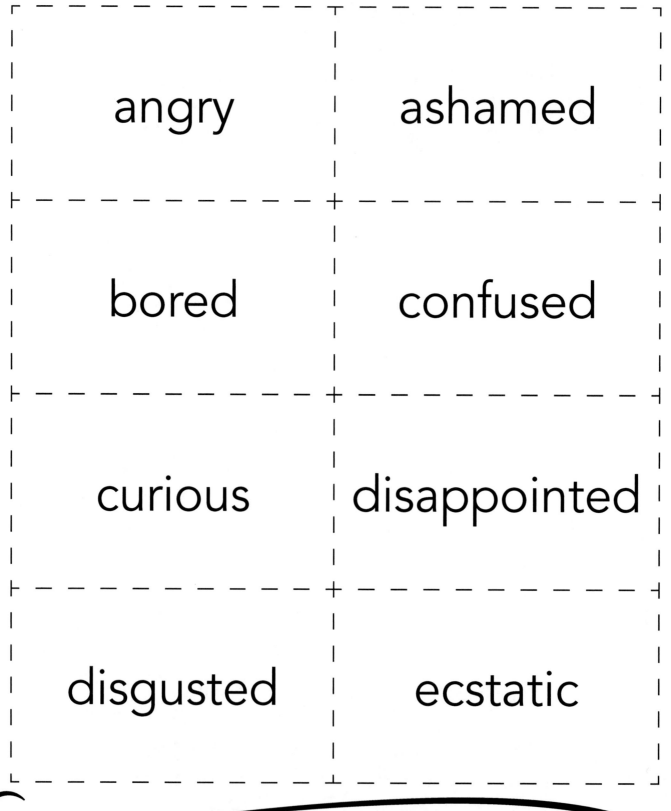

angry	ashamed
bored	confused
curious	disappointed
disgusted	ecstatic

Emotion Cards (cont.)

embarrassed	exhausted
frantic	frightened
guilty	happy
hopeful	lonely

Emotion Cards (cont.)

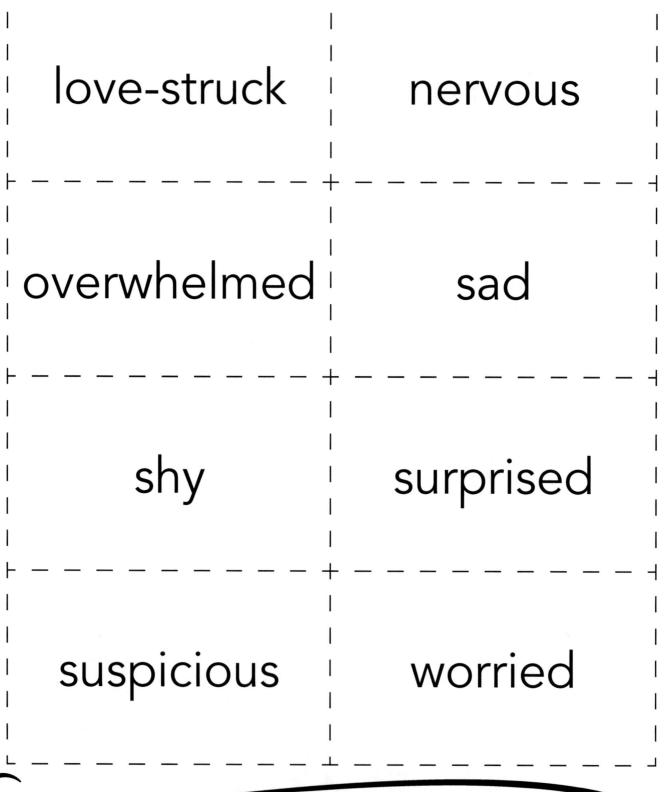

love-struck	nervous
overwhelmed	sad
shy	surprised
suspicious	worried

What's My Voice?

Standard

Writes expressive compositions

Materials

- *Emotions Cards* (pages 212–214; emotioncards.pdf)
- Chart paper
- Markers
- Writer's Notebooks

Mentor Texts

- *The Bee Tree* by Patricia Polacco
- *Bedhead* by Margie Palatini
- *Everybody Needs a Rock* by Byrd Baylor
- *The Memory String* by Eve Bunting
- See *Mentor Text List* in Appendix C for other suggestions.

Procedures

Note: Expose students to voice through all genres of literature. Use your core stories to discuss voice.

Think About Writing

1. Remind students that authors "show, not tell" about the characters and actions in their stories. Explain that authors often do not name the emotions. Authors show emotion through the use of descriptive words and characters' thoughts and actions.

2. Review mentor texts, if desired, and emphasize the author's use of voice.

Teach

3. Tell students, "Today I will show you how to write just like our favorite authors and show the feelings and action in your writing." Explain they are going to play a voice guessing game.

4. Select a card from the *Emotion Cards* (pages 212–214), but do not tell students what the emotion is. Write a short paragraph on chart paper that shows the emotion through the use of descriptive words, phrases, and actions without naming it. Have students try to guess what emotion you were showing.

5. Tell students that when they show emotion they should ask questions, such as, "What does this emotion look like, sound like, feel like?"

Engage

6. Display several *Emotion Cards*. Have students meet with partners to select an emotion. Students should discuss how they will show the emotions with their partners. Allow time for conversation.

What's My Voice? (cont.)

Apply

7. Remind students that there are many emotions that can be used in writing.

Write/Conference

8. Provide time for students to write. Be available to support students with the trait of voice. Make anecdotal notes in your Conferring Notebook for future reference and conferring.

Spotlight Strategy

9. Spotlight students who are using voice in their writing. For example, "Spotlight on Timothy and Gwen. These partners have the right idea. Listen in to see if you can hear the voice."

Share

10. Do a gallery share. Number students' papers and post them around the room so all students have the opportunity to read them. Provide students with additional paper to take with them as they read the posted work. Have students write down the number of the paper they read then write the emotion they think the author showed in the work.

Homework

Ask students to listen for voice in conversations and in books. Have students write the name of one emotion and the way it was shown.

The Voices on the Bus

Standard

Writes expressive compositions

Materials

- Chart paper
- Markers
- Writer's Notebooks
- *The Voices on the Bus Notebook Entry* (page 219; voicesonbus.pdf)

Mentor Texts

- *The Wheels on the Bus* by Maryann Kovalski
- *Sweet Tooth* by Margie Palatini
- *Yours Truly, Goldilocks* by Alma Flor Ada
- *Voices in the Park* by Anthony Browne
- See *Mentor Text List* in Appendix C for other suggestions.

Procedures

Note: The trait of voice cannot be taught step-by-step. Sharing literature with strong voice is the best means of exposing students to this trait. Model using *The Voices on the Bus Notebook Entry* (page 219) several times before asking students to work independently.

Think About Writing

1. Explain that authors add voice or their own personality to their writing. This is what makes us care about characters and adds personality to the stories.

2. Review mentor texts, if desired, and emphasize the author's use of voice.

Teach

3. Tell students, "Today I will show you how your writing can reflect different voices based on the characters that are in the story."

4. Create a table on chart paper such as the one shown below.

Think About	Character 1	Character 2
Mood: What tone/mood does the story have?		
Personality: What kind of personality does the character have? How does the author show the reader?		
Thoughts: What might the character be thinking?		
Senses: What is the character seeing, hearing, smelling, feeling?		
Actions: Do the actions reflect the character's personality?		

The Voices on the Bus *(cont.)*

5. Share a text that represents two or more voices. Identify two characters to study and write their names at the tops of the *Character* columns. Answer each of the questions for each of the characters. Discuss the completed table and any similarities and differences that you identified.

Engage

6. Ask students if they remember a story song from their younger years called, "The Wheels on the Bus." Remind students that the song had several characters. Explain that students will select a character from the bus and use the questions from the table (or notebook entry) to help develop their own tables about their characters. Then, have students create their own stories based on the voices of their characters. Ask students not to identify the characters by name and have the class guess who each character is based on the description in the stories.

Apply

7. Remind students to give their writing personality and voice to keep the reader interested. Provide students with *The Voices on the Bus Notebook Entry* to add to their Writer's Notebook. Have students work on the *Your Turn* section before proceeding to their writing folders.

Write/Conference

8. Provide time for students to write. Gather a small group of writers who may need additional support. Assist them with getting started and then rotate in order to support others. Note observations in your Conferring Notebook.

Spotlight Strategy

9. Spotlight students who are using voice to make their stories more interesting. For example, "Incredible! Just listen to the voice in Elena's writing. I can tell right away which character she selected for the story."

Share

10. Have students share their writing with partners. Ask students if they can identify their partner's characters based on the descriptive writing.

Homework

Ask students to listen to several commercials on television. Have them think about the voice the author is sharing. Ask students to list two examples of voice.

The Voices on the Bus Notebook Entry

The Voices on the Bus

Authors use **voice** to make stories more interesting. The voice can make us chuckle, sniffle, or even get goosebumps! We can show voice through the characters in our stories.

Think About
Mood: What tone/mood does the story have?
Personality: What kind of personality does the character have? How does the author show the reader?
Thoughts: What might the character be thinking?
Senses: What is the character seeing, hearing, smelling, feeling?
Actions: Do the actions reflect the character's personality?
Does the character seem real to you?

Your Turn:

Try using the chart above to develop a new character from "The Bus." Then, use the information to create a paragraph or story. Remember, do not tell who your character is, just give your character a voice.

Various Voices

Standard

Writes expressive compositions

Materials

- Chart paper
- Markers
- A variety of greeting cards

Mentor Texts

- *Feelings* by Aliki
- *How Are You Peeling? Foods with Moods* by Saxton Freymann and Joost Elffers
- *Dog Breath* by Dav Pilkey
- See *Mentor Text List* in Appendix C for other suggestions.

Procedures

Note: Remember to include e-cards in your discussion as well. You may want to have students create their own greeting cards through one of the many available publishing software products.

Think About Writing

1. Remind students that authors may write to a specific audience. Explain that they use a different voice based on the kind of writing and who the reader will be; authors also add voice based on the purpose of their writing.

2. Review mentor texts, if desired, and emphasize the author's use of voice.

Teach

3. Tell students, "Today I will show you how to match your voice to the purpose for your writing." Explain that the mood of an author's voice can be shown in the writing.

4. Share several greeting cards with students. Display the cards so students can see the illustrations or photographs. Read the cards and discuss the mood of each card and how the writer expressed the mood in the writing. Record the findings on an anchor chart. Be sure to model a variety of greeting cards so students can see specific characteristics of voice.

5. Sort the greeting cards by mood and reread the cards. Discuss if each card in a group expresses the mood in the same way.

Various Voices (cont.)

Engage

6. Provide student partners with greeting cards. Have students read the cards and then discuss what mood is being represented in the writing. Allow two minutes for discussion. Have several pairs of students share their findings aloud with the whole group.

Apply

7. Remind students to include emotions in their writing as a simple way to show voice. Challenge students to create a greeting card with voice. Have students decide what moods they want to show in their cards. Remind students to consider who the card is for. You may ask all students to create a card or make the activity optional, leaving students to explore voice in their own writing piece.

Write/Conference

8. Provide time for students to write. Monitor students for understanding and work ethic. Then, select a small group of students to support based on student needs. Record your observations in your Conferring Notebook for future planning purposes.

Spotlight Strategy

9. Spotlight students who are adding voice to their writing. For example, "The spotlight shines on Nina today. Wow! I noticed right away how she is revising her writing to reflect more voice. It sounds just like her."

Share

10. Have students meet in quads today and share a small section of their writing that they feel sounds just like them—it represents their voice.

Homework

Ask students to look for cards and other media, such as magazine ads and junk mail, that has voice. Have students bring the examples to class to share with the whole group.

Conventions

Checking Your Writing

Writing that does not follow standard conventions is difficult to read. The use of correct capitalization, punctuation, spelling, and grammar is what makes writing consistent and easy to read. Students need to have reasonable control over the conventions of writing. This section provides lessons that guide students and helps them internalize conventions as they write and check their work for conventions after they have written a piece. Lessons in this section include the following:

- Lesson 1: Capital Creations (page 225)
- Lesson 2: Super Spellers (page 228)
- Lesson 3: Common Comma Conventions (page 231)
- Lesson 4: The Color of CUPS (page 235)
- Lesson 5: Dandy Dialogue (page 239)
- Lesson 6: Show Me Editing (page 242)
- Lesson 7: Traits Team Checklist (page 245)
- Lesson 8: Digging into Editing (page 248)

The *Callie, Super Conventions Checker* poster (page 224) can be displayed in the room to provide a visual reminder for students that conventions is one of the traits of writing. You may wish to introduce this poster during the first lesson on conventions. Then, refer to the poster when teaching other lessons on conventions to refresh students' memories and provide them questions to help guide them as they make an effort to use correct conventions in their writing.

Callie

Super Conventions Checker

How do I edit my paper?

✔ Did I check my capitalization?

✔ Did I check my punctuation?

✔ Did I check my spelling?

✔ Did I use good spacing?

✔ Did I read over my story?

Capital Creations

Standard

Uses conventions of capitalization in written compositions

Materials

- Chart paper
- Markers
- Writer's Notebooks
- *Capital Creations Notebook Entry* (page 227; capital.pdf)

Mentor Texts

- *The Day I Swapped My Dad for Two Goldfish* by Neil Gaiman
- *If You Were a Writer* by Joan Lowery Nixon
- *What Do Authors Do?* by Eileen Christelow
- other CCSS and Core literature
- See *Mentor Text List* in Appendix C for other suggestions.

Procedures

Note: Revisit this lesson over several days and recite the capitalization chant regularly. Upon completion of the chant, have students write it in their notebook or type and duplicate for students. You may have student groups type their section before presentation. Be sure to include the authors' names for each section.

Think About Writing

1. Remind students that effective writing is a result of rereading, rewriting, and rereading again and again until the message is presented accurately. Explain that favorite authors revise and edit their work numerous times before sending it off for publication.

2. Review mentor texts, if desired, and emphasize the conventions used in the books.

Teach

3. Tell students, "Today I will show you a trick for remembering the rules for capitalization." Explain that capitalizing certain words guides the reader through your writing; for example, it lets your reader know when a new sentence begins or if a word is important or specific, such as a name.

4. Discuss the principles of capitalization. Write the following on chart paper for students to reference.

   Remember to always capitalize

   - *the beginning of a sentence;*
   - *the pronoun I;*
   - *major words in titles of movies, books, magazines, and songs;*
   - *letter salutations and closings; and*
   - *proper nouns.*

Capital Creations (cont.)

5. Explain that creating cheers or raps can help remind us of the principles of capitalization. Display or write the chant from the *Capital Creations Notebook Entry* (page 227) on chart paper. Teach students the chant by reading it several times.

Capitalization Chant

(*Clap, tap, or snap and get into the beat!*)
Capitalization is a skill, you see!
You'll be a better writer if you listen to me.
So, just remember these simple rules,
and add them to your writing tools!
(*Tap, Tap-Tap, Tap*)

The first word of a sentence and the pronoun I,
Always have a capital, so give it a try!
FIRST-WORD-PRONOUN I,
(*Tap-Tap, Tap-Tap-Tap*)
FIRST-WORD-PRONOUN I!

6. Select one of the capitalization rules to create the next stanza of your chant. Be sure to think aloud your process and demonstrate your capital creation for the students. Note the rhythm and flow, which will make it easy and memorable.

Engage

7. Divide students into quads and assign each group a capitalization rule. Have groups create stanzas of the chant for their assigned rules. Provide time for students to talk with their groups about their ideas for the chants.

Apply

8. Remind students that using correct capitalization creates signals that help your reader understand the meaning of your writing. Provide students with the *Capital Creations Notebook Entry* to add to their Writer's Notebook. Have students work on the *Your Turn* section before proceeding to their writing folders.

Write/Conference

9. Provide time for students to work with their groups to create, write, and practice their chant. Rotate from group to group to monitor noise level and to provide assistance and motivation.

Spotlight Strategy

10. Spotlight students who are working diligently on editing their writing. For example, "Spotlight! What an exceptional performance. Writers, you rock! You're well on your way to becoming exceptional editors. What genius!"

Share

11. Have students share and present their capitalization chants.

Homework
Ask students to notice the use of capitals in magazines, books, newspapers, or on TV ads and billboards. Tell them to be ready to share their findings tomorrow.

Capital Creations Notebook Entry

Capital Creations

Remember to always capitalize

- the beginning of a sentence;

- the pronoun *I*;

- first, last, and major words in titles of movies, books, magazines, and songs;

- letter salutations and closings; and

- proper nouns, such as, people, places, holidays, days, months, historic events, organizations, and product names.

Capitalization Chant

(*Clap, tap, or snap and get into the beat!*)
Capitalization is a skill, you see!
You'll be a better writer if you listen to me.
So, just remember these simple rules,
and add them to your writing tools!
(*Tap, Tap-Tap, Tap*)

The first word of a sentence and the pronoun I,

Always have a capital, so give it a try!

FIRST-WORD-PRONOUN I,
(*Tap-Tap, Tap-Tap-Tap*)
FIRST-WORD-PRONOUN I!

Your Turn:

Writers, practice these rules in your writing. Correct and write this sentence.

for dinner last night, jean and i had hamburgers for our main course and ice cream for dessert.

Super Spellers

Standard

Uses conventions of spelling in written compositions

Materials

- Chart paper
- Markers
- Writer's Notebooks
- *Super Spellers Notebook Entry* (page 230; superspellers.pdf)
- Grade level high frequency word list

Mentor Texts

- *Miss Alaineus: A Vocabulary Disaster* by Debra Frasier
- Core spelling program
- See *Mentor Text List* in Appendix C for other suggestions.

Procedures

Note: Teach this lesson frequently so that students have automaticity with grade level words.

Think About Writing

1. Explain that authors spell words quickly, accurately, and automatically from memory. Tell students that this is a skill that often comes with spelling study, practice and repetition.

2. Review mentor texts, if desired, and emphasize the author's use of conventional spelling and what may happen if words are not spelled correctly. For example, in Debra Frasier's story, *Miss Alaineus*, a vocabulary disaster in the making has a humorous twist when Sage misunderstands the word *miscellaneous* and spells *Miss Alaineus*.

Teach

3. Tell students, "Today I will show you how to build a core of known words you can write fast, smooth, and automatically. Explain that knowing these words will free students up to work on more difficult words that need to be stretched into word parts.

4. Model the following steps in order to learn how to spell high frequency words.

   - **Look!** Look at the word and notice the spelling.

   - **Say!** Say the word out loud.

   - **See!** Visualize the word so that you see it in your mind.

   - **Write!** Cover the word, and then write the word quickly and smoothly.

   - **Check!** Check your spelling with the spelling on the chart.

Super Spellers *(cont.)*

5. As students work, move around and observe, providing corrective feedback to any student making incorrect letter strokes.

6. Assign student partners that have been carefully selected with attention given to academics and social abilities. Provide students with individual white boards and markers or paper and pencils.

7. Write four or five words from a grade level high frequency word list on chart paper. Have students work with their partners using the procedures in Step 4 to practice these words.

Engage

8. Have students talk with partners to name the parts of the spelling strategy they learned today.

Apply

9. Remind students that their goal is to be able to spell with automaticity. Provide students with the *Super Spellers Notebook Entry* (page 230) to add to their Writer's Notebook. Have students work on the *Your Turn* section and edit spelling errors in their writing projects.

Write/Conference

10. Provide time for students to write. Scan the room for students who may need assistance getting started. Then, rotate among students to ask questions and give comments.

Spotlight Strategy

11. Spotlight students who are using spelling tools. For example, "What a genius! Terri is using the word chart and practicing a spelling strategy to avoid a spelling catastrophe! Good writers use tools and strategies to support them."

Sharing

12. Have students meet with partners to discuss how this strategy will improve their writing.

Homework
Ask students to practice spelling some of the words they practiced during Writer's Workshop today. Have them write each word two times using "Look! Say! See! Write! Check!"

Super Spellers Notebook Entry

Super Spellers

Expert writers have a core of words they know.

Look! Say! See! Write! Check!

- **Look!** Look at the word and notice the spelling.

- **Say!** Say the word out loud.

- **See!** Visualize the word so that you see it in your mind.

- **Write!** Cover the word, and then write the word quickly and smoothly.

- **Check!** Check your spelling with the spelling on the chart.

Frequently Misspelled Words

about	different	many	they're
again	every	neighbor	through
always	family	other	until
beautiful	favorite	outside	went
because	finally	people	what
become	friend	really	when
believe	gone	sometimes	where
children	it's vs. its	their	which
could	know	there	while

Your Turn:

Choose three words from the list above that you want to spell with automaticity. Practice the Look! Say! See! Write! Check! strategy with the words.

Common Comma Conventions

© Shell Education #50918—Getting to the Core of Writing—Level 4

Standard

Uses conventions of punctuation in written compositions

Materials

- Chart paper
- Markers
- *Common Comma Convention Cards* (page 234; commacards.pdf)
- Blank sentence strips
- Writer's Notebooks
- *Common Comma Conventions Notebook Entry* (page 233; commoncomma.pdf)

Mentor Texts

- *Eats, Shoots & Leaves: Why, Commas Really Do Make a Difference!* by Lynne Truss
- Core literature with evidence of comma conventions
- See *Mentor Text List* in Appendix C for other suggestions.

Procedures

Note: Provide repetition of this lesson over several days and repeat regularly so writers understand that commas clarify messages both in writing stories and compositions and when used with technology.

Think About Writing

1. Explain that most authors use standard conventions to make their writing easier for the reader to understand. Remind students that they have worked to edit for correct capitalization and spelling; explain that writers also have to be aware of the use of commas to add meaning to their sentences.

2. Review mentor texts, if desired, and emphasize the author's use of commas.

Teach

3. Tell students, "Today I will show you how to use commas to control your message to the reader." Explain that by using conventions, such as commas, the author tells the reader when to pause, slow down, speed up, or even deliver expression.

4. Review the following comma conventions with students. Write each comma rule on chart paper and an example sentence or two from the notebook entry.

   - **Dates and addresses:** Put a comma between the day and year in dates and between the city and state in addresses.

   - **Series:** Use a comma to separate items in a series of three or more.

   - **Introductory words and phrases:** Use a comma after an interjection or introductory word or phrase.

Common Comma Conventions *(cont.)*

- **Compound sentences:** Use a comma between two statements that are joined in the same sentence. Put the comma right before the coordinating conjunction: FANBOYS *(for, and, nor, but, or, yet, so)*

- **Direct address:** Use a comma to set off a name of someone being spoken to.

Engage

5. Place students in teams of three or four and provide each group with a blank sentence strip. Distribute the *Common Comma Conventions Cards* (page 234), one to each group. Ask the group to work together to write an example sentence using the assigned convention. Allow approximately three minutes for students to work.

Apply

6. Review with students that they should use correct conventions of written language so that their message is clear for their reader. Provide students with the *Common Comma Conventions Notebook Entry* (page 233) to add to their Writer's Notebook. Have students work on the *Your Turn* section before proceeding to their writing folders.

Write/Conference

7. Provide time for students to write. Rotate among students to conference with individual students. Make notes on your observations of student work.

Spotlight Strategy

8. Spotlight students who are using commas in their writing. For example, "Spotlight! Extraordinary comma use today! Your effort is a great example for all!"

Share

9. Have students meet with partners to share their writing. Then, have each partner team find another group of partners to meet with to share their writing.

Homework

Ask students to notice the conventions of print around them. Have students identify three places they see commas in use. Have students bring the examples or write them down.

Common Comma Conventions Notebook Entry

Common Comma Conventions

Authors use commas to tell the reader where to pause.

Dates and addresses: Put a comma between the day and year in dates and between the city and state in addresses.   *Gia was born on October 9, 2012 in Red Bud, Illinois.*
Series: Use a comma to separate items in a series of three or more.   *Rodger enjoys football, basketball, and hockey.*
Introductory words and phrases: Use a comma after an interjection or introductory word or phrase.   *Yes, I finally got my new puppy.*   *Oh, how is the puppy getting along?*   *After lunch, we will take her for a walk.*
Compound sentences: Use a comma between two statements that are joined in the same sentence. Put the comma right before the coordinating conjunction: **FANBOYS** (**f**or, **a**nd, **n**or, **b**ut, **o**r, **y**et, **s**o)   *Calee ran to the door, but the puppy quickly scampered out.*
Direct address: Use a comma to set off a name of someone being spoken to.   *Jasmine, did you feed the cat?*

Your Turn:

Create a sentence using each convention and write the sentences in your Writer's Notebook.

Common Comma Conventions Cards

Directions: Cut out cards. Distribute one card to each group to write a sentence using the convention on the card.

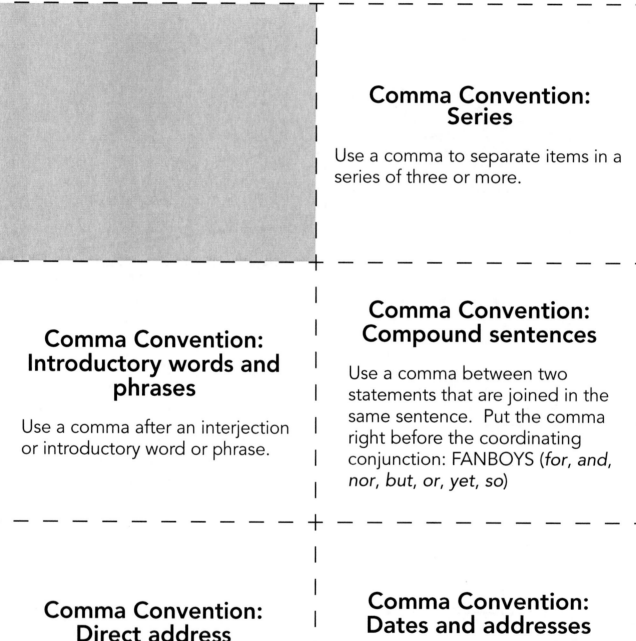

Comma Convention: Series

Use a comma to separate items in a series of three or more.

Comma Convention: Introductory words and phrases

Use a comma after an interjection or introductory word or phrase.

Comma Convention: Compound sentences

Use a comma between two statements that are joined in the same sentence. Put the comma right before the coordinating conjunction: FANBOYS (*for, and, nor, but, or, yet, so*)

Comma Convention: Direct address

Use a comma to set off a name of someone being spoken to.

Comma Convention: Dates and addresses

Put a comma between the day and year in dates and between the city and state in addresses.

The Color of CUPS

Standards

- Uses strategies to edit and publish written work
- Uses conventions of spelling in written compositions
- Uses conventions of capitalization in written compositions
- Uses conventions of punctuation in written compositions

Materials

- Student writing sample
- Different colored pens or pencils (green, orange, blue, red)
- Writer's Notebooks
- *The Color of CUPS Notebook Entry* (page 237; colorofcups.pdf)
- *Camping Trip Writing Sample* (page 238; camping trip.pdf)

Mentor Texts

See *Mentor Text List* in Appendix C for suggestions.

Procedures

Note: Repeat this mini-lesson over several days, demonstrating each component of *CUPS*. Using different color pens supports young writers as they learn to edit their papers.

Think About Writing

1. Explain that once authors are finished writing, they work on editing or fixing up the writing for publication. Remind students that the goal is to have writing that is easy for others to read.

Teach

2. Tell students, "Today I will show you how to use CUPS to edit your writing." Explain that *CUPS* stands for **C**apitalization, **U**sage of grammar, **P**unctuation, and **S**pelling.

3. Display a writing sample and write CUPS vertically down the left side of the paper.

4. Think aloud as you model editing the paper for each convention.

   C: Underline each capital letter in green. Make a green box around the first letter of each sentence.

   U: Check for subject/verb agreement, overused words, and that sentences make sense. Circle any problems in orange.

   P: Underline all punctuation in red. Make a red box around punctuation at the end of each sentence. Check to see if there are an equal number of green boxes and red boxes.

   S: Circle any words that are not spelled correctly in blue. Read your story backward to double check.

Initially, you may wish to do one step per day until students become familiar and comfortable with the editing process.

The Color of CUPS *(cont.)*

Engage

5. Have students name the word they can use to help check their work to make it presentable to the public. Have students work with partners to tell what each letter of *CUPS* stands for and how checking their work will improve it.

Apply

6. Remind students that editing is an important step in the writing process. Encourage students to use CUPS any time they write a story, so the reader will understand the story. Provide students with the *The Color of CUPS Notebook Entry* (page 237) to add to their Writer's Notebook. Have students work on the *Your Turn* section.

Write/Conference

7. Provide students with *Camping Trip Writing Sample* (page 238). Ask students to edit the page using *CUPS*. If necessary, break the task into small, manageable pieces so that students are not overwhelmed.

Spotlight Strategy

8. Spotlight students who are using CUPS to edit their writing. For example, "What remarkable editing! You are exciting me with your understanding of capitalization, usage, punctuation, and spelling."

Share

9. Have students meet with partners to share their editing results.

Homework

Ask students to discuss editing with their parents. Have students identify things that need editing and things that do not, for example: books, checkbooks, grocery lists, contracts, etc.

The Color of CUPS Notebook Entry

The Color of CUPS

Editing is an important step in the writing process. Use **CUPS** anytime you write a story, so your reader will better understand your writing.

C: Underline each capital letter in green. Make a green box around the first letter of each sentence.

✓ First word in a sentence and all proper nouns

U: Check for subject/verb agreement, overused words, and that sentences make sense. Circle any problems in orange.

✓ Does your writing sound right?

P: Underline all punctuation in red. Make a red box around punctuation at the end of each sentence. Check to see if green boxes = red boxes.

✓ Periods, question marks, exclamation points, commas, quotation marks

---

S: Circle any words that are not spelled correctly in blue. Read your story backward to double check.

✓ Use word walls, word list, and dictionary

Your Turn:

With a partner, CUPS the practice paragraph. Then, select one of your writing projects and work through it together.

Name: _____ Date: _____

Camping Trip Writing Sample

Directions: Use CUPS to edit the paragraph below.

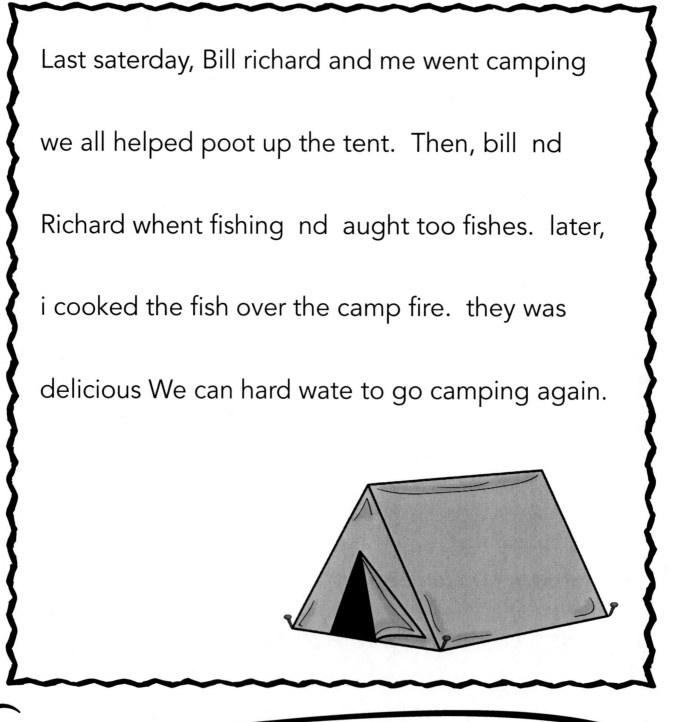

Last saterday, Bill richard and me went camping

we all helped poot up the tent. Then, bill nd

Richard whent fishing nd aught too fishes. later,

i cooked the fish over the camp fire. they was

delicious We can hard wate to go camping again.

Dandy Dialogue

Standard

Uses conventions of punctuation in written compositions

Materials

- Chart paper
- Markers
- Writer's Notebook
- *Dandy Dialogue Notebook Entry* (page 241; dandydialogue.pdf)

Mentor Texts

- *Grandpa's Teeth* by Rod Clement or other text with prominent dialogue
- See *Mentor Text List* in Appendix C for other suggestions.

Procedures

Note: Use this lesson over several days to show students the appropriate way to insert written conversation. Caution children to only use dialogue to extend the meaning of the story and not to overuse it.

Think About Writing

1. Explain that authors use strategies to show conversation and create interest in character development.

2. Review mentor texts, if desired, and emphasize the author's use of dialogue. For example, in the book *Grandpa's Teeth*, Rod Clement writes, *"HELP, I've been robbed!" We heard Grandpa shouting. "It'sth a disthasthter! Come quickly!"* Discuss how dialogue creates interest and shows character.

Teach

3. Tell students, "Today I will show you how to see and hear characters in action." Explain that well-written dialogue can draw readers quickly into story action.

4. Write the following sentence on chart paper:

   Sara exclaimed, "It is going to be a beautiful day!"

5. Model how to use two hands to show where dialogue begins and ends. Place palms upright, facing each other, close, but not quite touching (as if about to clap). Begin to read the sentence on the chart paper. When the beginning quotation mark indicates where Sara starts to speak, move your right hand up to the right side of your mouth. Keep your hand there as you say the words Sara spoke. When you get to the end quotation mark, move your left hand up to the left side of your mouth. This movement helps students better understand the beginning and ending of the quotation and aids in memory retention.

Dandy Dialogue (cont.)

6. Read additional snippets of dialogue from mentor text or other chosen texts. Use your hands to demonstrate the beginning and ending of dialogue. Use the chart paper to show the speaker's words in quotation marks. Remind students that commas, periods, and exclamation points go inside quotation marks.

Engage

7. Have students work with partners to practice the hand movements with the following sentences.

   - *Mom said, "What would you like for dinner tonight?"*

   - *"Okay," replied my friend, "we're going to the movies together."*

   Provide approximately two minutes for students to practice.

Apply

8. Remind students to insert dialogue into writing projects to increase interest and action. Provide students with the *Dandy Dialogue Notebook Entry* (page 241) to add to their Writer's Notebook. Have students work on the *Your Turn* section before proceeding to their writing folders.

Write/Conference

9. Provide time for students to write. Punctuating dialogue is an important skill, so plan to pull a small group and reteach for those students who need additional support.

Spotlight Strategy

10. Spotlight students who are using dialogue in their writing. For example, "What sophisticated writers! You continually amaze me! Just listen to how Lioni added dialogue to create interest and action."

Share

11. Have students meet with partners to share where they added dialogue in their writing. Provide approximately two minutes for students to share.

Homework

Ask students to listen to the flow of conversation around them. Have students write down the words spoken between two people to show dialogue.

Dandy Dialogue Notebook Entry

Dandy Dialogue

Authors use **dialogue** to create talk on paper. Dialogue should sound exactly how the character would talk.

We use quotations marks to identify the spoken words of a character or speaker. When writing dialogue, keep these points in mind.

- Put quotation marks before and after the spoken words.

- Place punctuation <u>inside</u> the quotation marks.

- Use an ellipsis (three periods) to show a pause in the dialogue.

Oliver, do you know what happened to my tie?

No, Dad... but, I saw Rover in your bedroom!

Your Turn:

Use these sentences to practice punctuating dialog in your notebook. Then, move into your own writing and reread and revise your dialogue.

- Never mind Oliver shouted as he fumbled with his hair.

- The photographer moaned Okay! One, two, three! Got it!

- Just look at his hair! howled Mom. We'll never get him ready in time for school.

Show Me Editing

Standards

- Uses strategies to edit and publish written work
- Uses conventions of spelling in written compositions
- Uses conventions of capitalization in written compositions
- Uses conventions of punctuation in written compositions

Materials

- Sentence strips
- Chart paper
- Markers
- Writer's Notebooks
- *Show Me Editing Notebook Entry* (page 244; showmeediting.pdf)

Mentor Texts

- *Sweet Tooth* by Margie Palatini
- *Twenty-Odd Ducks: Why, Every Punctuation Mark Counts!* by Lynne Truss
- See *Mentor Text List* in Appendix C for other suggestions.

Procedures

Note: Repeat this lesson and have fun with editing. Model and practice body movements on many occasions to create enthusiasm and motivation for editing for all conventions. Need a quick pick-me-up? Use *Show Me Editing* on a couple of sentences to give students a quick kick start.

Think About Writing

1. Explain that authors know that they must give readers a strategy to understand their messages. Nothing is more confusing for a reader than picking up a piece of writing with no capitalization or punctuation, poor meaning, and misspelled words. Explain that it is their responsibility to edit their writing for their readers.

2. Review mentor texts, if desired, and emphasize the role punctuation plays in developing the meaning.

Teach

3. Tell students, "Today I will show you a fun strategy called *Show Me Editing*." Explain that it will help with editing for capitalization and punctuation.

4. Ask one or two students some simple questions, such as, "What is your name?" and "Who are your friends?" Record students' answers on sentence strips without any capitalization or punctuation.

5. Tape the sentences up in one long line. Have students read the sentences without stopping. Discuss the difficulties in understanding the writing.

6. Display the *Show Me Editing Notebook Entry* (page 244) or write the movements on chart paper. Review each movement with students. Return to the sentence strips and perform the movements as you edit the sentences.

Show Me Editing *(cont.)*

Engage

7. Have students review the body movements for *Show Me Editing* with partners. Allow approximately two minutes for students to talk.

Apply

8. Remind students to use *Show Me Editing* as they edit their writing projects. Provide students with the *Show Me Editing Notebook Entry* to add to their Writer's Notebook. Have students rewrite the paragraphs on the *Your Turn* section before proceeding to their writing folders.

Write/Conference

9. Provide time for students to write. Observe students to check for understanding. Initiate individual or small group conferences. Plan for your next instructional strategy.

Spotlight Strategy

10. Spotlight students who are diligently editing their writing. For example, "Rahul did what good writers do! He made excellent observations and changes."

Sharing

11. Have students meet with partners to share their writing. Remind students to provide and get feedback.

Homework

Ask each student to look in a book to notice how writers clarify and create understanding with accuracy. Have each student copy two sentences from a book and circle examples of correct capitalization and punctuation.

Show Me Editing Notebook Entry

Show Me Editing

Authors **edit** for capitalization and punctuation to clarify the meaning of their writing.

Use movements to "show me" capitalization and punctuation editing.

- **Capital:** Stand tall with arms and hands together overhead

- **Period:** Grind right foot into the floor

- **Exclamation:** Right arm straight up, pull down, punch

- **Comma:** Karate chop

- **Quotation Marks:** Hands to each side of mouth, palms facing toward each other, to separate speaker's words.

- **Hyphen:** Slide hand across front of body

- **Ellipsis:** Silent finger count, 1–2–3.

Your Turn:

With a partner use *Show Me Editing* to correct capitalization and punctuation in the passage below. Then, rewrite the paragraph in your Writer's Notebook.

hello friends i'm jen and this is my partner dan we live in waco texas dan enjoys spending time riding horses roping steers and panning for gold my job…well i just catch all the bad guys we always say life in best in the west

Traits Team Checklist

Standard
Uses strategies to edit and publish written work

Materials
- *Traits Team Checklist Notebook Entry* (page 247; traitschecklist.pdf)
- Student writing samples
- Markers
- Writer's Notebooks

Mentor Texts
- *Amelia's Notebook* by Marissa Moss
- *Two Bad Ants* by Chris Van Allsburg
- See *Mentor Text List* in Appendix C for other suggestions.

Procedures

Note: If students are not familiar with the traits of writing, distribute this lesson over several days, so that students feel comfortable using the checklist with peer/adult support.

Think About Writing

1. Explain that authors check and double-check their work before they publish it. Reviewing writing to make it the best it can be is one of the last steps before publication.

2. Review mentor texts, if desired, and emphasize the author's use of all the traits of writing.

Teach

3. Tell students, "Today I will show you how to use a checklist of ideas to prepare a writing piece for display." Remind students that they have been using the Traits Team throughout the year. Tell them that the checklist they will use today will help them make sure each of the writing traits is included in their writing.

4. Display the *Traits Team Checklist Notebook Entry* (page 247) and a student writing sample. Be sure to get permission from the author in advance or use one from another class without a name.

5. Model how to review a piece of writing for each item on the checklist. Use a student partner to model how to review the paper. Think aloud as you pose problems, give your point of view, and reflect on strategies you see being used in the paper. Be an explicit model for asking deep, critical questions. Avoid asking questions that require simple, one-word answers.

Engage

6. Have students talk with partners about how the *Traits Team Checklist* will help them as they get ready to publish a piece of writing.

Traits Team Checklist *(cont.)*

Apply

7. Remind students to use the *Traits Team Checklist* as a resource to self-assess their writing projects. Provide students with the *Traits Team Checklist Notebook Entry* to add to their Writer's Notebook.

Write/Conference

8. Have each student select a piece of writing from his or her writing folder. Group students in triads and spread the groups around the room. Have students help each other review their writing using the *Traits Team Checklist* as a guide. Remind students to self-assess and use the support of the group. Provide approximately twelve minutes for students to work. Today you need to move around, look around, listen in, and provide encouragement. Keep your Conferring Notebook handy.

Spotlight Strategy

9. Spotlight one or two students. For example, find a student who represents what you would most like to see while working independently to assess work using the *Traits Team Checklist*.

Share

10. Have students meet with partners to share their writing. Encourage students to observe their partners' writing for deep reflection and self-assessment. Have students who have challenged their thinking perhaps share their thinking with the group. Sharing is crucial!

Homework

Ask students to tell their parents about each of the traits of writing. Have students write down all six traits and define them.

Trait Team Checklist Notebook Entry

Traits Team Checklist

Authors are part of a team that rereads their writing to make revisions and editing decisions.

This writing traits checklist can help you polish your writing.

Ideas ❑ I have a focused topic. ❑ I use supporting and interesting details.	**Word Choice** ❑ My words paint a picture in my reader's mind. ❑ I use words that are precise and expressive.
Sentence Fluency ❑ I include complete and correct sentences. ❑ I include a variety of sentence types and lengths. ❑ My sentences begin in different ways.	**Voice** ❑ My writing sounds like me. ❑ I "talk" to the reader/ audience in my writing.
Organization ❑ My introduction hooks the reader. ❑ I have a sequence with a beginning, middle, and end. ❑ I include transition words to link ideas. ❑ I have a strong conclusion.	**Conventions** ❑ I use correct capitalization, spelling, and punctuation. ❑ I use correct grammar.

Digging into Editing

Standards

- Uses strategies to edit and publish written work
- Uses conventions of spelling in written compositions
- Uses conventions of capitalization in written compositions
- Uses conventions of punctuation in written compositions

Materials

- Chart paper
- Markers
- Student writing samples
- Colored pens
- Writer's Notebooks
- *Digging into Editing Notebook Entry* (page 250; digging.pdf)
- *He's the Man Writing Sample* (page 251; hestheman.pdf)

Mentor Texts

- *Eleven* by Patricia Reilly Giff
- Other CCSS literature
- See *Mentor Text List* in Appendix C for other suggestions.

Procedures

Note: Editing marks are fairly generic and with the influx of technology, editing is fast becoming a lost art. Teach in a group so students can talk, listen, and reflect together. This lowers the level of concern and raises the level of support.

Think About Writing

1. Explain that professional authors use editors to check their writing projects for accuracy. Remind students that they do not have editors, so it is important that they find errors in their own writing. Reassure students that you will provide them two things to help as they edit—a checklist and a partner.

2. Review mentor texts, if desired, and emphasize the use of correct conventions.

Teach

3. Tell students, "Today I will show you how to use symbols to help you as you edit your writing." Explain that using editing symbols will make the job of editing easier than trying to erase and fix the writing.

4. Select several editing symbols to introduce and model each day for several days. Write the symbols for them on chart paper. Create sample sentences that are in need of editing or use the ones provided in the notebook entry. Model for students how to use the editing symbols to make corrections to the writing. When all the symbols have been introduced, proceed to the next step.

5. Display a piece of student writing. (Be sure to get the student's permission or use an unnamed piece of writing from another class.) With the help of a student partner, read through the piece and use the editing symbols where needed. Think aloud as you work so students have an explicit model of how you are going about editing the writing.

Digging into Editing *(cont.)*

Engage

6. Provide students with the *Digging into Editing Notebook Entry* (page 250) to add to their Writer's Notebook.

7. Provide students with *He's the Man Writing Sample* (page 251) and have them practice editing it using the editing symbols. Allow several minutes for students to practice editing and then review.

Apply

8. Ask students to think of a garden shovel for digging. Explain that they need to practice digging out errors so that their messages are clear.

Write/Conference

9. Provide time for students to write. Provide praise to students who move out and immediately began working on projects. Then, gather a small group that needs additional support. Keep a checklist with you, and help students practice editing work from their writing folders.

Spotlight Strategy

10. Spotlight students who are working on editing their writing. For example, "Writers! Great discovery! You're scooping out many errors and using great evidence by rereading."

Share

11. Have students meet with partners to tell how they dug out errors to clarify their messages. Encourage students to be explicit in their explanations. Allow approximately two minutes for students to share.

Homework

Ask students to be alert to errors in the world. Have them observe and listen for errors on signs, billboards, advertisements, and in newspapers. Encourage them to be editor detectives to see if they can catch mistakes.

Digging into Editing Notebook Entry

Digging into Editing

Authors scoop out errors to develop a clear message for their readers.

Dig into your writing and identify errors using these editing marks.

Editing Mark	Meaning	Example
☰	Capitalize	david gobbled up the grapes.
/	Change to lower case	My mother hugged Me when I Came Home.
⊙	Insert a period	The clouds danced in the sky ⊙
sp ◯	Check spelling	I (laffed) at the story.
∿	Transpose words or letters	How you are?
∧	Add a word or letter	Would you please pass the pizza?
∧,	Insert a comma	I have two cats, two dogs and a goldfish.
ℒ	Delete	Will you call call me on the phone tonight?
¶	New paragraph	… in the tree. ¶ After lunch, I spent the day…

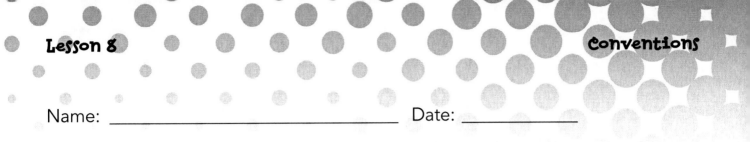

Name: _____ Date: _____

He's the Man Writing Sample

Directions: Dig into the errors in this writing sample. See if you can improve this piece by using editing symbols from your Writer's Notebook.

He's the Man!

you've got to be kidding me. eli manning, exciting quarterback

or the New York iants makes $8,500,000 a year. by the time you add in

money for dvertisements, his salary is "over the moon," With a passing

eficency rate of 110%, and the most valuable playr award at the Super

Bowl, perhaps he is erning his dinner. One thing for sure, every year he

continus too grab heedlines, his value will increase.

#50918—Getting to the Core of Writing—Level 4 © Shell Education

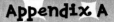

Essential Materials

Create a toolkit of items you can carry around with you as you conference with students. The toolkit can be a shoebox, a plastic tote, or anything you are comfortable carrying around from student to student. Any supplies that will help make your conference run smoothly are appropriate to put in the tote. Suggested items are listed below:

- Teacher Conferring Notebook
- Mentor text used for daily writing lesson (changes regularly)
- Highlighters or highlighting tape (to draw attention to words)
- Scissors, glue, tape, or a small stapler for revision, cutting, pasting, and moving around
- Sticky notes for making suggestions
- Colored pens for editing (green, red, blue, black, orange)
    - Green—capitalization
    - Red—ending punctuation
    - Blue—spelling
    - Black—inserting
    - Orange—usage
- Rubber band for stretching sentences
- Whiteboard or magnetic board with markers for modeling
- Magnetic chips or large colored buttons
- 1 package of correction tape or correction fluid
- Assorted paper

Conferring Notebook
Getting to the Core of Writing

Mini-Lesson Log

Date	Mini-Lesson Instructional Focus

Conference Log

P: Praise—What strategies did I notice the child using independently?

TP: Teaching Point—What teaching point will move this child forward in his or her development as a writer?

Name: Date: P: TP:	Name: Date: P: TP:	Name: Date: P: TP:	Name: Date: P: TP:
Name: Date: P: TP:	Name: Date: P: TP:	Name: Date: P: TP:	Name: Date: P: TP:
Name: Date: P: TP:	Name: Date: P: TP:	Name: Date: P: TP:	Name: Date: P: TP:

Conference Countdown

10 Conversation—The conversation should feel like a friendly chat with the student doing the most talking. Keep in mind, the person doing the most talking is doing the most learning.

9 It's about the WRITER, not the Writing—Teach the strategy that will support the writer after he or she is finished with this particular piece of writing. For example, do not just spell a word for a child, but teach him or her to segment the sounds to spell many words.

8 Focus on the Content—You are not there to simply fix up the conventions of a writing piece. When possible, have the student read the piece aloud before you even look at it and focus purely on the content. It's a challenge!

7 Observe, Praise, Guide, Connect—Establish a routine to become effective and efficient.

6 Begin with Praise!—Everyone likes a compliment. Beginning with a compliment gives students a sense of joy and pride in their work as well as recognizes developing writing skills.

5 Talk Like a Writer to a Writer—Use the language and vocabulary of a writer and respect the student's developmental level of writing.

4 Connect or not to Connect?—When conferring, only make connections to your daily mini-lesson when appropriate for the student's piece of writing.

3 Record and Reflect—Use your Conferring Notebook to monitor the progress of writing in your classroom and individual students. The information is valuable in defining your focus for writing instruction.

2 Variety—Incorporate a variety of activities that meet the multiple learning modalities of your students, like varying your conferring group sizes and using manipulatives.

1 Be There!—Your face and eyes tell it all. Let students know you truly care about the writing they are sharing with you.

Conferring Step-by-Step

The four phases of a conference structure are:

1. Observe
2. Praise
3. Guide
4. Connect

Observe—Use observation as a chance to build your background knowledge of the writer. During this element of the conference, you will determine what the writer knows and can do independently, and what the writer can do with support, called the zone of proximal development (Vygotsky 1978). Begin by asking yourself:

- What do I already know about this student's developmental level of writing and past writing from my conference notes and previous observations?
- What can I learn from the student's current writing piece and writing behaviors?
- What can I learn through questioning and listening to the writer?

When asking students about their writing work, open-ended questions provide guidance and support for students to begin reflecting on their writing. A close-ended question, such as, "Is this you in the picture?" elicits a simple one- or two-word response. An open-ended question, such as, "What can you tell me about your picture?" offers opportunities for the writer to explain and describe ideas, motives, and feelings about his or her work, ultimately gaining clarity and developing a deeper understanding of his or her writing. You might ask the writer:

- So, what are you working on in your writing today?
- What can you tell me about your important writing work?

Through your observation, you should determine a successful writing point and one teaching point that will help this child become a more independent writer. Selecting a teaching point can be daunting as we analyze a young writer's work. Teachers often ask, "How do you know what to work on when there are so many things?" The truth is there is no right answer. Here are some ideas to guide you as you select teaching points:

- Use what you know about the growth of this writer. Where is this writer developmentally?
- Consider what the student is working on at this time. What is the student's focus in his or her writing?
- Use the current writing curriculum and the Common Core State Standards.
- Use what is being taught in mini-lessons and whole-group instruction.

Where we ourselves are as writers, as well as where we are as teachers of writing, greatly affect our decisions. As you become more knowledgeable about the developmental phases of writers and the understanding of quality writing instruction, your decisions become more sophisticated. The more you confer with your writers, the more effective you become at making decisions during conferring. Most importantly, select one teaching point that will support each writer during your conference. Calkins, Hartman, and White (2003) reminds us to teach to the writer and not to the writing.

Conferring Step-by-Step *(cont.)*

Praise—Recognize the writer for work well done. Always begin a conference with a positive comment. This praise provides positive feedback intended to identify what the student is doing correctly and to encourage the writer to repeat that accomplishment in future writing. Isolate and identify the successful writing strategy in the student's writing piece. When praises are authentic and specific, they become a teachable moment. Below are some examples of powerful praise:

- "Something I really like that you've done is how you shared the setting with your reader. That's exactly what good writers do!"

- "I see here in your writing you chose to use color words to give your reader more details in your story. Wonderful words!"

- "Just like the authors we have been studying, you have an excellent picture that helps your reader visualize exactly what is happening in your story."

- "I am so impressed with the way you just got right to work and accomplished so much writing in such a short amount of time."

Guide—Personalize and scaffold instruction to meet the writer's needs. The instruction includes sharing the writing strategy you will teach the writer, demonstrating the strategy, and then guiding the writer through practicing the process. Teach the writer a personalized strategy based on your earlier decisions. When the decision is based on a previously taught mini-lesson, writers make additional connections and greater achievement is gained. As part of the routine of the mini-lesson, you must explicitly state what you will teach the student.

- Mentor texts and writing samples are excellent resources to weave into your conference instruction. Writers can visualize the craft you are teaching when they are exposed to concrete examples, particularly from real literature.

- Initial teaching remarks may include, "Let me show you something that good writers do…" and, "Sometimes in my writing, I try to…"

By offering support while the student practices the strategy, you increase the chances of success. Any time you engage students in the application of new strategies, you enhance the probability they will recall that strategy in future writing. Once the writer is engaged in practice, you may move on to confer with another writer. However, leave the writer with expectations until you return, such as, "When I get back, I want to see …" Upon your return, provide specific feedback relative to your expectations. For example, "Well done! Now I really have a picture in my mind of your character."

conferring Step-by-Step *(cont.)*

Connect—Make connections between teaching and future writing. First, clearly restate what the writer learned and practiced. Then, remind and encourage the writer to use the strategy in future writing. As students become familiar with the conference structure, you may ask the student to share the new learning to get a sense of his or her understanding of your teaching. Making connections may begin as follows:

- "Remember, good writers always…"

- "Tell me what you just learned as a writer."

Writer's Workshop conferences will vary in length and type based on the time of year and the needs of your class. Conferences are most successful when routines and expectations have been established and young writers can manage their own writing time. At the beginning of the year, while establishing routines, drop-by conferences provide a quick glimpse into what each student is working on and what kind of help is needed. Once routines are established, meet with students in individual and/or small group conferences that are focused around specific needs. You may also include peer conferences, but this requires modeling, experience, and practice. For young writers, we use *Compliment and Question*. The compliment should be more than a general statement, such as, "I like your story." It should be specific to the writing, for example, "I like the way you ask a question to begin your story." A question should be something the peer would like to know more about or something that needs clarification.

The conference should be brief and reflect the child's age and development. Small group conferences may be as long as 8–10 minutes as you will be checking in with each student. Hold the conference wherever you prefer. Some teachers prefer moving desk to desk or table to table while others prefer that students join them at a small conference table or on the floor. Remember these two points:

- *Have a seat!* Wherever you decide to hold your conferences, it is important that students know you are committed to giving them your attention. By sitting down, you are sending the message that you are there with them at that moment.

- *Be prepared!* Have materials readily available to you during the conference. You may wish to compile a Conferring Toolkit of essential materials (see page 253 of Appendix A) that can be carried with you or placed in your conference area.

Continuing to provide meaningful and relevant conferences requires some form of keeping notes during your writing conferences. A simple, but thorough conference summary can identify areas of writing deficiencies and strengths as you plan future mini-lessons, select students for small group conferences, and report student progress to parents. To support you as you make conferring a priority in Writer's Workshop, pages for the *Conferring Notebook* are included on pages 254–257.

Benchmark Assessment Overview

Administering a Benchmark (page 262) is a guide to assist you as you begin giving benchmarks. It is important that the prompt is uniform across classrooms when measuring growth at a school level. Fourth grade benchmark prompts should be simple and attainable, for example:

- Sometimes it is fun to imagine what might happen if you found something while walking to school. What might happen if you found a bag and a shoe? Reveal the sequence in a natural way. Use dialogue to add interest.

- Eating healthy foods is important. Think about why it is important to eat healthy. What food do you consider to be healthy? Provide details and examples to support your topic.

- Your school is considering changes in the dress code, including requiring students to wear uniforms. What suggestions would you make concerning the dress code? Write an essay to convince your readers to agree with your recommendations.

The Writing Rubric (pages 263–264; writingrubric.pdf) is a tool to analyze student writing skills.

The Writing Report (page 265; writingreport.pdf) serves as a summative report of a student's writing benchmarks. The completed form along with the beginning-, middle-, and end-of-year benchmarks are placed in the student's record folder at the end of the year.

The Grouping Mat (page 266; groupingmat.pdf) is an at-a-glance chart showing which students in your classroom have attained particular benchmarks. Simply circle the current benchmark period, and complete the chart by recording your students' names in the boxes. Your goal is to see the students' names progressively move upward on the rubric report.

The core of writing instruction is the desire to support young writers as they explore, discover, and learn the writing process. It also involves determining what knowledge and skills young writers have developed over a period of time. Assessment is a continuous process and, when used properly, benefits teachers as well as students.

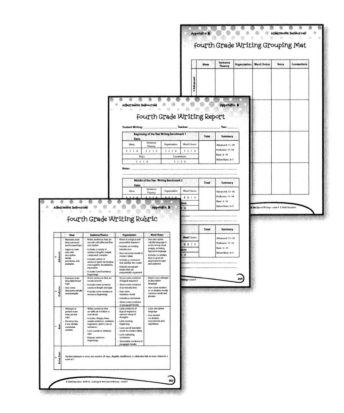

Administering a Benchmark

Writing Benchmarks are usually administered at the beginning, middle, and end of the school year to measure improvements and determine the writer's strengths and deficits in writing development. To get started, follow these guidelines:

- Administer the Writing Benchmark Prompt in small groups. This allows the teacher to observe and take anecdotal notes of individual student behaviors.

- It is important not to practice the prompt prior to the writing benchmark session.

- Do not provide teacher support. Your goal is to determine what students are able to do independently. If a student demonstrates frustration, he or she may just draw a picture, but you may wish to redirect the student to the prompt. Compliment the drawing and invite the student to write something about the drawing as best he or she can.

- Allow students to use classroom displays such as word walls. Note words copied from the word wall.

- Distribute paper to each student. Use paper familiar to the students. Students should write their name and the date on the back so that it is not seen prior to scoring the writing. This will help you to stay objective as you grade the writing piece .

- Supply pencils and crayons when necessary.

- Explain to your class that this process will show how much they have grown as writers and that a prompt will be given at the beginning, middle, and end of the year.

- Read the prompt to your students. Paraphrase the prompt when necessary to clarify understanding. You may wish to display the prompt on chart paper or on a whiteboard.

- Have each student read you his or her story upon completion. Keep a record of what each student wrote in your own writing so that you will be able to identify the words that he or she used. If some words are unreadable due to invented spelling, write them down at the bottom of the writing piece or on a sticky note.

Fourth Grade Writing Rubric

		Ideas	Sentence Fluency	Organization	Word Choice
3	**Advanced**	• Maintains main idea; narrowed and focused topic • Supports main idea with descriptive details, anecdotes, and examples	• Writes sentences that are smooth with effective flow and rhythm • Includes a variety of sentence lengths: simple, compound, complex • Includes variety of sentence types: declarative, interrogative, exclamatory, imperative • Includes varied sentence beginnings	• Writes in a logical and purposeful sequence • Includes an inviting introduction • Uses transition words to connect ideas • Includes a conclusion that satisfies the reader • Includes paragraph breaks that are purposefully organized	• Uses descriptive, colorful language to evoke strong visual images, including figurative language • Includes vocabulary that is varied yet purposeful to topic and audience
2	**Proficient**	• Expresses main idea; fairly broad topic • Uses some descriptive details and examples	• Writes sentences that are mostly smooth • Includes some sentence variety in length and type • Includes some variation in sentence beginnings	• Shows some evidence of logical sequence • Shows some evidence of an introduction • Uses some transition words • Includes a conclusion • Shows some evidence of paragraph breaks	• Makes some attempts at descriptive language • Uses some variation in vocabulary; mostly common words and phrases
1	**Basic**	• Attempts to present main idea; unclear topic • Develops few, if any, details; somewhat random	• Writes sentences that are difficult to follow or read aloud • Includes choppy, basic, simple sentences, sentence fragments, and/or run-on sentences • Lacks variety in sentence type • Repeats sentence beginnings	• Lacks evidence of logical sequence; random string of thoughts • Lacks inviting beginning • Lacks use of transition words to connect ideas • Lacks satisfying conclusion • Shows little evidence of paragraph breaks	• Lacks descriptive language • Uses limited vocabulary; monotonous and repetitious
0	**Below Basic**	Student attempts to write, but result is off-topic, illegible, insufficient, or otherwise fails to meet criteria for a score of 1			

Fourth Grade Writing Rubric *(cont.)*

		Voice	Conventions
3	**Advanced**	• Shows originality, excitement, and commitment to topic • Speaks to and connects with audience and purpose; engages reader	• Little, if any, need for editing • Capitalization is correct, errors may be minor • Consistently correct usage of grammar • Effective and correct use of punctuation • Few errors in spelling
2	**Proficient**	• Shows some originality, excitement, and commitment to topic • Writes with some sense of the audience	• Some need for editing • Capitalization may be inconsistent • Correct grammar usage is fairly consistent • Inconsistent use of punctuation • Most common words spelled correctly
1	**Basic**	• Shows little of writer's personality or commitment to topic • Reads rather dull and mechanical; connecting to no particular audience	• Extensive editing necessary • Capitalization appears random; sparse • Grammar and usage interfere with readability • Little use of correct punctuation • Frequent spelling errors
0	**Below Basic**	Student attempts to write, but result is off-topic, illegible, insufficient, or otherwise fails to meet criteria for a score of 1	

Fourth Grade Writing Report

Student Writing: _____ **Teacher:** _____ **Year:** _____

Beginning of the Year Writing Benchmark 1 Date:				Total	Summary
Ideas	Sentence Fluency	Organization	Word Choice		Advanced: 15–18
3 2 1 0	3 2 1 0	3 2 1 0	3 2 1 0		Proficient: 11–14
Voice		Conventions			Basic: 6–10
3 2 1 0		3 2 1 0			Below Basic: 0–5

Notes: _____

_____

Middle of the Year Writing Benchmark 2 Date:				Total	Summary
Ideas	Sentence Fluency	Organization	Word Choice		Advanced: 15–18
3 2 1 0	3 2 1 0	3 2 1 0	3 2 1 0		Proficient: 11–14
Voice		Conventions			Basic: 6–10
3 2 1 0		3 2 1 0			Below Basic: 0–5

Notes: _____

_____

End of the Year Writing Benchmark 3 Date:				Total	Summary
Ideas	Sentence Fluency	Organization	Word Choice		Advanced: 15–18
3 2 1 0	3 2 1 0	3 2 1 0	3 2 1 0		Proficient: 11–14
Voice		Conventions			Basic: 6–10
3 2 1 0		3 2 1 0			Below Basic: 0–5

Notes: _____

_____

Fourth Grade Writing Grouping Mat

	Ideas	Sentence Fluency	Organization	Word Choice	Voice	Conventions
3 Advanced						
2 Proficient						
1 Basic						
0 Below Basic						

Benchmark Writing Samples

Beginning of the Year

Prompt: Sometimes it is fun to imagine what might happen if you found something while walking to school. What might happen if you found a bag and a shoe? Reveal the sequence in a natural way. Use dialogue to add interest.

One cold fall morning at seven-thirty, I was walking to school, and when I wasn't paying attention I tripped over something! When I got up, I found I had tripped over a bag. My mother says I am very cuorious, so I looked in the bag. There was one moccasin in it. I tried it on and a golden window appeared! I could not believe my eyes.

I went through the window and at first it was very dark. Once it got brighter, I realized that I was in a castle! Before I knew it, I had both of the mocassins on! First, I passed the kitchen. Then, the living room. Next the bathroom, the atic, the basement, and the storage room. Once I got into the hallway, I opened a door that led me to a HUGE BEDROOM!!!!! It was so beautiful that I was almost blinded by the wonderful sight.

I saw a king-sized bed! I saw fantastic flowers. I even saw giant leaves for rugs! The bed had sheets made of silk! I loved it.

I noticed three princesses calling there three maids. They had a tray of food for the princesses. They even gave me a cookie. Before I even got to eat it, kidnappers broke into the castle and took the princesses! Before they could get away, I started to fight them. Without even knowing how, I knocked them out just by punching them! After the kidnappers were gone and put in prision, I took the princesses back to their castle where their father was. He thanked me and the golden window appeared again.

At first I climed through it and everything was so bright I could not see a thing! Once I could see, my teacher said that we would be studying science. Nobody in my class was happy about that. I looked in my desk and saw a golden mirror! Was it not a dream?

Benchmark Writing Samples (cont.)

Beginning of the Year (cont.)

Beginning of the Year Writing Benchmark 1 Date:				Total	Summary
Ideas	Sentence Fluency	Organization	Word Choice		Advanced: 15–18
3 ② 1 0	3 ② 1 0	3 ② 1 0	3 ② 1 0	13 Proficient	Proficient: 11–14
Voice		Conventions			Basic: 6–10
3 ② 1 0		③ 2 1 0			Below Basic: 0–5

Notes:

- Uses some descriptive details and examples (Ideas)
- Includes some sentence variety in length and type (Sentence Fluency)
- Includes some variation in sentence beginnings (Sentence Fluency)
- Shows some evidence of logical sequence (Organization)
- Shows some evidence of an introduction (Organization)
- Includes a conclusion (Organization)
- Shows some evidence of paragraph breaks (Organization)
- Makes some attempts at descriptive language (Word Choice)
- Shows some originality, excitement, and commitment to topic (Voice)
- Writes with some sense of the audience (Voice)
- Little, if any, need for editing (Conventions)
- Capitalization is correct, errors may be minor (Conventions)

Benchmark Writing Samples (cont.)

Middle of the Year

Prompt: Eating healthy foods is important. Think about why it is important to eat healthy. What food do you consider to be healthy? Provide details and examples to support your topic.

Mom, Dad and I searched the field for the best beef so we could butcher it for a healthy food. The healthy food, a delicious steak, gives the body muscle and energy. I enjoy my steak bloody, rare in the middle. Steak is fun to make and I love going to restaurants to taste all of the different flavors.

First, steak is mouth watering and scrumptious. It is juicy and tastes good with A1 sauce. I like my awesome steak with a side of baked potato with ranch. Steak is also good served with broccoli and cheese. I love it rare in the middle, but my brother likes his medium rare, which is pink in the middle, but brown on the outside. My dad likes his rare like me.

Secondly, steaks are fun to make. You have to grain your beef for 2 months, which means you buy grain from the store. You haul it to the slaughter house where it will hang for two weeks to draw out the flavor. Next, you have to call and tell the butcher how you want it cut. Finally, you will pick it up when it is ready, and put it in a freezer, so it won't thaw.

Third, I like to eat fabulous steak at a restaurant. My favorite restaurant is the Steer Steakhouse in Elkins, West Virginia. I can get a side of salad from the bar. I can also get a hot bar that comes with a roll, mashed potatoes, green beans and corn. I only wait 30 minutes to get my tremendous steak. I have a delicious steak meal spread out before me.

In conclusion, steak is my healthy food choice, juicy and tasty. It is fun to make. Just throw it on the grill, season it with A1 sauce, flip it and it is ready to eat. Come on over and eat a rare steak with me.

Benchmark Writing Samples (cont.)

Middle of the Year (cont.)

Middle of the Year Writing Benchmark 2 Date:				Total	Summary
Ideas	Sentence Fluency	Organization	Word Choice	14 Proficient	Advanced: 15–18
3 ② 1 0	3 ② 1 0	③ 2 1 0	3 ② 1 0		Proficient: 11–14
Voice		Conventions			Basic: 6–10
3 ② 1 0		③ 2 1 0			Below Basic: 0–5

Notes:

• Uses some descriptive details and examples (Ideas)

• Includes some sentence variety in length and type (Sentence Fluency)

• Includes some variation in sentence beginnings (Sentence Fluency)

• Writes in a logical and purposeful sequence (Organization)

• Uses transition words to connect ideas (Organization)

• Includes paragraph breaks that are purposefully organized (Organization)

• Makes some attempts at descriptive language (Word Choice)

• Shows some originality, excitement, and commitment to topic (Voice)

• Writes with some sense of the audience (Voice)

• Little, if any, need for editing (Conventions)

• Capitalization is correct, errors may be minor (Conventions)

Benchmark Writing Samples (cont.)

End of the Year

Prompt: Your school is considering changes in the dress code, including requiring students to wear uniforms. What suggestions would you make concerning the dress code policy at your school? Write an essay to convince your readers to agree with your recommendations.

Dress To Impress!

I have concise thoughts about instilling a dress code in my school. Would a dress code be accepted in my school? My answer is both yes and no, depending upon the type of code introduced. In my opinion, some dress codes in West Virginia are quite frivolous. These codes include: no skulls on clothing, no spaghetti straps, no tank tops, and no flip-flops. Students tattle frequently at my school on those who wear skulls on their clothing and try to conceal them. This results in controversy between students, punishments such as changing clothes or turning the clothing inside-out, and humiliation of the offending student. We should have a dress code in my school, just not the current one. We should have one that works for everyone!

My first thought about instilling a dress code in my school is that clothes need to be secure. Students should not be allowed to wear clothes that fit improperly, such as shirts that are too large or shirts that are too small and too short. Large shirts could slide, exposing what should not be exposed; while shorter, smaller shirts could lift, revealing what should not be revealed. I do not want to see private parts or belly buttons! Baggy pants should not be permitted in school. The school should make students wear belts, buttons, zippers, or elastic waistbands on their pants. If a student's pants fall down, it is inappropriate and could be embarrassing not only for that student, but also for anyone who may observe the occurrence! Shoe choice could also be problematic. Students should not be granted permission to wear open-toe or high-heel shoes. For example, my school has an abundance of stairs and students could stumble and fall. This is especially dangerous for kindergarten students. Students should instead wear shoes that allow them to walk carefully and gracefully. These would include tennis shoes and flats.

My second thought about instilling a dress code in my school is that students should not have to wear uniforms. Students need to express their individual style. We should have a right to dress in at least some things we want to wear. Individuality allows a student to establish their own personality and gives them an outlet for expression. This also helps to promote a positive self-esteem! We could incorporate at least one school color in every outfit. If we wear one school color in each ensemble, we could represent our school and be somewhat allied. This could be accomplished by providing students with school colorful buttons, hair ribbons, patches, socks, and/or shoelaces. Girls should not be permitted to wear heels over one and a half inches high. High-heels could be very treacherous in school. A girl in my class fell while wearing three inch heels. This resulted in a sprain to her ankle and a week of walking with crutches.

My final thought about instilling a dress code in my school is to simply dress appropriately. Girls should not be allowed to wear more than three make-up items per day. Some girls are envious of others who wear make-up which could cause an unnecessary rivalry. Also, at a young age, some girls are not taught how to apply make-up in a tasteful manner and may appear trashy.

Writing Analysis (cont.)

End of the Year (cont.)

Students should not wear mini skirts, strapless shirts, or shorts that are too short. These items of dress look very unbecoming for school. Everyone with long hair, girls as well as boys, should pull it away from his or her face. This is more suitable for school, in my viewpoint, because it would be easier to see and focus on schoolwork.

In summary, my thoughts about instilling a dress code in my school are: stable, fitted clothing, reliable shoes, and no uniforms. I would also instill the promotion of school spirit, through color selections, attractive and age-appropriate make-up choices, and well-groomed hair. I think this is an excellent plan and should be implented in my school. Send this to the school board for approval immediately! I am like a fashion guru; some say I am a member of the fashion police. I suspect I am just insightful about design and fashion. What are your ideas for a dress code at your school? I'm listening!

End of the Year Writing Benchmark 3 Date:				Total	Summary
Ideas	Sentence Fluency	Organization	Word Choice	18 Advanced	Advanced: 15–18
③ 2 1 0	③ 2 1 0	③ 2 1 0	③ 2 1 0		Proficient: 11–14
Voice		Conventions			Basic: 6–10
③ 2 1 0		③ 2 1 0			Below Basic: 0–5

Notes:

- Maintains main idea; narrowed and focused topic (Ideas)
- Supports main ideas with descriptive details, anecdotes, and examples (Ideas)
- Writes sentences that are smooth with effective flow and rhythm (Sentence Fluency)
- Includes a variety of sentence types (Sentence Fluency)
- Writes in a logical and purposeful sequence (Organization)
- Uses transition words to connect ideas (Organization)
- Uses descriptive, colorful language to evoke strong visual images (Word Choice)
- Uses vocabulary that is varied yet purposeful to topic and audience (Word Choice)
- Shows originality, excitement, and commitment to topic (Voice)
- Speaks to and connects with audience and purpose; engages reader (Voice)
- Little, if any, need for editing (Conventions)
- Capitalization is correct, errors may be minor (Conventions)
- Effective and correct use of punctuation (Conventions)

Mentor Text List

Managing Writer's Workshop

DiSalvo, DyAnne. 2008. *The Sloppy Copy Slipup*. New York: Holiday House.

Fletcher, Ralph. 1996. *A Writer's Notebook: Unlocking the Writer Within You*. New York: HarperCollins.

Lionni, Leo. 1973. *Swimmy*. New York: Dragonfly Books.

McGovern, Ann. 1992. *Too Much Noise*. Boston: Sandpiper.

Moss, Marissa. 2006. *Amelia's Notebook*. New York: Simon & Schuster.

Schotter, Roni. 1999. *Nothing Ever Happens on 90th Street*. New York: Scholastic.

Ideas

Allen, Susan. 2006. *Read Anything Good Lately?* Minneapolis, MN: Millbrook Press.

Allen, Susan. 2010. *Written Anything Good Lately?* Minneapolis, MN: Millbrook Press.

Baylor, Byrd. 1985. *Everybody Needs a Rock*. New York: Aladdin.

———. 1995. *I'm in Charge of Celebrations*. New York: Aladdin.

———. 1998. *The Table Where Rich People Sit*. New York: Aladdin.

Brinckloe, Julie. 1986. *Fireflies*. New York: Aladdin.

Brown, Margaret W. 1990. *The Important Book*. New York: HarperCollins.

Bunting, Eve. 1990. *The Memory String*. New York: Clarion Books.

———. 1990. *The Wall*. Boston: Sandpiper.

Crews, Donald. 1996. *Shortcut*. New York: Greenwillow Books.

Cronin, Doreen. 2003. *Diary of a Worm*. New York: HarperCollins.

Denenberg, Dennis. 2005. *50 American Heroes Every Kid Should Meet*. Minneapolis, MN: Millbrook Press.

DiCamillo, Kate. 2009. *The Miraculous Journey of Edward Tulane*. Somerville, MA: Candlewick.

Ewald, Wendy. 2002. *The Best Part of Me*. New York: Little, Brown Books for Young Readers.

Fletcher, Ralph. 1996. *A Writer's Notebook: Unlocking the Writer Within You*. New York: HarperCollins.

———. 2005. *Marshfield Dreams: When I Was A Kid*. New York: Henry Holt and Company.

Harris, Caroline. 2006. *I Wonder Why Whales Sing and Other Questions About Sea Life*. Boston: Kingfisher.

Horowitz, Ruth. 2004. *Crab Moon*. Somerville, MA: Candlewick.

Johnson, Angela. 1995. *Shoes Like Miss Alice's*. New York: Scholastic.

Kalman, Bobbie. 1997. *How a Plant Grows*. New York: Crabtree Publishing Company.

Kellogg, Steven. 1988. *Johnny Appleseed*. New York: HarperCollins.

———. 1992. *Pecos Bill*. New York: HarperCollins.

MacLachlan, Patricia. 1994. *All the Places to Love*. New York: HarperCollins.

Mentor Text List (cont.)

Ideas (cont.)

MacLachlan, Patricia. 1998. *What You Know First*. New York: HarperCollins.

McLeod, Sandra. 2005. *Dare to Dream! 25 Extraordinary Lives*. Amherst, NY: Prometheus Books.

Moss, Marissa. 2005. *Amelia's Most Unforgettable Embarrassing Moments*. New York: Simon & Schuster.

———. 2006. *Amelia's Notebook*. New York: Simon & Schuster.

———. 2012. *Amelia Writes Again*. New York: Simon & Schuster

Munsch, Robert. 1995. *Love You Forever*. Ontario: Firefly Books Ltd.

Polacco, Patricia. 1998. *Chicken Sunday*. New York: Puffin.

———. 1998. *My Rotten Redheaded Older Brother*. New York: Aladdin.

———. 1999. *My Ol' Man*. New York: Puffin.

———. 2001. *Thank You, Mr. Falker*. New York: Philomel Books.

Rosenthal, Amy K. 2006. *One of Those Days*. New York: Putnam Juvenile.

Rylant, Cynthia. 1993. *When I Was Young in the Mountains*. New York: Puffin.

———. 2000. *The Old Woman Who Names Things*. Boston: Sandpiper.

———. 2004. *The Relatives Came*. Pine Plains, NY: Live Oaks Media.

Schaefer, Carole. 1999. *The Squiggle*. New York: Dragonfly Books.

Schotter, Roni. 1999. *Nothing Ever Happens on 90th Street*. New York: Scholastic.

Simon, Seymour. 1992. *Our Solar System*. New York: William Morrow and Company.

———. 2001. *Tornadoes*. New York: HarperCollins.

Spinelli, Eileen. 2008. *The Best Story*. New York: Dial.

Stevens, Janet. 1999. *From Pictures to Words: A Book about Making a Book*. New York: Holiday House.

Viorst, Judith. 2009. *Alexander and the Terrible, Horrible, No Good, Very Bad Day*. New York: Atheneum Books for Young Readers.

Wiesner, David. 1997. *Tuesday*. Boston: Sandpiper.

———. 2006 *Flotsam*. New York: Clarion Books.

William, Vera B. 1984. *A Chair for My Mother*. New York: Greenwillow Books.

Wong, Janet S. 2002. *You Have to Write*. New York: New York: Margaret K. McElderry Books.

Yolen, Jane. 1987. *Owl Moon*. New York: Philomel.

Sentence Fluency

Allen, Debbie. 2003. *Dancing in the Wings*. New York: Puffin.

Bunting, Eve. 1993. *Fly Away Home*. Boston: Sandpiper.

Mentor Text List *(cont.)*

Sentence Fluency *(cont.)*

Bunting, Eve. 2004. *Whales Passing*. New York: Scholastic Inc.

Cleary, Brian P. 2001. *To Root, To Toot, To Parachute: What Is a Verb?* Minneapolis, MN: Carolrhoda Books.

Clement, Rod. 1999. *Grandpa's Teeth*. New York: HarperCollins.

Dahl, Roald. 2007. *The Twits*. New York: Puffin.

Fletcher, Ralph. 1997. *Twilight Comes Twice*. New York: Clarion Books.

MacLachlan, Patricia. 1994. *All the Places to Love*. New York: HarperCollins.

Palatini, Margie. 2003. *Bedhead*. New York: Simon & Schuster Books for Young Readers.

Paulson, Gary. 1995. *Dogteam*. New York: Dragonfly Books.

Polacco, Patricia. 2001. *Thank You, Mr. Falker*. New York: Philomel Books.

Rylant, Cynthia. 1993. *When I Was Young in the Mountains*. New York: Puffin.

———. 2004. *The Relatives Came*. Pine Plains, NY: Live Oaks Media.

Smucker, Anna. 1994. *No Star Nights*. New York: Dragonfly Books.

Steig, William. 2009. *Amos & Boris*. New York: Square Fish.

———. 2010. *Shrek!* New York: Farrar, Straus and Giroux.

Walton, Rick. 2011. *Just Me and 6,000 Rats: A Tale of Conjunctions*. Layton, UT: Gibbs Smith.

William, Vera B. 1984. *A Chair for My Mother*. New York: Greenwillow Books.

Yolen, Jane. 1987. *Owl Moon*. New York: Philomel.

Organization

Ada, Alma Flor. 1997. *Dear Peter Rabbit*. New York: Aladdin.

———. 2001. *Yours Truly, Goldilocks*. New York: Atheneum Books for Young Readers.

Arnosky, Jim. 2009. *Slither and Crawl: Eye to Eye with Reptiles*. New York: Sterling Publishing Company.

———. 2011. *Thunder Birds: Nature's Flying Predators*. New York: Sterling Publishing Company.

Aylesworth, Jim. 1998. *The Gingerbread Man*. New York: Scholastic Press.

Blackburn, Ken. 1996. *Kid's Paper Airplanes*. New York: Workman Publishing Company.

Bolin, Frances S. 2008. *Poetry for Young People: Emily Dickinson*. New York: Sterling Publishing Company.

Brett, Jan. 1996. *Goldilocks and the Three Bears*. New York: Puffin.

Buehner, Caralyn. 2004. *Snowmen at Night*. New York: Scholastic.

Cassidy, John. 1987. *The Klutz Yo-Yo Book*. Palo Alto, CA: Klutz.

Mentor Text List (cont.)

Organization (cont.)

Cherry, Lynne. 1990. *The Great Kapok Tree: A Tale of the Amazon Rain Forest*. Boston: Harcourt Children's Books.

Cobb, Vicki. 2003. *I Face the Wind*. New York: HarperCollins.

Creech, Sharon. 2003. *Love That Dog*. New York: HarperCollins.

———. 2008. *Hate That Cat: A Novel*. New York: HarperCollins.

Crews, Donald. 1996. *Shortcut*. New York: Greenwillow Books.

Dahl, Roald. 2007. *The Twits*. New York: Puffin.

Denenberg, Dennis. 2005. *50 American Heroes Every Kid Should Meet*. Minneapolis, MN: Millbrook Press.

Diaz, David. 2000. *Wilma Unlimited: How Wilma Rudolph Became the World's Fastest Woman*. Boston: Sandpiper.

Fagerstrom, D., and L. Smith. 2008. *Show Me How: 500 Things You Should Know*. New York: HarperCollins.

Fletcher, Ralph. 2005. *Marshfield Dreams: When I Was A Kid*. New York: Henry Holt and Company.

Frazee, Marla. 2003. *Roller Coaster*. Boston: Harcourt Children's Books.

Galdone, Paul. 1979. *The Three Bears*. New York: Clarion Books.

Gibbons, Gail. 2006. *Owls*. New York: Holiday House.

Harley, Avis. 2012. *African Acrostics: A Word in Edgeways*. Somerville, MA: Candlewick.

Henson, Heather. 2008. *That Book Woman*. New York: Simon & Schuster.

Houston, Gloria. 1997. *My Great Aunt Arizona*. New York: HarperCollins.

James, Simon. 1997. *Dear Mr. Blueberry*. New York: Aladdin.

Janeczko, Paul. 2009. *A Kick in the Head: An Everyday Guide to Poetic Forms*. Somerville, MA: Candlewick.

Jenkins, Steven. 2003. *What Do You Do With a Tail Like This?* Boston: Houghton Mifflin Books for Childr.

Johnson, Steve. 1994. *The Salamander Room*. New York: Dragonfly Books.

Keats, Ezra Jack. 2005. *Whistle for Willie*. Pine Plains, NY: Live Oak Media.

Kellogg, Steven. 1992. *Pecos Bill*. New York: HarperCollins.

Kloske, Geoffrey. 2005. *Once Upon a Time, The End*. New York: Atheneum Books for Young Readers.

Laminack, Lester. 1998. *The Sunsets of Miss Olivia Wiggins*. Atlanta, GA: Peachtree Publishers.

———. 2004. *Saturdays and Teacakes*. Atlanta, GA: Peachtree Publishers.

———. 2007. *Snow Day!* Atlanta, GA: Peachtree Publishers.

Lester, Julius. 1999. *John Henry*. New York: Puffin.

Loewen, Nancy. 2009. *Sincerely Yours: Writing Your Own Letter*. Mankato, MN: Picture Window Books.

Mentor Text List *(cont.)*

Organization *(cont.)*

Lollis, Sylvia and Joyce Hogan. 2003. *Should We Have Pets?: A Persuasive Text*. New York: Mondo Publishing.

Marshall, James. 1993. *Red Riding Hood*. New York: Picture Puffins.

Moss, Marissa. 2006. *Amelia's Notebook*. New York: Simon & Schuster.

Nelson, Julie. 2006. *Families Change: A Book for Children Experiencing Termination of Parental Rights*. Minneapolis: Free Spirit Publishing, Inc.

Orloff, Karen Kaufman. 2010. *I Wanna New Room*. New York: Putnam Juvenile.

Palatini, Margie. 2003. *Bedhead*. New York: Simon & Schuster Books for Young Readers.

Pallotta, Jerry. 1990. *The Ocean Alphabet Book*. Watertown, MAL Charlesbridge Publishing.

———. 1993. *The Extinct Alphabet Book*. Watertown, MA: Charlesbridge Publishing.

Pilkey, Dav. 1999. *The Paperboy*. New York: Scholastic.

Polacco, Patricia. 2001. *Thank You, Mr. Falker*. New York: Philomel Books.

Prelutsky, Jack. 2008. *Pizza, Pigs, and Poetry: How to Write a Poem*. New York: Greenwillow Books.

Routman, Regie. 2000. *Kids' Poems: Teaching Third & Fourth Graders to Love Poetry*. New York: Scholastic.

Rylant, Cynthia. 2004. *The Relatives Came*. Pine Plains, NY: Live Oaks Media.

Schmidt, Gary D. 2008. *Poetry for Young People: Robert Frost*. New York: Sterling Publishing Company.

Schnur, Steven. 1997. *Autumn: An Alphabet Acrostic*. New York: Clarion Books.

Scieszka, Jon. 2008. *Knucklehead: Tall Tales and Almost True Stories of Growing Up*. New York: Viking Juvenile.

Silverstein, Shel. 2004. *Where the Sidewalk Ends*. New York: HarperCollins.

Steig, William. 2010. *Shrek!* New York: Farrar, Straus and Giroux.

Stevens, Janet. 1989. *The Princess and the Pea*. New York: Holiday House.

Stewart, Sarah. 2007. *The Gardener*. New York: Square Fish.

Teague, Mark. 2002. *Dear Mrs. LaRue: Letters from Obedience School*. New York: Scholastic.

Torres, Laura. 1996. *Friendship Bracelets*. Palo Alto, CA: Klutz.

White, E. B. 2004. *Charlotte's Web*. New York: HarperCollins.

Wood, Audrey. 2006. *The Bunyans*. New York: Scholastic.

Yolen, Jane. 1987. *Owl Moon*. New York: Philomel.

Young, Ed. 1996. *Lon Po Po: A Red Riding Hood Story from China*. New York: Puffin.

Mentor Text List (cont.)

Word Choice

Arnold, Tedd. 2003. *More Parts*. New York: Puffin.

———. 2007. *Even More Parts*. New York: Puffin.

Bauer, Marion D. 1996. *When I Go Camping with Grandma*. New York: Troll Communications.

Brennan-Nelson, Denise. 2011. *My Teacher Likes to Say*. Chelsea, MI: Sleeping Bear Press.

Cannon, Janell. 1993. *Stellaluna*. Boston: Harcourt Children's Books.

Cherry, Lynne. 2003. *How Groundhog's Garden Grew*. New York: Blue Sky Press.

Cleary, Brian. 2001. *Hairy, Scary, Ordinary: What Is an Adjective?* Minneapolis, MN: Carolrhoda Books.

Coffelt, Nancy. 2009. *Big, Bigger, Biggest!* New York: Henry Holt and Company.

Cook, Julia. 2008. *It's Hard to be a Verb!* Chattanooga, TN: National Center for Youth Issues.

Dahl, Michael. 2007. *If You Were a Synonym*. Mankato, MN: Picture Window Books.

Dahl, Roald. 2007. *The Twits*. New York: Puffin.

———. 2011. *James and the Giant Peach*. New York: Puffin.

dePaola, Tomie. 1998. *The Knight and the Dragon*. New York: Puffin.

DiCamillo, Katie. 2003. *The Tale of Desperaux*. Somerville, MA: Candlewick.

Edwards, Pamela. 1998. *Some Smug Slug*. New York: Katherine Tegen Books.

Fox, Mem. 1994. *Tough Boris*. Boston: Harcourt Children's Books.

Frasier, Debra. 2000. *Miss Alaineus: A Vocabulary Disaster.* Boston: Harcourt Children's Books.

Haseley, Dennis. 2002. *A Story for Bear*. Boston: Harcourt Children's Books.

Heller, Ruth. 1998. *Kites Sail High*. New York: Puffin.

———. 1998. *Many Luscious Lollipops*. New York: Puffin.

———. 1998. *Merry-Go-Round*. New York: Puffin.

———. 1998. *Up, Up and Away: A Book About Adverbs*. New York: Puffin.

Juster, Norton. 2010. *The Odious Ogre*. New York: Michael di Capua Books.

Kellogg, Steven. 1987. *Chicken Little*. New York: HarperCollins.

Leedy, Loreen. 2003. *There's a Frog in my Throat! 400 Animal Sayings a Little Bird Told Me*. New York: Holiday House.

———. 2009. *Crazy Like a Fox: A Simile Story*. New York: Holiday House.

Loewen, Nancy. 2011. *Stubborn as a Mule and Other Silly Similes*. Mankato, MN: Picture Window Books.

MacLachlan, Patricia. 1994. *All the Places to Love*. New York: HarperCollins.

———. 1998. *What You Know First*. New York: HarperCollins.

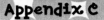

Mentor Text List *(cont.)*

Word Choice *(cont.)*

MacLachlan, Patricia. 2004. *Sarah, Plain and Tall*. New York: HarperCollins.

Noble, Trinka. 1992. *Meanwhile Back at the Ranch*. New York: Puffin.

Palatini, Margie. 2000. *Zoom Broom*. New York: Hyperion Paperbacks for Children.

———. 2003. *Bedhead*. New York: Simon & Schuster Books for Young Readers.

Parish, Peggy. 2003. *Amelia Bedelia*. New York: Greenwillow Books.

Pinkney, Andrea. 2006. *Duke Ellington: The Piano Prince and His Orchestra*. New York: Hyperion.

Piven, Hanoch. 2007. *My Dog Is as Smelly as Dirty Socks*. New York: Schwartz & Wade.

Polacco, Patricia. 1998. *Chicken Sunday*. New York: Puffin.

Pulver, Robin. 2007. *Nouns and Verbs Have a Field Day*. New York: Holiday House.

Raschka, Christopher. 1997. *Charlie Parker Played Be Bop*. New York: Scholastic.

Rylant, Cynthia. 1996. *An Angel for Solomon Singer*. New York: Scholastic.

———. 2001. *The Relatives Came*. Pine Plains, NY: Live Oaks Media.

Schotter, Roni. 1999. *Nothing Ever Happens on 90th Street*. New York: Scholastic.

Steig, William. 2010. *Shrek!* New York: Farrar, Straus and Giroux.

———. 2011. *Brave Irene*. New York: Square Fish.

Terban, Marvin. 1993. *It Figures! Fun Figures of Speech*. Boston: Sandpiper.

———. 2007. *In a Pickle and Other Funny Idioms*. Boston: Sandpiper.

Walton, Rick. 2011. *Suddenly Alligator: Adventures in Adverbs*. Layton, UT: Gibbs Smith.

———. 2011. *Why the Banana Split*. Layton, UT: Gibbs Smith.

Wood, Audrey. 1996. *Quick as a Cricket*. Swindon, London: Child's Play International.

———. 2006. *The Bunyans*. New York: Scholastic.

Yashima, Taro. 1987. *Umbrella*. Pine Plains, NY: Live Oak Media.

Yolen, Jane. 1987. *Owl Moon*. New York: Philomel.

Voice

Ada, Alma Flor. 2001. *Yours Truly, Goldilocks*. New York: Atheneum Books for Young Readers.

Aliki. *Feelings*. 1986. New York: Greenwillow Books.

Baylor, Byrd. 1985. *Everybody Needs a Rock*. New York: Aladdin.

Bridges, Ruby. 1999. *Through My Eyes: Ruby Bridges*. New York: Scholastic.

Browne, Anthony. 2001. *Voices in the Park*. New York: DK Publishing.

Mentor Text List (cont.)

Voice (cont.)

Bunting, Eve. 1992. *The Wall*. Boston: Sandpiper.

———. 1993. *Fly Away Home*. Boston: Sandpiper.

Bunting, Eve. 2000. *The Memory String*. New York: Clarion Books.

———. 2000. *Train to Somewhere*. Boston: Sandpiper.

Cain, Janan. 2000. *The Way I Feel*. Seattle, WA: Parenting Press.

Cronin, Doreen. 2003. *Diary of a Worm*. New York: HarperCollins.

Forward, Toby. 2005. *Wolf's Story: What Really Happened to Little Red Riding Hood*. Somerville, MA: Candlewick.

Freymann, Saxton and Joost Elffers. 2004. *How Are You Peeling! Foods with Moods*. New York: Scholastic.

Gantos, Jack. 2011. *Joey Pigza Swallowed the Key*. New York: Square Fish.

Hall, Donald. 1994. *I Am the Dog I Am the Cat*. New York: Dial.

Heller, Ruth. 2000. *Fantastic! Wow! and Unreal! A Book About Interjections and Conjunctions*. New York: Puffin.

Kirk, Daniel. 2003. *Dogs Rule!* New York: Hyperion.

Kotzwinkle, William. 2001. *Walter the Farting Dog*. Berkeley, CA: Frog Children's Books.

Kovalski, Maryann. 1990. *The Wheels on the Bus: An Adaptation of the Traditional Song*. Tonawanda, NY: Kids Can Press Ltd.

Loewen, Nancy. 2007. *If You Were An Interjection*. Mankato, MN: Picture Window Books.

Moss, Marissa. 2006. *Amelia's Notebook*. New York: Simon & Schuster.

O'Malley, Kevin. 2006. *Straight to the Pole*. New York: Walker Children's.

O'Neill, Alexis. 2002. *The Recess Queen*. New York: Scholastic.

Palatini, Margie. 2003. *Bedhead*. New York: Simon & Schuster Books for Young Readers.

———. 2004. *Sweet Tooth*. New York: Simon & Schuster Books for Young Readers.

Pilkey, Dav. 2004. *Dog Breath*. New York: Scholastic.

Polacco, Patricia. 1994. *Pink and Say*. New York: Philomel.

———. 1998. *The Bee Tree*. New York: Puffin.

———. 1998. *My Rotten Redheaded Older Brother*. New York: Aladdin.

———. 2001. *Thank You, Mr. Falker*. New York: Philomel Books.

———. 2012. *The Art of Miss Chew*. New York: Putnam Juvenile.

Ryder, Joanne. 1999. *Earthdance*. New York: Henry Holt and Company.

Rylant, Cynthia. 2001. *The Relatives Came*. Pine Plains, NY: Live Oaks Media.

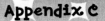
Mentor Text List (cont.)

Voice (cont.)

Scieszka, Jon. 1996. *The True Story of The Three Little Pigs*. New York: Puffin.

Shannon, David. 1998. *No, David!* New York: Blue Sky Press.

Shannon, David. 2006. *Good Boy, Fergus!* New York: Blue Sky Press.

Viorst, Judith. 2009. *Alexander and the Terrible, Horrible, No Good, Very Bad Day*. New York: Atheneum Books for Young Readers.

Ware, Cheryl. 1999. *Flea Circus Summer*. New York: Scholastic.

Conventions

Buzzeo, Toni. 2006. *Our Librarian Won't Tell Us Anything!* Madison, WI: Upstart Books.

Christelow, Eileen. 1995. *What Do Authors Do?* New York: Clarion Books.

Clement, Rod. 1999. *Grandpa's Teeth*. New York: HarperCollins.

Crews, Donald. 1996. *Shortcut*. New York: Greenwillow Books.

Frasier, Debra. 2000. *Miss Alaineus: A Vocabulary Disaster*. Boston: Harcourt Children's Books.

Gaiman, Neil. 2004. *The Day I Swapped My Dad for Two Goldfish*. New York: HarperCollins.

Giff, Patricia R. 2009. *Eleven*. New York: Yearling.

Hall, Pamela. 2009. *Punk-tuation Celebration*. Minneapolis, MN: Magic Wagon.

Leedy, Loreen. 2005. *Look at My Book: How Kids Can Write & Illustrate Terrific Books*. New York: Holiday House.

Moss, Marissa. 2006. *Amelia's Notebook*. New York: Simon & Schuster.

Nixon, Joan L. 1995. *If You Were a Writer*. New York: Aladdin.

Palatini, Margie. 2003. *Bedhead*. New York: Simon & Schuster Books for Young Readers.

———. 2004. *Sweet Tooth*. New York: Simon & Schuster Books for Young Readers.

Polacco, Patricia. 2001. *Thank You, Mr. Falker*. New York: Philomel Books.

Pulver, Robin. 2008. *Punctuation Takes a Vacation*. Pine Plains, NY: Live Oak Media.

Raschka, Chris. 2007. *Yo! Yes?* New York: Scholastic.

Shulevitz, Uri. 2003. *On Monday Morning*. New York: Farrar, Straus and Giroux.

Truss, Lynne. 2006. *Eats, Shoots & Leaves: Why, Commas Really Do Make a Difference!* New York: Putnam Juvenile.

———. 2007. *The Girl's Like Spaghetti: Why, You Can't Manage without Apostrophes!* New York: Putnam Juvenile.

———. 2008. *Twenty-Odd Ducks: Why, Every Punctuation Mark Counts!* New York: Putnam Juvenile.

Van Allsburg, Chris. 1988. *Two Bad Ants*. Boston: Houghton Mifflin Books for Children.

Sample Home Connections Letter

Dear Parents,

One of our first writing projects is to decorate our Writer's Notebook. The notebook is a very important part of our writing time together. In the notebook, students will practice the many skills learned during Writer's Workshop. The notebook serves as an ongoing resource as your child becomes a writer.

Over the weekend, students are asked to decorate the cover of their Writer's Notebook in the form of a collage, and return them to school on Monday. The notebook decorations should reflect your child's interests. Here is a list of possible items you might include on the notebook:

- photographs
- magazine clippings
- stickers
- scrapbooking items

- shapes and letters
- printed clipart
- construction paper
- illustrations and drawings

Attached is a copy of the cover of the notebook that I made last year. Some of the items that I have on it are pictures of my close family members and my pet, music notes, a picture of an mp3 player (because I love music), a picture of a book by my favorite author, roses (because that is my middle name), airplanes and sandals (because I like to travel), and credit cards (because I love to shop). I also used some various scrapbooking items to decorate.

Remember these ideas should reflect your child's interests, hobbies, family, favorites, etc. Take the next step! Share stories and memories and record a list of writing ideas to give your child a jump start.

Please contact me if you have any questions or concerns about the notebook project.

Thank you in advance for your support!

Sincerely,

Ms. Olivito

Supporting with Technology

Whether communicating via cell phones, texts, blogs, tweets, Facebook, email or gathering information via Internet, Google, and eBooks, today's students will live in a world increasingly shaped by technology. For this reason, Common Core State Standards highlight the effective use of technology-integrated instruction across the curriculum. Incorporating technology into instruction increases opportunities for students to be active learners, rather than passive receivers of information, and offers new ways of learning and sharing information.

The challenge for most teachers is how to seamlessly integrate technology use so that it does not take time away from writing instruction but enhances that instruction and increases students' interest and involvement. While uses of technology are seemingly limitless and constantly being updated, here are seven important ways teachers are successfully integrating technology into Writer's Workshop:

1. Digital and flip cameras can add excitement to any writing project. Student projects that capture pictures of the life cycle of a chick or a class field trip instantly invite students into a writing project. Digital photos can be used to generate a photo album of writing ideas, organize storyboards, promote language and vocabulary, illustrate student writing, and even be included in slide show presentations.

2. Document cameras are easily integrated in writing lessons and activities by both teachers and students. The benefits of using mentor texts for modeling are sometimes lost on students who may not be close enough to see the specific texts. Whether presenting photographs to gather writing ideas, sharing multiple beginnings from mentor texts, or displaying leaves and fossils to model descriptive language, the document camera offers a myriad of opportunities for modeling writing instruction for all students to see. Using the document camera allows you to zoom in on specific text features and details in illustrations. Students frequently volunteer to display their writing with the document camera and gather feedback from classmates on revising and editing. Teachers and students also enjoy presenting examples of good writing work and highlighting quality features in writing using the document camera.

3. Interactive whiteboards can serve a number of purposes for writing instruction. They provide the opportunity for student engagement and involvement of almost any materials or activity that can be viewed on a computer screen. Consider using the interactive whiteboard to teach whole group keyboarding skills, revising word choice by highlighting verbs or adjectives, using editing marks, building story webs, or reinforcing skills by accessing interactive websites. Of course, whiteboards are an excellent source to demonstrate and model lessons, present presentations and create class books and word banks.

Supporting with Technology *(cont.)*

4. Publishing tools abound in the technology realm. Students may be involved in illustrating their writing with Microsoft® Paint or a software program like KidPix®. Through word processing, students can create letters, essays, brochures, and even class newsletters. Many teachers use Microsoft® PowerPoint for publishing individual, team, or class writing projects, which can easily be printed and bound into classroom books or saved as eBooks. Podcasts are used to record students as they read their writing. This can support the revising and editing process as they listen carefully to their writing and add a special touch to a final published project. Technology enhances the writer's options for publishing their work. For example, parents and students enjoy viewing and listening to final projects on the school website.

5. Research has never been easier. Though writing teachers must be cognizant of Internet safety, misuse, plagiarism, and follow district policies, they know technology allows for new and purposeful ways to gather and synthesize research. Writing teachers demonstrate technology-driven research procedures and help students locate and bookmark trusted websites. Collaborating with colleagues about their student research websites can make research easy and accessible.

6. URLs (Uniform Resource Locator) are great to include in your classroom newsletter. Offer links for students to practice skills, view presentations, or learn about future topics like Arbor Day. And don't forget the authors! With activities like Ralph Fletcher's

Tips for Young Writers, Patricia Pollacco's *Who Am I*, or *Poetry Writing with Jack Prelutsky*, author websites are filled with an assortment of information and activities to engage and motivate student writing. Visit author sites while teaching students how to create their own Author's Page. The possibilities are limitless.

7. Collaborative writing projects like ePals and virtual field trips open classroom boundaries to endless learning opportunities. EPals is a modern pen pal project in which students can collaborate on academic and cultural projects as well as establish everlasting friendships in other districts, states, or countries. Virtual field trips (VFT) offer learning opportunities that might otherwise be limited by distance and funding. Writing projects may be further enhanced by a virtual visit to the San Diego Zoo to learn about animal characteristics and habitats or to the National Aeronautics and Space Administration (NASA) to interview an astronaut.

Terminology Used

In order to adequately implement the lessons included in *Getting to the Core of Writing*, it is necessary to understand the terminology used throughout the resources.

Analytics—In order to be consistent with National Assessment of Educational Progress (NAEP) standards, the following analytics are used when describing writing proficiency:

- **Below Basic/Score 0**—Writing demonstrates an attempt to write, but the result is illegible, insufficient, or otherwise fails to meet the criteria for a score of 1.

- **Basic/Score 1**—Writing demonstrates little or marginal skill in responding to the writing benchmark tasks. Few traits of quality writing are present.

- **Proficient/Score 2**—Writing demonstrates developing skills in responding to the writing benchmark tasks. Most traits of quality writing are evident.

- **Advanced/Score 3**—Writing demonstrates effective skills in responding to the writing benchmark tasks. All traits of quality writing are obvious.

Anchor Charts—Anchor charts are used to track student thinking. In this resource, anchor charts are created cooperatively by the teacher and students. The charts are used to scaffold learning and chart key concepts of writing such as ideas for writing, vocabulary words, and examples of sentence structure. Anchor charts are displayed throughout the room to support a print-rich environment that promotes literacy acquisition.

Anecdotal Observations—Throughout Writer's Workshop, teachers practice the art of becoming astute observers of student writing behaviors. The teacher's Conferring Notebook is an excellent resource to store observations for the entire year of instruction (See Appendix A). As you observe, remember to present a statement of praise and develop a teaching point as this will guide future instructional decisions.

Author's Chair—Students are selected to share their writing with classmates. Usually students sit in a designated chair/stool. Classmates provide feedback to authors in the form of a question or a compliment.

Author's Tea/Author's Luncheon—An author's tea can be held anytime to support student writing efforts. Students invite parents and special loved ones to join them, sometimes with refreshments, to celebrate accomplishments in writing. Each student writes, illustrates, publishes, and presents a favorite piece of writing from the past year. It is important that every student has someone to listen to his or her especially planned presentation. You might invite the principal, cafeteria cook, librarian, or teacher specialists as part of the celebration.

Benchmark Assessments—The beginning-of-the-year benchmark serves as baseline information about a student's writing. Middle-of-the-year and end-of-the-year benchmarks represent a student's progress toward state, district, and/or school benchmark goals.

Terminology Used (cont.)

Heads-up, Stand-up, Partner-up—This is an activity in which the teacher gains students' attention, they stand up and quickly move to find partners, and they begin a discussion of focused writing talk. Partners can be assigned based upon the needs of the class or they can be chosen spontaneously. However, it is crucial that students move quickly and in an orderly fashion without any wasted time.

Mentor Texts—A mentor text is a book that offers multiple learning opportunities as both teacher and student develop writing skills. Mentor texts contain explicit and strong examples of the author's craft and are visited repeatedly to explore the traits of quality writing. Your favorite books to share often make the best mentor texts. You may wish to use the recommended mentor text as a read-aloud during your reading block with spirited discussions or quickly review it during Writer's Workshop. During writing block, focus on small samples of text that match the mini-lesson skill. A recommended list of mentor texts is provided as part of each lesson and additional titles are provided in Appendix C.

Notebook Entry—Notebook entries are pages that students will cut out and glue into their Writer's Notebook. They reinforce the lesson with the key points for students to remember. At the bottom of most notebook entries is a *Your Turn* section where students can practice the skill taught in the lesson.

Turn and Talk—*Turn and Talk* is a management tool for giving opportunities to students to have partner conversations. This procedure may take place at the meeting area or at desks. Students make eye contact, lean toward their partner, talk quietly, or listen attentively.

Triads and Quads—These are terms used to quickly divide the class into groups of three or four.

References

Anderson, Carl. 2000. *How's It Going? A Practical Guide to Conferring with Student Writers.* Portsmouth, NH: Heinemann.

Bjorklund, David F. 1999. *Children's Thinking: Developmental Function and Individual Differences.* New York: Brooks/Cole Publishing Company.

Buckner, Aimee. 2005. *Notebook Know How: Strategies for the Writer's Notebook.* Portland, ME: Stenhouse Publishers.

Calkins, Lucy M. 1994. *The Art of Teaching Writing* (New ed.). Portsmouth, NH: Heinemann.

Calkins, Lucy, Amanda Hartman, and Zoe White. 2003. *The Conferring Handbook.* Portsmouth, NH: Heinemann.

———. 2005. *One to One: The Art of Conferring with Young Writers.* Portsmouth, NH: Heinemann.

Culham, Ruth. 2003. *6 + 1 Traits of Writing: The Complete Guide (Grades 3 and Up).* New York: Scholastic.

———. 2005. *One to One: The Art of Conferring with Young Writers.* Portsmouth, NH: Heinemann.

———. 2008. *6 + 1 Traits of Writing: The Complete Guide for the Primary Grades.* New York: Scholastic.

———. 2008. *Using Picture Books to Teach Writing With the Traits K–2.* New York: Scholastic.

Cunningham, Patricia M. and James W. Cunningham. 2009. *What Really Matters in Writing: Research-Based Practices Across the Curriculum.* Boston, MA: Allyn & Bacon/Pearson.

Davis, Judy, and Sharon Hill. 2003. *The No-Nonsense Guide to Teaching Writing: Strategies, Structures, Solutions.* Portsmouth, NH: Heinemann.

Dolch, Edward W. 1941. *Teaching Primary Reading.* Champaign, IL: The Garrard Press.

Dorn, Linda J., and Carla Soffos. 2001. *Scaffolding Young Writers: A Writers' Workshop Approach.* Portland, ME: Stenhouse Publishers.

Ehri, Linnea C. 1997. "Learning to Read and Write Are One and the Same, Almost." In *Learning to Spell: Research, Theory, and Practice Across Languages.* Edited by Charles A. Perfetti, Laurence Rieben, and Michael Fayol. London: Lawrence Erlbaum Associates.

Erlauer, Laura. 2003. *The Brain-Compatible Classroom: Using What We Know About Learning to Improve Teaching.* Alexandria, VA: Association for Supervison and Curriculum Development.

Fletcher, Ralph. 1996. *A Writer's Notebook: Unlocking the Writer Within You.* New York: HarperCollins.

———. 1999. *Live Writing: Breathing Life Into Your Words.* New York: HarperCollins.

———. 2000. "Craft Lessons to Improve the Quality of Student Writing." Presentation at the 28th Annual Conference of The Maryland International Reading Association. Baltimore, MD.

———. 2002. *Poetry Matters: Writing a Poem From the Inside Out.* New York: HarperCollins.

Fletcher, Ralph, and JoAnn Portalupi. 1998. *Craft Lessons: Teaching Writing K–8.* Portland, ME: Stenhouse Publishers.

Fletcher, Ralph, and JoAnn Portalupi. 2001. *Writing Workshop: The Essential Guide.* Portsmouth, NH: Heinemann.

References (cont.)

Frayer, Dorothy, Wayne Frederick, and Herbert Klausmeier. 1969. *A Schema for Testing the Level of Cognitive Mastery.* Madison, WI: Wisconsin Center for Education Research.

Freeman, Marcia. 1998. *Teaching the Youngest Writers: A Practical Guide.* Gainesville, FL: Maupin House Publishing, Inc.

———. 2001. *Non-Fiction Writing Strategies: Using Science Big Books as Models.* Gainesville, FL: Maupin House Publishing, Inc.

Gentry, J. Richard. 2000. *The Literacy Map: Guiding Children to Where They Need to Be (K–3).* New York: Mondo Publishing.

———. 2002. *The Literacy Map: Guiding Children to Where They Need to Be (4–6).* New York: Mondo Publishing.

———. 2004. *The Science of Spelling: The Explicit Specifics That Make Greater Readers and Writers (and Spellers!).* Portsmouth, NH: Heinemann.

———. 2006. *Breaking the Code: New Science of Beginning Reading and Writing.* Portsmouth, NH: Heinemann.

———. 2007. *Breakthrough in Beginning Reading and Writing.* New York: Scholastic, Inc.

———. 2008. *Step-by-Step: Assessment Guide to Code Breaking.* New York: Scholastic, Inc.

———. 2010. *Raising Confident Readers: How to Teach Your Child to Read and Write—from Baby to Age 7.* Cambridge, MA: Da Capo Lifelong Books.

Gentry, J. Richard, and Jean Gillet. 1993. *Teaching Kids to Spell.* Portsmouth, NH: Heinemann.

Ginott, Hiam G. 1972. *Teacher & Child: A Book for Parents and Teachers.* New York: Macmillan Publishing Company.

Gould, Judith. 1999. *Four Square Writing Method: A Unique Approach to Teach Basic Writing Skills for Grades 1–3.* Carthage, IL: Teaching and Learning Company.

Graham, Steve, and Michael Hebert. 2010. *Writing to Read: Evidence for How Writing Can Improve Reading. A Carnegie Corporation Time to Act Report.* Washington, DC: Alliance for Excellent Education.

Graham, Steve, Virginia Berninger, and Robert Abbott. 2012. "Are Attitudes Toward Writing and Reading Separable Constructs? A Study with Primary Grade Children." *Reading & Writing Quarterly, 28* (1), 51-69.

Graves, Donald H. 1994. *A Fresh Look at Writing.* Portsmouth, NH: Heinemann.

———. 2003. *Writing: Teachers and Children at Work 20th Anniversary Edition.* Portsmouth, NH: Heinemann.

Jensen, Eric. 2009. *Different Brains, Different Learners: How to Reach the Hard to Reach* (Second ed.). Thousand Oaks, CA: Corwin Press.

Mann, Jean. 2002. "Writing in Grades Four, Five, and Six." In *The Literacy Map: Guiding Children to Where They Need to Be (4–6).* New York: Mondo Publishing.

References *(cont.)*

McKenna, Michael C., and Dennis J. Kear. 1990. "Measuring attitude toward Reading: A new tool for teachers." *The Reading Teacher, 43* (9), 626–639.

McMahon, Carolyn, and Peggy Warrick. 2005. *Wee Can Write: Using 6 + 1 Trait Writing Strategies with Renowned Children's Literature.* Portland, OR: Northwest Regional Educational Laboratory.

Murray, Donald. 2004. *Write to Learn.* Independence, KY: Cengage Learning.

National Governors Association Center for Best Practices and Council of Chief State School Officers. 2011. *Common Core State Standards Initiative: The Standards.* Retrieved June 2011, from Common Core State Standards Initiative: http://www.corestandards.org

Pearson, P. David, and Margaret C. Gallagher. 1983. "The instruction of reading comprehension." *Contemporary Educational Psychology*, 8, 317-344

Ray, Katie W. 2001. *The Writing Workshop: Working Through the Hard Parts (And They're All Hard Parts).* Urbana, IL: National Council Of Teachers of English.

Ray, Katie W., and Lisa Cleaveland. 2004. *About the Authors: Writing Workshop with Our Youngest Writers.* Portsmouth, NH: Heinemann.

Rog, Lori Jamison, and Paul Kropp. 2004. *The Write Genre: Classroom Activities and Mini-Lessons That Promote Writing with Clarity, Style, and Flashes of Brilliance.* Ontario, Canada: Pembroke Publishers.

Routman, Regie. 1999. *Conversations: Strategies for Teaching, Learning and Evaluating.* Portsmouth, NH: Heinemann.

———. 2000. *Kids' poems: Teaching Third & Fourth Graders to Love Writing Poetry.* New York: Scholastic.

———. 2005. *Writing Essentials: Raising Expectations and Results While Simplifying Teaching.* Portsmouth, NH: Heinemann.

Shanahan, T. (In Press). *College and Career Readiness Standards for Reading, Writing, and Speaking and Listening-Draft for Review and Comment.*

Spandel, Vicki. 2001. *Books, Lessons, Ideas for Teaching the Six Traits: Writing in the Elementary and Middle Grades.* Wilmington, MA: Great Source Education Group.

———. 2005. *Seeing with New Eyes: A Guidebook on Teaching and Assessing Beginning Writers Using the Six-Trait Writing Model* (6th Edition.) Portland, OR: Northwest Regional Educational Laboratory.

———. 2008. *Creating Young Writers: Using the Six Traits to Enrich Writing Process in Primary Classrooms* (2nd Edition.). New York: Allyn & Bacon.

Sprenger, Marilee B. 2007. *Becoming a "Wiz" at Brain-Based Teaching: How to Make Every Year Your Best Year.* Thousand Oaks, CA: Corwin Press.

Vygotsky, Lev. 1978. *Mind in Society: The Development of Higher Psychological Processes.* Edited by Michael Cole, Vera John-Steiner, Sylvia Scribner, and Ellen Souberman. Cambridge, MA: Harvard University Press.

Yates, Elizabeth. 1995. *Someday You'll Write.* Greensville, SC: Bob Jones University Press.

Contents of the Teacher Resource CD

Teacher Resources

Page Number	Title	Filename
N/A	The Traits Team	traitsteam.pdf
N/A	Year-at-a-Glance	yearataglance.odf
12–13	Suggested Pacing Guide	pacingguide.pdf
24–30	Correlation to Standards	standards.pdf
254	Conferring Notebook Cover	cover.pdf
255	Mini-Lesson Log	minilessonlog1.pdf
256	Conference Log	conferencelog.pdf
257	Conference Countdown	conferencecountdown.pdf
263–264	Fourth Grade Writing Rubric	writingrubric.pdf
265	Fourth Grade Writing Report	writingreport.pdf
266	Fourth Grade Grouping Mat	groupingmat.pdf
273–281	Mentor Text List	mentortextlist.pdf
282	Sample Home Connections Letter	samplehomeletter.pdf

Managing Writer's Workshop

Page Number	Title	Filename
37	Components of Writer's Workshop Notebook Entry	writersworkshop.pdf
40	Sample Looks Like, Sounds Like, Feels Like Anchor Chart	lookssoundsfeelschart.pdf
43	Student Mini-Lesson Log	minilessonlog2.pdf
44	Dolch Sight Word List	dolchwordlist.pdf
45	Fry Sight Word List	frywordlist.pdf
46–47	Short and Long Vowel Charts	shortlongvowelcharts.pdf
48–49	Vowel Teams Chart	vowelteamschart.pdf
54	Traits of Writing Notebook Entry	traitswriting.pdf
55–57	Traits Team Mini Posters	traitsteamposters.pdf
60	Sharing Notebook Entry	sharing.pdf
61	Compliment and Comment Cards	complicommentcards.pdf
64	Turn and Talk Notebook Entry	turntalk.pdf
67	Guidelines for Writer's Workshop Notebook Entry	guidelineswritersws.pdf
70	Peer Conference Notebook Entry	peerconference.pdf
73	The Five-Step Writing Process Notebook Entry	fivestepprocess.pdf

Contents of the Teacher Resource CD (cont.)

Ideas

Page Number	Title	Filename
76	Ida, Idea Creator	ida.pdf
79	My Authority List Notebook Entry	myauthoritylist.pdf
82	Authors as Mentors Notebook Entry	authorsmentors.pdf
85	Interesting Places Notebook Entry	interestingplaces.pdf
88	The Best Times! The Worst Times! Notebook Entry	bestworst.pdf
91	Brainstorming Boxes Notebook Entry	brainstormbox.pdf
94	What Should We Write? Notebook Entry	write.pdf
97	Pocket of Picture Topics Notebook Entry	pocketpictures.pdf
100	I Wonder List Notebook Entry	iwonder.pdf

Sentence Fluency

Page Number	Title	Filename
102	Simon, Sentence Builder	simon.pdf
105	Circle and Count Notebook Entry	circlecount.pdf
108	Subject + Predicate = Sentence Notebook Entry	subjpred.pdf
109	Sentence Puzzle Pieces	sentencepuzzle.pdf
112	Sentence Search Notebook Entry	sentencesearch.pdf
113–116	Sentence Type Posters	sentencetype.pdf
119	Appositive Action Notebook Entry	appositiveaction.pdf
120	Appositive Action Puzzle Sentences	appositivepuzzle.pdf
123	Compound Sentences Notebook Entry	compoundsentences.pdf
124–125	Coordinating Conjunction Cards	conjunctioncards.pdf
128	Writing Complex Sentences Notebook Entry	writingcomplex.pdf
129–130	Subordinating Conjunction Cards	subconjunctioncards.pdf
133	Stepping Up Sentences Notebook Entry	steppingup.pdf
136	Building Triangle Sentences Notebook Entry	trianglesentences.pdf

Contents of the Teacher Resource CD (cont.)

Organization

Page Number	Title	Filename
138	Owen, Organization Conductor	owen.pdf
141	Creating Cinquains Notebook Entry	cinquains.pdf
144	Powerful Paragraphs Notebook Entry	powerful.pdf
147	Narrative Notes Notebook Entry	narrativenotes.pdf
150	Build-a-Character Notebook Entry	buildcharacter.pdf
153	Story Building Blocks Notebook Entry	storyblocks.pdf
156	It's a Bear Beginning Notebook Entry	bearbeginning.pdf
157	Three Bears Hook Cards	3bearscards.pdf
160	Don't You Agree? Notebook Entry	dontyouagree.pdf
163	It's Your Business Notebook Entry	itsyourbusiness.pdf
164	Dear Pen Pal Notebook Entry	dearpenpal.pdf
167	How-To Writing Notebook Entry	howtowriting.pdf
170	Composition Planner Notebook Entry	compplanner.pdf
171	All About Owls Writing Sample	allaboutowls.pdf
174	A Cache of Poetry Notebook Entry	cachepoetry.pdf

Word Choice

Page Number	Title	Filename
176	Wally, Word Choice Detective	wally.pdf
179	Stupendous Similes Notebook Entry	similes.pdf
182	Be a Word Wizard Notebook Entry	wordwizard.pdf
185	Connecting Ideas Notebook Entry	connectideas.pdf
186	Transition Words Practice Paragraph	transitionwords.pdf
189	Put "Said" to Bed Notebook Entry	saidtobed.pdf
192	COW to WOW Notebook Entry	cowtowow.pdf
195	Auspicious Adjectives Notebook Entry	auspicious.pdf
198	Be Explicitly Specific Notebook Entry	bespecific.pdf
201	Adverb Alert Notebook Entry	adverbalert.pdf
202	Adverb Cards	adverbcards.pdf
205	Alliteration Action Notebook Entry	alliteration.pdf

Contents of the Teacher Resource CD *(cont.)*

Voice

Page Number	Title	Filename
208	Val and Van, Voice	valvan.pdf
211	Show Me Your Voice Notebook Entry	showme.pdf
212–214	Emotion Cards	emotioncards.pdf
219	The Voices on the Bus Notebook Entry	voicesonbus.pdf

Conventions

Page Number	Title	Filename
224	Callie, Super Conventions Checker	callie.pdf
227	Capital Creations Notebook Entry	capital.pdf
230	Super Spellers Notebook Entry	superspellers.pdf
233	Common Comma Conventions Notebook Entry	commoncomma.pdf
234	Common Comma Conventions Cards	commacards.pdf
237	The Color of CUPS Notebook Entry	colorofcups.pdf
238	Camping Trip Writing Sample	campingtrip.pdf
241	Dandy Dialogue Notebook Entry	dandydialogue.pdf
244	Show Me Editing Notebook Entry	showmeediting.pdf
247	Traits Team Checklist Notebook Entry	traitschecklist.pdf
250	Digging Into Editing Notebook Entry	digging.pdf
251	He's the Man Writing Sample	hestheman.pdf